CW01499938

Disinherited

Edward Myles
2025

Copyright © 2025 by Edward Myles.

All rights reserved.

No part of this book may be reproduced, distributed, transmitted or modified in any form, including photocopying, recording, or other electronic or mechanical methods, or by any information storage and retrieval system, without permission in writing from the Author.

For the avoidance of doubt, the Author reserves the rights, and publishers/platforms have no rights to, reproduce and/or otherwise use the Work in any manner for purposes of training artificial intelligence technologies to generate text, including without limitation, technologies that are capable of generating works in the same style or genre as the Work, unless such publisher/platform obtains the Author's specific and express permission to do so.

Nor do publishers/platforms have the right to sub-license others to reproduce and/or otherwise use the Work in any manner for purposes of training artificial intelligence technologies to generate text without the Author's specific and express permission.

Disinherited is a literary and analytical reckoning focussing on the slow, often silent, unravelling of modern Britain.

Structured as a novel-in-stories, this work presents thirteen fictional accounts drawn from a fractured national landscape — council estates, maternity wards, failing schools, border posts, and beyond. Each story stands alone, yet together they reveal a country grappling with institutional paralysis, cultural confusion, and the quiet rage of those left behind.

Every fictional story is followed by a critical essay. These essays do not explain or moralise the fiction. Instead, they excavate it — drawing connections to public policy, cultural theory, and the long, slow corrosion of trust between people and the systems that once held them.

This is not a manifesto. It is not nostalgia. It is not a call to arms.

It is a testament to grief, to failure, to the human cost of political cowardice and ideological silence.

It is also a literary experiment — a work that invites readers to feel *before* they analyse, and to reflect *after* they judge.

Whether read as literature, critique, or both, *Disinherited* is a response to one question.

What happens when a nation disinherits its own people — not through force, but through forgetting?

Contents

There is no revolution here. Only rooms. Flats. Corridors. Paper trails.

What follows is not fiction in the traditional sense. It is fiction built from fragments — overheard, half-remembered, footnoted and then erased. Names have changed. Systems have not.

This book began with a single question: *What happens when a nation disinherits its people, not through violence, but through forgetting?*

That forgetting doesn't look like fire or collapse. It looks like letters not answered. A bin that never gets collected. A child who stops speaking. It is a kind of soft violence — ambient, deniable, slow. And because it rarely announces itself, it requires a different form of recording.

This work uses fiction not to escape reality, but to reach it sideways. Each story is written as a refusal — to accept the lie that these lives are too minor to matter, that their complaints are isolated, their failures individual. They are not.

The accompanying essays do not explain the stories. They are their second breath. Together, the two forms try to do what neither can alone — hold a moment open long enough to name it.

Nothing in this book is extraordinary.

That's the point.

Some names are invented. All silences are real.

Part 1: The Council Flat Ghost

Old Light

The light in the stairwell had changed. It wasn't just the bulbs — though those were dimmer now, yellow instead of white, flickering like tired eyes. No, it was the light itself. The way it fell across the walls. In the eighties, Nora remembered, it used to catch on the gloss-painted handrails, pick out the red stencilled numbers on each landing. It made the place feel permanent. Now the light sank instead of shining. It settled low and dull, as if the building were trying to disappear.

She stood by the kitchen window, kettle boiling behind her, and watched the breeze play with a torn curtain three floors up. Someone had wedged a bit of cardboard in the broken frame. No one fixed anything anymore. The communal sense of care — gone. She remembered the neighbours who used to polish the stairwell tiles on Saturdays, who painted the doorframes every other year without being asked. Most of them were dead. Or moved. Or moved and then died.

The estate had a name once: Beverley Rise. It was printed on the original tenancy documents in cursive font, with a small logo of a robin. People used to say it with pride. "I'm up Beverley Rise, pet," they'd say at the butcher or in the queue at the post office. Now, the name had been dropped from signage. Maps labelled it "Zone 17." The robin was long gone — scrubbed from the wall during a refurb that never finished.

Nora poured hot water into her chipped mug and sat. She didn't drink tea anymore — too bitter. But she still liked the ritual. Hands around warmth. Something to do. Her flat smelt faintly of lavender and mildew. The radio whispered from the other room, some panel show where no one let anyone finish a sentence.

She reached for the photo frame on the table. Her son, age eight, holding a football and missing his front teeth. She remembered that day — summer, bright sun, sound of radios from open windows, ice cream from the van that parked by the bins. She remembered the whole estate spilling out like a single family. No fences then. No locked doors.

Now, people passed each other like shadows. Eyes down. Voices low. She sipped and waited for the light to change back. It never did.

Two weeks ago, the first board came down.

It had been over Flat 3B for years — thick plywood, painted council grey, nailed hard against the frame. No one touched it, not even the kids with spray cans and boredom. Everyone knew 3B was sealed. After the overdose, no one wanted to live there anyway. Too much memory, too much talk. But then, on a Thursday morning, Nora woke to the sound of drills. Two men in high-vis jackets. One carrying a toolbox, the other filming on his phone.

By evening, the flat had light. Real light — new bulbs, strong and white. Someone had washed the windows. The smell of fresh paint drifted down the corridor, sharp and citrusy. Nora stood at her door for a long time, pretending to struggle with her keys, just to watch.

Three days later, a van pulled up. Not a moving van — smaller, branded with the logo of a housing association she didn't recognise. Four men climbed out, one of them holding a clipboard. They didn't speak English. The youngest had a child on his hip, maybe two years old, silent and wide-eyed.

They moved in that evening. No furniture came with them. Just duffel bags, a cot, and a flatscreen TV that looked newer than anything Nora owned. She watched from her window as they struggled with the lift — broken, as always — and then climbed the stairs, breathless, apologising in a language she didn't understand.

By the following week, two more flats were unboarded. 4A and 2C. Same process. Same vans. Nora asked the housing officer about it, during a routine inspection of her bathroom leak — the one that had gone unresolved for six months. He looked uncomfortable. Said the council had new obligations now. Emergency intake. "Different funding stream," he muttered, writing nothing down.

She nodded. She didn't argue. She rarely did. But later, she found herself walking the halls more often. Listening. Watching. Counting. The rhythms were different now — doors opening at odd hours, cooking smells she couldn't place, shoes left in the hallway. No names on the buzzers yet. Just blank metal plates.

One night she caught her reflection in the stairwell glass — pale, still, barely there. Behind her, Flat 3B glowed with warm light. Laughter floated down the corridor, and a child cried, briefly, then stopped. Nora stood there for a long time, not sure if she was watching life arrive...or watching herself vanish.

Doors that Don't Knock

Nora tried, at first.

A simple hello when they passed in the stairwell. A polite smile at the woman with the pushchair. A nod toward the man who sometimes smoked on the landing. They nodded back — shy, deferential — but never spoke. Not even a "hiya." Just brief eye contact, then a retreat into the flat.

One morning, she knocked on 3B's door. She'd baked banana bread, an old recipe that used to make the whole building smell like childhood. She thought the boy might like it. She thought maybe the woman would smile. But when the door opened, the man who answered looked startled. Younger than she'd thought. Thin. Barefoot. He stared at the tin in her hands like it was a trap.

"Gift," she said gently, holding it out.

He looked over his shoulder, then back at her. "No... English," he said, very slowly, enunciating each syllable like a borrowed phrase.

She smiled, just as slowly. "That's all right."

He took the tin, bowed awkwardly, and shut the door without another word.

The next day, the tin was left on her doormat. Empty. Washed. No note.

After that, Nora stopped trying. Not out of malice — just exhaustion. Conversation had become translation, and she had no tools for it. The estate was full of tongues now — Arabic, Somali, Polish, maybe more. She recognised none of them. The lift was a babel of sound. Even the children, who once roared down the corridor in accents that mirrored her own, now played in languages she couldn't place.

The noticeboard in the lobby used to advertise local clubs — bingo nights, repair cafés, pensioner lunches. Now it was blank except for one poster in five languages: *"Need Housing*

Help? Scan Here." She didn't know how to scan. She wasn't sure her phone could.

One afternoon, a little girl dropped her toy rabbit in the stairwell. Nora picked it up, tried to catch the child before she turned the corner. "Love," she called softly. "You dropped—"

The girl stopped. Looked up at her. Said nothing.Then turned and ran.

Nora held the rabbit for a moment, then placed it carefully on the bottom step. It sat there for two days before disappearing.

In her own flat, she turned on the radio and listened to voices she could still understand — clipped, chatty, confident — and for the first time in years, she turned the volume up.

It started with sirens that never came.

Nora was halfway through peeling potatoes when she heard the shouting — two voices, sharp and rising, bouncing off the tiled corridor like thrown dishes. A child's name repeated over and over. Then the heavy thud of a door, and footsteps running down the stairs.

She moved to the spyhole. A man — the younger one from 4A — was pacing the landing in circles, shouting into a phone in his own language, gesturing wildly at nothing. A woman stood near the lift, crying, her headscarf half fallen, her arms open as if expecting something to fall into them.

Nora opened her door an inch. "Everything all right, love?"

Neither looked at her.

The man turned and ran back up. The woman sank to the floor.

She stayed there for twenty minutes.

That night, the estate felt pinched — the kind of silence that hummed with things unsaid. No one spoke in the stairwell. No one cooked. The lights on the third floor flickered in and out like a dying signal. Nora waited for the police. For an ambulance. For the shrill burst of authority that used to arrive when something went wrong.

It never came.

The next morning, Nora passed the woman from 4A sitting by the bins, face blank. In her lap, a child's jumper. Red with a cartoon bear. Nora nodded gently as she passed. No reply.

That evening, two council workers came with clipboards. They stood by the lift, speaking in low tones, glancing occasionally toward the upper floors. One of them took photos of the hallway. The other took notes.

Nora opened her door.

"Excuse me," she said. "Was there an incident? A child?"

The younger of the two turned to her. Smiled. "We can't comment on individual cases, sorry."

"I understand. But... was it serious?"

He paused, professionalism tightening like a drawstring. "We've passed everything on to the appropriate services."

Nora nodded. She closed her door and didn't speak again that day.

That night, she thought she heard footsteps — small ones, soft ones — outside her flat. A child, maybe. A boy. But when she opened the door, the hallway was empty. Just the sound of the extractor fan in someone's kitchen. And a single red sock, damp and abandoned, halfway down the stairwell.

Housing Officer

The ceiling in Nora's bathroom had begun to sag. It had started with a faint stain — like a bruise just beneath the plaster — and spread slowly into a dark, swollen ellipse. Water gathered there after every rain, pooling quietly above her head, cold and invisible. She kept a mop and bucket ready in case it gave way mid-shower.

When the housing officer finally arrived, she was ready. Notes written. Letters printed. Photos taped to the fridge. She had even dusted the living room.

He was younger than she expected — maybe thirty, polite, smiling, wearing the uniform of someone who had learned to nod and escape.

"Right," he said, tapping at a tablet. "Nora Elsey?"

"That's me."

He glanced around the flat as if measuring its fatigue. "We're here about the ceiling?"

She led him to the bathroom, stepping carefully over a bowl she'd placed beneath the newest drip. He stood beneath the sag, hands on hips, and whistled softly.

"How long's it been like this?" he asked.

"Seven months. Reported three times. I called again last week. Again yesterday."

He tapped his tablet. "Yeah… I can see those. It's just that we've got quite a backlog at the moment."

"I understand. But that's my ceiling."

He didn't look at her. "The upper flat's drainage has been rerouted. It'll take a few weeks to dry. Then we can assess the plastering."

"It could collapse."

He nodded thoughtfully, noncommittally. "If it does, keep the area clear. Don't stand under it."

Nora blinked. "This is council housing, isn't it?"

"Yes, but this block's been reallocated under emergency provision. Some units are managed differently now."

"What does that mean?"

He hesitated. "Different funding stream. Emergency in-take. Repairs are triaged according to tenancy type."

"So I wait, because I've lived here longer?"

"I didn't say that."

"No. You didn't."

He smiled again — the kind that meant the visit was ending — and typed something into his tablet. "We'll log it again. If anything changes, ring the out-of-hours number."

Nora walked him to the door. He didn't take the photos she'd prepared. Didn't ask to see the stained towels. She closed the door quietly behind him, leant against it for a long time, and looked up at the ceiling.

It hadn't dripped in hours.But she didn't trust it anymore.

Two days later, Nora called the housing office.

She pressed through five automated menus, entered her tenancy number twice, waited thirteen minutes on hold, and was finally connected to someone named Callum. Young voice. Upbeat. The kind that apologised before you even spoke.

"I'm just following up on a maintenance visit," she said. "My ceiling. Bathroom. It's sagging."

He made listening sounds. She could hear typing in the background.

"Right... yes. Looks like you're in a mixed-allocation block. Emergency-use units included, so repairs fall under two separate budget codes. That can delay things."

"Why?"

"Just how the funding's structured. Emergency tenants come under a different stream — managed partly by Home Office resources."

"But I've been here forty-seven years."

"I understand, Mrs. Elsey. But allocations are need-based now."

"I don't have a ceiling."

He chuckled softly, then caught himself. "Sorry. I just meant — we prioritise cases where a health risk has been formally assessed."

"Is water over your head not a health risk?"

"I can escalate it. But I should say: due to capacity pressures, legacy tenants may face longer lead times for non-critical issues."

Nora sat in silence, holding the phone to her ear like a brick.

"Legacy tenant?" she said finally.

"Long-term occupancy."

"You say it like I'm expired."

"Not at all. You're absolutely on record. But newer tenancies — asylum dispersals, at-risk families — those are coded urgent."

"And what am I coded?"

He hesitated. "Standard. Category four."

Nora said nothing.

"We do appreciate your patience."

"Don't," she said, softly. "Don't appreciate me. Just fix the ceiling."

"I'll log another request. And if anything changes —"

"I know. Call the out-of-hours number."

He thanked her for her call. She hung up before he could finish.

Later, she sat at the table with her old folder of documents — rent receipts, council letters, notes from housing meetings. She flipped through them slowly, hands dry against the pages. At the back, she found the original lease agreement. 1976. Two signatures, her husband's in blue ink, hers in black.

This tenancy shall be held in trust for the wellbeing of the tenant and the security of the dwelling.

She stared at that sentence for a long time.

Then folded the paper back into its sleeve and turned on the kettle.

The Corridor That Sings

It started just after midnight.

A low, rhythmic hum — soft and slow, rising and falling like a lullaby. At first, Nora thought it was the wind in the vents. Then she recognised the cadence: **a voice**. Male, young, unhurried. Singing in a language she didn't know, words like water sliding over stone.

She rose, shuffled to the door, and pressed her ear to the wood.

The corridor beyond was empty. But the voice drifted closer, not louder, just clearer — like it was being carried, not projected. She unlocked the chain and opened the door a crack.

Nothing. No one.

The hallway lights were on — two flickering, one out entirely. She saw no feet under the other doors, no movement. The singing continued. No footsteps. Just the sound, hovering like fog. It curled around her.

She stepped into the corridor barefoot, her robe pulled tight, her heart louder than she'd admit.

Then — suddenly — the voice stopped.

Silence swallowed the space, thick and quick, like a curtain dropping.

She waited. Listened.

A creak behind her. The sound of a door settling. Then — from somewhere above — footsteps. Deliberate. Measured.

One after the other. But too slow for anyone in a hurry. Too soft for steel-capped boots. They moved across the ceiling, then along the wall, then—

There's no flat there, she thought.

She turned back to her door. Stepped inside. Closed it gently, then quickly locked the bolt.

In the living room, the radio was still on — shipping forecast murmuring in its strange, poetic code. She turned it off. The silence felt even louder.

She sat in her armchair and stared at the ceiling.

She didn't believe in ghosts. But she knew presence when she felt it. And this wasn't a haunting in the traditional sense. It wasn't dread. It wasn't malevolent. It was alienation with a melody. A voice she couldn't reach, occupying a place she once knew.

She thought of her son's bedroom, long since cleared. She remembered his cassette player, his awful music, his heavy-footed dance steps. She remembered yelling at him to keep it down. And now here she was — straining to hear someone else's song, alone in a flat that felt less hers each night.

She reached for the light switch.

But didn't turn it on.

The next night, the singing returned — louder this time, and layered. More than one voice. Male and female. A low chant threaded with something higher, almost mournful. It echoed faintly through the vents, like a hymn carried by rust.

Nora waited an hour. Then picked up the phone.

She didn't call 999. She wasn't mad. But she'd kept the number for the neighbourhood policing team — a printout pinned to the fridge beside the takeaway menus and her grandson's last drawing. A smiley face in blue crayon. Four fingers on each hand.

A woman answered after seven rings. Tired voice. Polite, but impatient.

Nora explained: the noise, the time, the strange movement in the corridor. Not threatening, but unsettling. Not an emergency, but... not nothing.

"Have you approached the neighbours directly?" the woman asked.

"They don't speak English. I've tried. And it's late."

"Well, it's not a criminal matter unless there's disturbance or damage."

"I didn't say it was criminal. I said it's frightening."

There was a pause. A click of keys. "We're stretched thin this week. If there's no violence, we log it as non-urgent. Environmental noise goes to council now. You can submit an online report."

"I'm 76."

"Of course, sorry. I understand. But unless there's immediate danger..."

"There never is," Nora said. "Until there is."

Another pause. Softer this time. "We'll note the concern. If it escalates, don't hesitate to call back."

Nora hung up.

Later, as she stood at her door again — just barely ajar — she heard the voices fade. Then footsteps again, heavier this time, purposeful. They stopped just outside 3B. She held her breath.

A child's voice, quick and breathy, spoke something she couldn't parse. A hush followed. Then a door clicked shut.

Nora waited.

The hallway held still.

The next morning, she checked the estate's WhatsApp group. She rarely posted, but she read. There were no complaints. No mentions. Just a video of someone's cat and a notice about bin day.

She typed a message — "Anyone else hear singing last night?" — and hovered her thumb over send.

Then deleted it.

Instead, she walked to the front door, opened it wide, and stared down the corridor.

The walls were the same.

But they no longer felt like hers.

Ghost in Flat 3B

It had been a Thursday.

She remembered that because the bin men came early, rattling down the back lane, and her son, Mark, had been sleeping on the sofa again. Not because there wasn't a bed — but because he couldn't stand the quiet in his old room. Said it made his thoughts go funny.

She'd made tea. Told him to get up. He grunted. Said later. She kissed the top of his head, just once. Hair greasy, warm. Then she went to the market.

When she came back, the door was ajar.

Flat 3B had always been the neighbour's — Mr. Gittins, then old Mrs. Patel, then no one. It was empty when Mark started sneaking in there. Nora knew it. The door didn't lock properly, and he liked the silence, the space. Said it helped him think. She warned him — drugs and danger go hand in hand with emptiness. But he smiled. Said she worried too much.

She found him there at half-past one.

He was curled against the wall, head resting on a cushion he must've carried from her flat. One shoe off. Mouth open.

The packet was beside him. Silver foil, faintly torn. Empty blister pack, some chalked lines on the floor, barely smudged.

She didn't scream. She dropped the bags. Knelt. Checked his chest. Cold, yes. But breath — maybe. She called for help.

The ambulance took twenty minutes.

He was gone by the time they arrived.

The paramedic — kind, grey-bearded, calm — told her it might've been peaceful. That he didn't look afraid. That sometimes, when the body gives up slowly, the brain makes it easier.

She didn't believe him. Not then. Not now.

Flat 3B had been sealed after that. Boards across the door. Official notices about contamination, danger, renovation. No one had entered for five years. Until last month.

Now it was home again. A new family. A boy about the same age Mark had been when the headaches started. The same dark hair. The same silence behind the eyes.

She sometimes thought she heard Mark in the pipes — his heavy footfall, his too-loud music, the slam of his laugh. But then it would fade. The pipes settled. The flat went quiet.

She didn't tell anyone. Who would she tell?

In this place, ghosts weren't news.

They were neighbours.

She saw him again the next night.

Not clearly — not as flesh. More like a suggestion in the corner of her vision, a shadow too still, a shape too familiar. He stood by the stairwell, just outside the lift, where the light from the ceiling flickered on a delay. Arms at his sides.

Head tilted slightly, like he was trying to hear something far off.

She didn't move. Just stared.

Mark.

Not as he'd been in the end — pale, slack, lost — but younger. Thirteen, maybe. The year he made her laugh every day and stole biscuits when he thought she wasn't looking. He wore that ridiculous bomber jacket from the market. The one with the peeling Union Jack on the back.

She blinked. He was gone.

She didn't scream. Didn't call anyone. She simply turned, walked back inside, and sat in the dark.

It wasn't the first time. Just the clearest.

Over the years, he'd shown himself in pieces. A cough from an empty room. The thud of a football on the balcony. Once, a brief reflection in the microwave door — her face beside his, just for a second.

She'd told no one. Grief was meant to fade. Talking about ghosts invited eye-rolls, pills, letters marked "Wellbeing Services." But she knew the truth.

The ghost wasn't him. Not really.It was hers.

Her memory. Her past. Her presence, flickering like the stairwell bulb. This estate was full of new faces, new lives. But she walked its corridors like someone caught between frames — not quite gone, not quite needed. A glitch in the system. A remnant.

The irony gnawed at her. Everyone talked about newcomers not integrating. But who had integrated her? Who had come to her door and asked her name, her story, what this place used to be? No one. She was the ghost. And like all ghosts, she haunted out of habit, not malice.

She stayed up that night, listening to the hum of the building — pipes and vents and lives lived loudly on the other side of thin walls. She heard a child cry, briefly. A man shout. A door slam. Then quiet.

She stood. Went to the mirror. Looked hard.

Still here.

Just not seen.

Eviction Letter

The envelope was cream-coloured and heavy, unlike the usual council post.

Nora found it on her doormat just after breakfast, partially crumpled where the letterbox had tried to swallow it. No window, no plastic. Just her name in printed capitals and the council's emblem stamped in red in the corner. She knew what it was before she opened it.

She didn't tear. She slid her finger beneath the flap like opening a wound.

Dear Ms Elsey,

We regret to inform you...

She read it once. Then again.

Reallocation. Emergency housing needs. No alternative.

They were offering her a unit in a sheltered complex three miles away — newer, smaller, closer to "health resources." Her name was on a list. Her transfer would be arranged. Boxes would be provided.

No timeline. No apology. Just process.

She sat at the table, letter in her lap, and looked at the flat around her. She knew every creak. Every stain. The line on the wall where Mark had measured his height in biro. The chip in the kitchen counter from the night she dropped a tin of peas. The scorch mark on the sill from her husband's old ashtray.

This wasn't a property. It was a chronology.

She rose. Walked room to room, touching objects like relics. The kettle. The curtain hooks. The framed school photo from 1989. She stopped at the hallway — stared down at the once-blue carpet, now grey and thinning. How many steps had she taken here? How many nights had she paced, waiting for Mark to come home?

They were evicting her from her own life.

She opened the airing cupboard and pulled out a half-melted candle. Vanilla-scented. A leftover from a power cut years ago. She placed it on the kitchen counter. Lit it. Watched the flame settle into a steady, patient flicker.

Outside, children ran down the corridor, laughing in a language she didn't recognise.

She didn't pack. She didn't call the number on the letter.She just sat in her chair and listened. One last time.

At some point, she stood.Put on her coat.Turned off the radio.

She left the door unlocked.Left the candle burning.

And stepped into the corridor, as quiet as the air behind her.

By the time the housing liaison knocked, the candle had burned down.

He waited the regulation two minutes, clipboard in hand, eyes scanning the doorframe for signs of movement. There was no answer. No sound. No note pinned to the wood. Just the faint smell of vanilla drifting into the corridor.

He logged it: "No response. Attempted contact."Moved on to Flat 2A.

Inside, the flat was silent.

The candle stub on the kitchen counter sat in a puddle of wax, pooled in slow spirals. The room was clean — not scrubbed, just *settled*. A cup in the sink. Chair pushed in. Radio unplugged.

In the bedroom, the wardrobe stood open. Clothes gone. Not all, but enough. One drawer left ajar. Her dressing gown still hung from a hook on the door, limp and weightless.

On the hallway table sat the eviction letter, folded once. On top of it, a single house key.

No suitcase. No sign of movers. No van on the street. Just absence. Soft. Total.

Later, the new tenant — a man from Eritrea, with two children and a wife who never left the bedroom — would comment on the smell. Said it reminded him of something from his grandmother's house. Couldn't explain it. Sweet. Dry. Like a memory waiting to be lit again.

The housing office closed Nora's file after six weeks of no contact. Mail returned. Phone number disconnected. A single welfare check conducted — nothing suspicious found. "Assumed relocated."

Some said she moved into the sheltered flats as assigned. Others said she'd gone to live with a niece up north. One neighbour insisted she saw Nora in town, near the war memorial, talking to a man who wasn't there.

But no one knew for sure.

The estate carried on. More flats unboarded. More languages in the corridor. More forms pushed under more doors.

No one removed the candle. Its wax hardened into the form of its final flicker.

And at night, when the hallway lights guttered, and the lift moaned up from the ground floor without stopping, a few tenants swore they heard a voice — not angry, not lost, just... present.

Soft as breath.

Saying nothing.

Saying everything.

Part 1: Critical Essay

The Collapse of the Commons

There was a time when a council flat meant more than a roof — it meant belonging. A right earned by generations who had contributed, paid in, stayed put. These bricks and concrete walkways, ugly to some, were once monuments to postwar egalitarianism — the physical embodiment of a state that saw housing not as a commodity, but as a covenant.

That covenant is broken.

Today, the language of public housing has shifted from entitlement to emergency. Once, applicants were seen as participants in a shared system; now, they are triaged through a moral algorithm that prioritises perceived vulnerability over accumulated investment. The local grandmother who raised her children in the same estate for forty years competes for shelter against newly arrived families whose trauma is real but whose ties to place are zero. This is not their fault. But the system now treats everyone as if history doesn't matter.

The commons — that old British idea of mutual interest — has withered under the weight of unacknowledged change. In estates from Hull to Haringey, former tenants whisper about "fast-tracking," about "the list going missing," about "being skipped." Their suspicions aren't always wrong. Emergency asylum allocations and resettlement quotas are managed outside traditional channels. Local councils, bound by statutory duty but drained by political pressure, bend criteria quietly. The result is resentment with no paper trail.

This is the soil in which ghosts grow. When people who feel they've played by the rules are displaced by those who simply arrived more recently — however needy — they don't riot. They recede. They fall silent. They let the walls rot. And when their children ask why Nana never complains, she just says: *"It's not for us anymore."*

This shift has created a post-commons Britain — where public goods are no longer shared, but partitioned. The ideal of reciprocal duty is gone, replaced by competitive desperation. And in this climate, the council flat becomes not a home but a symbol of betrayal. A reminder that the system remembers the crisis — but forgets its own citizens.

We are no longer a society of neighbours, but a queue of claimants.

And no one tells the woman at the back of the line that the gate has already closed.

Entitlement vs. Emergency

There is a moral chasm in British housing policy, though it rarely speaks its name: entitlement versus emergency. One is built on continuity — a life lived in one place, taxes paid, children raised, roots put down. The other is rooted in displacement — sudden need, trauma, flight. But the bureaucracy cannot hold both with equal weight. And so it chooses: the urgent over the patient.

This triage mentality is not inherently unjust. Of course, those fleeing war or persecution require urgent shelter. But the deeper injustice lies in the erasure of the conversation. The native poor — white, working-class, static — have been told, sometimes explicitly, that their suffering is less morally compelling. They are not tragic. They are not victims of geopolitics. They are merely unlucky.

The policy framework has quietly evolved to bypass visible fairness in favour of politically insulated mechanisms. "Section 95 support," "dispersal housing," "non-local priority listings" — each of these routes inserts newly arrived individuals directly into housing stock, sometimes ahead of those who have waited years. The criteria are real. The justifications are plausible. But the optics are corrosive. Residents don't see the spreadsheet — they see the new family moving into a freshly refurbished unit while their own bathroom ceiling caves in.

This dynamic breeds not just resentment, but political disengagement. The older tenants stop voting. They stop writing letters. They stop believing their voice means anything — because it hasn't meant anything for years. In that vacuum, myth rushes in. Conspiracy theories, Telegram whispers, bitterness that calcifies into alienation. And all the while, policymakers insist the system is working — as if perception were irrelevant to legitimacy.

Worse still is the way this tension is morally policed. To question the fairness of allocation is to risk being branded racist, reactionary, or cruel. So people stay quiet. And that silence builds into something heavier — a kind of psychic eviction. One day, they look at the estate they helped build, and they no longer see themselves in it.

The state has not merely reprioritised — it has redefined who the state is for. It now sees its role not as balancing duties, but as managing optics and avoiding backlash. And in doing so, it has triggered the very backlash it fears.

The entitlement of the long-resident is not bigotry. It is memory.

And memory, when denied, becomes something else entirely.

Historical Memory and Estate Identity

An estate is more than a cluster of buildings. It is a story told over generations — a geography of effort, failure, and belonging. The trees planted by tenants who once worked in the dockyards. The football posts welded by a dad long dead. The mural of a miner painted during the strikes. These are not sentimental tokens. They are civic relics, living artefacts of the working-class idea of Britain — communal, stable, proud.

But that idea is fading. Gentrification never arrived in places like Nora's estate. What arrived instead was a quiet, creeping reassignment: not redevelopment, but reallocation. The working-class memory that once animated these places is being overwritten — not by new life, but by neutrality. Emergency housing schemes do not preserve murals. They do not understand the tree was planted for someone's son. They do not care about the names carved into the concrete benches. To them, the estate is just a unit — a vessel for temporary placement, a line on a government spreadsheet.

There is a kind of violence in this forgetting. When new residents are moved in with no sense of the place's history — and when existing tenants are told to make space, be patient, stop complaining — a cultural rupture opens. The physical buildings remain, but the emotional infrastructure collapses. No more summer barbecues. No more key-swapping when someone's lost theirs. The old codes of the block — who knocks where, which door stays unlocked — vanish.

Nora watches this unfold not with rage, but with a sorrow so deep it has stopped needing words. She remembers the estate in the 1980s: the Christmas lights strung across balconies, the sound of her son's bike wheels against the railings, the neighbour who kept bees illegally on the roof. That world is gone. Not because people changed — but because the system stopped caring about memory.

Housing policy today is ahistorical by design. It is responsive, transient, ideologically sanitised. It pretends that space is empty until it is filled. But in estates like Nora's, space is haunted. It carries grief, pride, lineage. When policy arrives with no recognition of that, it doesn't just displace bodies. It disinherits memory.

And in that vacuum, even the living begin to feel like ghosts.

Dignity Deferred

There is a particular kind of humiliation that comes not from being poor, but from being poor in public — and being expected to be grateful for it. Council tenants like Nora are not only made to wait for basic repairs or live in mould-infested flats — they are also expected to keep quiet, to be patient, to understand that things are difficult for everyone. Their pain must remain quiet, bureaucratic, and clean.

But there is nothing clean about waking up to black mould above your bed. Or stepping over syringes in the stairwell. Or watching, year after year, as the communal garden you once pruned turns into a fly-tipping site. Dignity dies in small increments: the call that never gets returned, the repair job that never gets done, the neighbour you once knew moved out without warning. And when you complain — if you complain — you're told it's not a priority.

Dignity, in this context, is not about pride. It's about recognition. Acknowledgement that your life has value, that your time matters, that your past is worth preserving. But in the age of perpetual emergency, that recognition is reserved for others — those with greater needs, more dramatic backstories, or those backed by advocacy networks with legal teeth. The native elderly, the long-resident poor, have no such lobby. They have only memory, and the slow erosion of place.

In this atmosphere, even time feels stolen. Nora waits six weeks for the council to send someone to fix her radiator. The man arrives, looks at it, shrugs, and leaves. "Budget cap," he says. Meanwhile, two doors down, a new family arrives. The flat has been painted, refitted, given new locks. Nora is told she must be understanding. She is. But something inside her folds in on itself — a quiet resignation that no one sees.

This is what it means to be deprioritised by policy and depersonalised by discourse. The state no longer says, "This is your home." It says, "You are lucky to still be here." And so people like Nora begin to internalise a kind of institutional self-loathing. They shrink. They simplify. They make fewer calls. They start preparing to leave long before the letter arrives telling them to go.

The state never tells them they're not welcome. It just stops answering the phone.

Visibility and Invisibility

Ghosts are not supernatural in places like Nora's estate. They are aesthetic facts. They move through stairwells unacknowledged. They exist in the form of unanswered emails, peeling paint, flickering hallway lights. In this context, to become a ghost is not to die — it is to be seen less, heard less, mattered less.

Visibility in Britain has become a matter of narrative legitimacy. The more your pain can be translated into a policy priority — refugee status, minority protection, victimhood within a defined legal frame — the more the state and its institutions will respond. But the pain of the long-resident working class is illegible. It does not trend. It cannot be filmed. It carries no novelty. It is an ache, not a spectacle.

Nora exists in this twilight — watched, yet unseen. Her complaints are logged, but unanswered. Her presence is recorded on tenancy rolls, but erased from discourse. She is not poor enough to be rescued, nor visible enough to be feared. She is simply residual — the last remnants of a civic order that no longer fits the national script.

Meanwhile, the new arrivals are hyper-visible. This is not their fault. But the contrast is stark. They are assigned case workers, translators, escorted access. And they are spoken about — by politicians, by NGOs, by journalists. They are, if not welcomed, at least *engaged*. Nora is not. The only time someone knocks on her door is when something has gone wrong — a fire alarm, a leak from upstairs, a missing child. She is no longer seen as a neighbour. She is seen as a witness — someone who must testify, not participate.

This imbalance breeds a strange spiritual effect: a sense of being *dead in place*. Nora doesn't feel envy. She feels evaporation. A gradual shedding of identity, purpose, and narrative weight. And as the estate fills with new voices, new languages, new rhythms, her own presence begins to feel not just marginal but haunting — a relic that should have been cleared out long ago.

Policy did not do this deliberately. But its logic, compounded by decades of neglect and silence, created a new social category:The administratively undead.

And they do not howl. They just wait.

Non-response and Bureaucratic Fog

There is no dramatic refusal in the way the modern British state neglects its citizens. No one slams a door. No one sends a letter that says "You don't matter." Instead, it practises something more insidious: non-response. A constant, silent buffering. You call, and no one picks up. You write, and no one replies. You escalate, and the portal times out.

For tenants like Nora, this bureaucratic fog is not frustrating — it's maddening. She isn't asking for luxury, just maintenance. Safety. A sense that someone, somewhere, is accountable. But the system now is a relay of deferral. The housing officer blames the council. The council blames central policy. The MP offers sympathy but no solutions. Everyone is polite. Everyone apologises. No one acts.

This polite inaction is how responsibility dies. It's also how power sustains itself. Because in the fog, no one is quite to blame. And in the absence of blame, there can be no redress. So Nora keeps her notes — dates of calls, names of staff, reference numbers. She reads them like a sacred text, a ledger of broken promise. But still, the repairs don't come.

And then something worse happens: the category of "emergency" is redefined. When she calls to report screaming in the corridor, she's told it's not urgent unless someone is bleeding. When the hallway lights go out, it's not a safety issue unless someone has already fallen. When a child disappears, she is advised not to speculate. The burden of proof has shifted — not to those causing the problem, but to those noticing it.

This redefinition is bureaucratic euthanasia. It doesn't kill the body. It kills civic faith. Nora begins to wonder what kind of danger she'd have to be in before anyone would come. She begins to suspect the answer is simple: the kind of danger that produces paperwork.

The estate has become a space governed not by law or trust, but by systemic latency. Things don't get better. They just get unlogged. And over time, Nora realises something awful — the estate isn't being neglected. It's being abandoned.

The system has not failed. It has evolved.And its evolution has no space for those who ask for nothing more than to be remembered.

Cultural Impasse and Speechlessness

The modern British estate is no longer just a place of low income. It has become a site of linguistic and cultural impasse — where shared space does not mean shared understanding. For tenants like Nora, the sounds in the corridor are no longer familiar. The greetings are gone. The small talk has evaporated. She walks past new neighbours with whom she shares walls but no words.

This is not about hostility. It's about mutual unintelligibility. And it creates a kind of civic aphasia — where everyday language fails to do its old work: to negotiate, to comfort, to include. Without a shared tongue, even basic neighbourliness collapses. The woman two doors down cannot explain why her baby cries all night. The man above cannot apologise for the banging. No one is rude. They are simply silent — a silence born not of malice, but of estrangement.

And into this silence enters fear. Not overt, but ambient — the kind that accumulates over time. Nora does not fear her neighbours as individuals. She fears the feeling that her world is slipping beyond legibility. That if something were to happen — an argument, a break-in, a fire — she could not explain, be explained to, or be helped.

The multicultural dream promised enrichment, diversity, colour. And sometimes, that promise is real. But in the unmanaged spaces of modern Britain — the overstretched schools, the under-patrolled estates, the reclassified ghettos — what emerges is not richness, but isolation within proximity. People live beside one another without ever entering each other's realities.

This is especially cruel for the elderly. Language is one of the last bastions of autonomy. To lose the ability to communicate is to become a child again — dependent, anxious, peripheral. Nora feels this acutely. The council once sent interpreters for new tenants. Now they send forms in sixteen languages but none with a human face. The bureaucracy has adapted. The community has not.

And so the estate becomes a place of unspoken tensions. No conflict, no community. Just a hallway where doors close quickly and the air hums with what no one can say. Nora begins to speak to herself — just to hear her own voice.

It is not racism. It is not xenophobia.It is a grief that has no vocabulary.

Symbolic Inheritance

In a society where so many feel they own nothing tangible — no house, no savings, no mobility — what remains is symbolic inheritance. Memory. Place. The right to say: *"I was here, and this meant something."* When even that is taken — or erased through neglect — what's left behind is not just emptiness, but a profound haunting.

Nora's council flat is not valuable by market standards. It's not desirable. But it is hers, in the only way that matters: it holds her son's laughter, her late husband's radio, the plant that never bloomed but she kept anyway. These things are not sentimental clutter. They are the proof of presence — the record of a life sustained in place.

When Nora receives the notice to vacate, there is no outrage. Only silence. She knew it was coming. The council needs the unit for emergency placement. The flats have been reclassified. She is no longer "essential." The logic is airtight. The moral cost is not even registered.

And so she leaves what little she has: a single candle burning on the kitchen counter, a gesture both ritualistic and defiant. The ghost she sees in the hallway — is it her son? Is it herself? It doesn't matter. What matters is that her exit is unrecorded. There will be no obituary. No council report that says she lived there for 47 years. No story filed under "displaced." She is simply gone.

This is what the modern British state does with its long-timers, its obedient citizens, its quiet pillars: it repurposes their homes and forgets their names. The physical inheritance — the flat — is recycled. But the symbolic inheritance — the memory, the rootedness, the web of meaning — is incinerated in a furnace called necessity.

And so we end with a paradox. A flat meant to provide stability becomes a vehicle for erasure. The home meant to shelter the loyal instead expels them. And the state — in trying to house the homeless — manufactures a new kind of exile: the native ghost, displaced not by bombs, but by bureaucratic gravity.

Nora leaves nothing behind except the unlit echo of her presence.And in that echo, a final bequest: loss, unacknowledged.

Part 2 : The Midwife's Silence

Night Ward

The sixth birth began before she'd even finished charting the fifth.

Amira rinsed her hands at the sink, rubbing between each finger with the same mechanical precision she'd learned twelve years ago. The gloves she peeled off made a sound like paper tearing. She blinked twice to clear the sting of sweat from her eyes and glanced at the wall clock. 02:47.

The labour bay was full again. One woman on her back, silent tears streaking her cheeks. Another kneeling, groaning low, the monitor cable half-torn from her belly. A third shouting at her partner, who stood against the wall filming with a phone angled too high.

Amira checked her list. Bed six — primigravida, twenty-two, thirty-nine weeks. No pain relief. No interpreter. Notes written in fractured English.

She stepped into the bay. The woman was clutching her abdomen, panting, her eyes wide and wet.

Amira knelt beside her.

"My name is Amira. I'm your midwife tonight. You're doing well, okay?"

The woman said something in Arabic — or maybe Farsi. Amira couldn't tell. The tone was panic, though. That much was universal. Her partner stood nearby, saying nothing, just watching the space between Amira's hands and the woman's thighs.

A quick assessment: crowning. No time for epidural. No time for the translator, still en route. No time, full stop.

She spoke slowly, calmly.

"Breathe. Push with the next contraction. I'm here."

The woman didn't respond. Just clenched her jaw and turned away.

The next contraction came like a thunderclap. The woman screamed — not just in pain, but in terror — and Amira moved instinctively, guiding, checking, catching. The baby came fast, shoulders sticky, cord loose.

"Girl," Amira whispered, more to herself than anyone else.

She held the newborn for a breathless second. Still. Pale. Slippery.

Then — a cry.

The room exhaled.

The partner put his phone down. The woman sobbed into the pillow. Amira placed the baby on the mother's chest, adjusted the blanket, checked for blood.

Just another one.Six down. Two waiting. Possibly three.

She peeled her gloves off. Tossed them in the bin. Picked up the chart.

Didn't write anything.

There wasn't time.

Amira noticed the phone before she noticed the father's face.

It hovered just above shoulder height, screen turned landscape, lens fixed on her hands. He wasn't filming the baby. He was filming *her*. The way she moved. The way

she touched. The way she worked. She knew the feeling —
being watched not as a person, but as a process.

"Sir," she said quietly. "Could you please lower the
phone?"

He said nothing. Just blinked, then adjusted the angle.

She tried again. "Please. It's hospital policy. No unautho-
rised filming."

Still no response. The mother — slick with sweat and
tears — didn't look up. She was whispering something in a
language Amira didn't understand, clutching the child like
an anchor.

The interpreter hadn't arrived. Again. She was probably covering three wards. Or had been rerouted. Or never
booked properly in the first place. Amira had filled out the
request form at the start of the shift. It meant nothing.

She turned to the father. "If you'd like to speak to someone, we can arrange it. But not now. Not like this."

The man lowered the phone, finally. Slowly. His eyes
didn't meet hers.

Amira stepped out of the bay and leant against the wall,
letting her head fall back for a second. The corridor light
buzzed overhead, pale and jittery. Her skin smelt like latex
and bleach. Her feet ached.

When she returned, the woman was asleep, or pretending. The baby mewled softly against her chest. The father
sat on the plastic chair by the bed, scrolling through the
video with his thumb, watching her hands in slow motion.

Amira picked up the chart. Wrote down the Apgar. Estimated blood loss. Logged the delivery time.

She didn't note the filming. There was no point.

It would be her word against his.

Later, she stood by the staff station, sipping cold tea from
a Styrofoam cup. A junior nurse leant over, whispered:

"They're all recording now. It's like they want to catch you slipping."

Amira nodded, but said nothing.

She looked through the glass toward the bays. Each one glowing with its own pale light, each one a sealed chamber of pain and expectation.

She didn't feel angry.

Just filmed.And replaceable.

Overload

The silence hit before the realisation.

No cry. No squirm. No intake of breath. Just weight.

Amira held the baby in her hands, slippery and too still. She turned gently, checking cord placement, cleared the nose, stimulated the back. Nothing. The mother — a girl, barely out of her teens — looked up, confused, waiting for the sound. The partner stood frozen at the foot of the bed.

A second passed. Then another.

Then Amira whispered: "Call the registrar."

The junior nurse moved. Quiet. Efficient. Head low.

Amira placed the baby on a sterile towel. Hands moving by memory. The mother had begun to shake, her lips forming a question Amira couldn't answer — not yet, not now. She reached out, touched the girl's arm gently, not reassuring but *anchoring*. You are still here. You are still breathing.

The father was filming.

She saw it again — the small red light of the phone screen, half-concealed. Not focused on the baby. Focused on her.

She said nothing.

The registrar arrived, gloved and wordless, nodding once before beginning the checks. Monitors unplugged. Blankets drawn up. The baby was taken away. The partner finally lowered the phone, his hand trembling slightly.

The girl began to wail — not loud, but long. The sound of something tearing that couldn't be stitched.

Amira stayed with her for twenty minutes. She said the words she was trained to say — *"There are people you can talk to. We'll explain everything. It's not your fault."* She hated them all. Not the woman. Not the man. The words. Their emptiness.

When she finally left the bay, she walked straight past the station, into the sluice room, locked the door, and sat on the bin lid.

Her hands shook. Not from grief. From accumulation.

That was the third stillbirth this month. The eighth this year. The numbers meant nothing to anyone but her. They were never patterns. Never trends. Just incidents. Isolated. Tragic. Unavoidable.

She washed her hands again. Slowly. As if scrubbing away something that might spread.

Outside, the ward buzzed with a steady hum — machines, footsteps, muffled voices. Business as usual.

She looked at her hands under the light.

They were clean.

But she didn't feel it.

It was just a sigh.

Not a groan. Not a snap. Just a breath, audible and sharp — the kind of exhale that leaks out when everything is too loud, too fast, too broken.

It came during handover. The registrar had asked why the stillbirth report wasn't logged yet. Amira was still in scrubs, still had the smell of antiseptic in her nose, and was still holding the image of the girl's empty arms in her head.

She said, "I'll file it after the next set." And then, without thinking, she sighed.

The room stopped.

The registrar tilted his head slightly. "Are we... inconveniencing you?"

Amira blinked. "No. Just tired."

He didn't reply. He made a note in his pad.

Later that day, she was called into the matron's office. The room smelt of lemon-scented wipes and reheated food. The matron didn't look up from her screen.

"I've received a note about your attitude on shift."

"My attitude?"

"A staff member observed you sighing during a clinical exchange. It was interpreted as dismissive."

"I'd just come from a stillbirth."

"I understand. But tone matters. Especially in diverse teams. We're under scrutiny, Amira. You know that."

The word hung in the air. Scrutiny.

It didn't mean safety. It meant surveillance.

Amira nodded once. "Noted."

The matron softened slightly. "I'm not saying you did anything wrong. Just... be aware of how things come across. Families are sensitive. Colleagues are sensitive."

She didn't mention the phone that filmed her. Or the father who never made eye contact. Or the girl's face when they took the baby away.

She said nothing.

Back on the ward, a new patient had arrived. Screaming in a language Amira couldn't place. The notes were missing. The interpreter was already in theatre.

The junior nurse asked, "Should we wait?"

Amira stared at the woman. At the monitor. At the hallway beyond.

"Wait for what?"

She went into the bay.

Later, during the post-shift debrief, no one mentioned the stillbirth. No one asked how she was. The registrar reminded them to complete their incident logs "promptly and with professionalism."

Amira said nothing.

The sigh stayed in her throat this time. Unbreathed. Folded into silence.

Supervision

The room was too warm.

Three people sat across from her — a senior midwife from another unit, a liaison from HR, and someone from "staff support services" whose name Amira forgot as soon as it was said. The table was laminated pine, the clock ticked too loudly, and the meeting had the tone of something already decided.

They used gentle voices. Phrases like "concerns raised" and "patterns emerging."

She listened, hands folded in her lap, as they described her behaviour: abrupt tone. Inflexibility. One patient report of "feeling judged." No formal complaints — just observations. A pattern. A shadow.

"Is there anything going on in your personal life that might be affecting your professional demeanour?" the HR liaison asked. She smiled as she said it. A performance of care.

Amira shook her head. "I'm tired. That's it."

"We understand," said the staff support officer. "This is a high-pressure environment. But some of your colleagues have noted tension — especially in culturally sensitive situations."

"What does that mean?"

"Well," the senior midwife leant forward slightly, "you've been involved in three cases recently where communication broke down with patients from non-English-speaking backgrounds."

"There was no interpreter," Amira said.

"Yes, but tone and body language still matter."

"I was delivering a stillborn baby."

A pause.

"We're not questioning your clinical ability," the HR woman said. "But it's important to recognise how we're perceived. Particularly when working with vulnerable groups."

Amira looked at them, one by one. "Am I being accused of racism?"

"No one said that," came the answer, almost in chorus.

"You're here because we want to support you. Help you reflect."

That word again. *Reflect.*

She said nothing. Just nodded once. Enough to end it.

Later, they sent her an action plan: attend a cultural sensitivity workshop. Arrange a check-in with the wellbeing team. Avoid taking solo high-risk cases until further notice.

No mention of the missing interpreter.No mention of the phone that filmed her.No mention of what it costs to hold life in your hands when no one helps you carry it.

She deleted the email.Then deleted the draft she'd written in reply.

When she returned to the ward, she didn't look anyone in the eye.

She just went back to work.

The scream still lived in her ears.

Not loud — not a scream of pain. It was *quiet*. A rippling moan that began deep in the chest and unravelled into silence. The kind that didn't rise — it *collapsed*.

Amira had been in theatre four minutes. The woman on the table — Syrian, nineteen, no notes, suspected placenta previa — had arrived mid-shift, unbooked, barely conscious. There was no family. No translator. Just a folded piece of paper with a name and date of birth. Everything else was blank.

The registrar made the call fast. Foetal distress. Category one. They moved as they'd been trained — efficient, clean, sterile. Amira held the woman's hand while the mask came down, lips mouthing words neither of them understood.

She remembered the woman's eyes — wide and glassy, darting between faces she couldn't name. Panic, even under anaesthetic. Trust offered only by force.

The baby was born limp. Seconds passed. Then a cry.

The woman never heard it. She was unconscious by then, stitched in silence, her body a battlefield claimed by strangers.

Afterward, Amira stayed late. She sat in the supply cupboard and cried — not loud, not performative, just the kind of tears that fall when your body refuses to carry one more moment.

No one asked about the case. There was no debrief. The baby survived. That was enough.

Two weeks later, Amira saw the woman again — wheeled into the postnatal ward, eyes blank, holding her newborn like a foreign object. She didn't smile. She didn't cry. She just stared.

Amira approached her gently. Tried a greeting in Arabic she'd practised online.

The woman flinched. Then turned away.

That night, Amira dreamt of the scream again. But it wasn't the woman's voice anymore.

It was hers.

She woke with her hands clenched into fists, her jaw aching.

The next day, a patient's husband accused her of being abrupt.

The day after that, she called in sick.First time in five years.

She said it was a virus.She didn't say it was the memory of a cut made too fast, too clean, and too necessary.

A cut that never healed.

Empty Cots

They ran out of blankets before dawn.

Not a catastrophe — just another quiet failure. The sort that didn't make headlines or trigger alerts. Just a blank shelf in the supply room and a shrug from the auxiliary nurse folding the last two into thirds to make them stretch.

Amira stood at the cabinet, fingers grazing the empty rack. She didn't move for a moment, staring at the metal grid as though something might materialise. But nothing did. It never did anymore.

She returned to the neonatal bay with one of the remaining blankets draped over her arm. Two infants waited in incubators. One wrapped in a towel. The other still in the scratchy white linen from delivery.

A mother stood nearby, anxious, rocking slightly.

Amira smiled — soft, tired — and offered the folded blanket like an apology.

"Sorry," she said. "Short this morning."

The mother didn't respond. Just clutched her baby and looked away.

On the whiteboard above the desk, someone had drawn a cartoon duck beside the note:*Please return blankets to Laundry A — NOT B. B is contaminated.*

It was meant to be funny.It wasn't.

Amira made a mental note to check the linen request form. She wouldn't. There was no point. Supplies came late, if at all. The shortage had become routine. She had delivered four babies in the last forty-eight hours and wrapped each one in something reused.

Once, that would've horrified her.

Now it was just logistics.

Behind her, monitors beeped in rhythm. A baby cried — high and thin. Another slept under blue light, tiny feet twitching. The ward felt like a factory running on its last bolts. Machines fine. Soul empty.

She caught her reflection in the glass: pale, dark-eyed, mask sliding off one ear.

She didn't recognise the woman looking back.

Across the bay, a colleague leant against the wall, face in her hands. Not crying. Just breathing. Too long. Too hard.

Amira turned away. Gently tucked the blanket tighter around the newborn.

The baby stared at her — wide-eyed, unspeaking — as if it already knew the language of quiet disappointment.

It was around 05:30 when Rachel walked out.

Not with drama. Not in a storm. Just quietly, in the middle of a handover. One moment she was standing at the nurses' station, tapping notes into the system. The next, her ID badge was on the desk, and the double doors were swinging closed behind her.

Amira saw it happen but said nothing. She'd known it was coming.

Rachel had been fraying for weeks — jaw clenched too often, laughter replaced with that brittle kind of silence people wear like armour. She was good. Steady hands. Clear voice. The kind of midwife you'd want in your worst hour. But the shifts had stretched her. The stillbirth last Tuesday. The family that accused her of favouritism. The missing interpreter. The broken heater in delivery room two.

It all stacked up.

They were all stacking up.

Amira followed her into the corridor, caught up with her by the stairwell. Rachel was leaning against the railing, one hand over her mouth, the other clenching and unclenching.

"I'm not doing this anymore," she said without turning.

Amira stepped closer. "You want me to call someone?"

Rachel shook her head. "They'll just log it as stress leave. Tell me to do a survey. Meditate. Take a breather."

Her voice cracked on the word *breather*.

Amira didn't try to comfort her. There was nothing to say that hadn't already been said a hundred times, in locker rooms and tea breaks and tearful toilets. Words didn't hold weight here anymore.

"They'll cover me, won't they?" Rachel asked, more bitter than hopeful.

Amira nodded.

"Someone always covers."

Rachel wiped her eyes with the sleeve of her scrub top, then straightened.

"Tell them I had to go. That I wasn't well. Make it sound clinical."

"I will."

She didn't say goodbye.

She just left.

When Amira returned to the ward, no one asked where Rachel had gone. The notes were completed. The shift staggered forward. The next delivery was already beginning.

There would be an email later. A rota change. A vague update.

No one would mention the tears. Or the silence. Or the fact that Rachel was the fourth midwife this quarter to walk out before breakfast.

Amira adjusted her mask. Took a breath.

And went back in.

Exit

She stood at the sink long after her shift ended.

Hot water. Soap. Lather. Rinse. Repeat.

The ward behind her buzzed like a dying machine — low, constant, filled with the clicks of keyboards and the hollow drone of fluorescent lights. But here, in the small side room off the corridor, there was quiet. Just the rhythmic scrape of soap against skin.

Her hands were raw. The backs of them cracked, thin red lines opening under the lather. But she didn't stop. She rubbed until the water turned cool. Then hot again.

She wasn't thinking of germs. Not this time.

She was thinking of weight. Of skin. Of every infant she'd held in the last seventy-two hours. The living ones, wriggling and loud. The still ones, heavy with absence. The ones who came too early. The ones who came too late.

She was thinking of the mother who didn't scream, who just stared. Of the registrar who rolled his eyes when she asked for support. Of the interpreter who never showed. Of the apology email that said *"We regret the delay and appreciate your patience."*

She was thinking of Rachel's eyes.

She was thinking of hers.

She washed until the soap dispenser clicked empty.

Then she just stood there, palms open, water rushing over skin as if it could erase the memory of what her hands had done. Or failed to do.

A junior doctor passed by the doorway, glanced in, said nothing.

Amira turned off the tap.

Dried her hands with a paper towel. Slowly. Tenderly. As if preparing them for burial.

She didn't go to the locker room. She didn't check the board. She didn't swipe out.

She just walked.

Past the nurses' station. Past the vending machine with the out-of-order sign. Past the noticeboard with smiling photos of staff who had "gone above and beyond."

She moved like a ghost through a place that once called her essential.

At the lift, she hesitated.Then took the stairs.

All the way down.

No one saw her leave.

The front desk was unmanned. The security guard was deep in conversation with a paramedic about football scores. The revolving door turned once, twice, then stilled.

Amira stepped into the cold without her coat. She didn't feel it. Her scrubs clung damp against her arms, her shoes squelched faintly with each step — a sound that, for a brief moment, made her want to laugh.

She didn't.

The car park was half-empty. Early blue light was beginning to edge the horizon. Birds called out from somewhere near the bins. She paused at the edge of the pavement, unsure whether to cross or stand still.

She wasn't expected home. No one waited for her. No children. No partner. Her flat was a silent box two bus rides away — white walls, tea-stained mugs, and a pile of unopened post. A life shrunk to necessity.

She turned left.

There was no plan. Only motion. Her bag was still in her locker. Her ID, her phone charger, the little lunchbox with yesterday's uneaten sandwich. None of it mattered now. She had nothing on her but her name badge and a memory she could no longer carry.

As she passed the staff garden, she paused — out of habit more than interest. The benches were wet. The cigarette butts piled in a corner bucket. Someone had scribbled a message on the side of the planter in Sharpie: *WE DON'T TALK ABOUT THE ONES WHO LEAVE.*

She traced the words with her eyes.

No one called out after her. No footsteps behind. No overhead announcement asking for Nurse Amira to return to Station 3.

She crossed the road. The city opened in front of her, grey and quiet. Traffic lights blinked without purpose. A fox slipped into an alley.

She kept walking.

She didn't cry. Didn't pause. Didn't second-guess.

Not because she felt strong — but because everything that could've broken her already had.

And now, what remained was silence.

Not numbness.

Not rage.

Just... the sound of nothing pulling her forward.

CCTV

The footage was reviewed two days later.

A formality, they said. "Just to complete the incident report."

A junior administrator clicked through the frames — timestamped, grainy, unremarkable. Amira appeared on screen at 06:04, exiting through the main doors. No rush. No distress. Just a slow, steady pace. She didn't glance back. She didn't speak to anyone. She walked straight out of frame and out of the system.

"Was she meant to be on the early shift?" someone asked.

"No. Night cover. Finished at six."

"She didn't clock out."

"Must've forgotten."

The file was saved, logged under a folder marked *Staff Irregularities*. A digital ghost shelved among rota gaps and HR alerts.

In the days that followed, staff filled in the blanks. They always did.

"She seemed tired lately."

"She was solid — never thought she'd just go."

"Probably burnout. Or something personal. Maybe she'll come back after some time off."

But she didn't.

No formal resignation came. No fit note. No voicemail. Just the echo of absence — her name crossed off the rota, her locker cleared by someone else, her ID badge quietly deactivated.

A new starter was assigned to her shifts the following week.

At a safety meeting, the matron mentioned "retention concerns" and urged colleagues to speak up early if they were struggling. A handout was passed around titled *Managing Fatigue in High-Pressure Environments*. No one read it.

Someone stuck a Post-it on the shelf above the staff room kettle:*Leave before the silence gets too loud.*

No one took it down.

Amira's image — frozen mid-step on the CCTV — lived briefly in the admin cloud, downloaded once, then overwritten.

She never contacted the ward again.

She never explained.

She didn't need to.

The footage said it all:No panic.No protest.No drama.

Just a woman in blue scrubs, walking away like it was the most ordinary thing in the world.

And maybe it was.

The ward went on.

Babies cried. Machines beeped. The smell of antiseptic lingered beneath the metallic tang of blood and bleach. The new shift arrived — yawning, adjusting masks, checking clipboards. The rhythm resumed as if nothing had shifted.

No one mentioned the empty chair at the nurses' station. Or the notes unfinished. Or the locker left unlocked, its door ajar like a breath held too long.

At 06:11, one of the infants in bay four began to wail — thin and high and insistent. Then another. By 06:14, the whole ward echoed with need. Newborns calling out with the single, undeniable demand that they be seen. Held. Met.

Amira wasn't there to answer.

A junior nurse moved between cots, trying to keep up. A bottle dropped. A monitor alarmed. The warmth of a hand was replaced by the cool swipe of a device. None of it was cruel. Just stretched.

A few of the mothers sat up slowly, confusion still soft behind their eyes. The long, blood-smeared hours of labour had blurred into fluorescent morning. Some reached for their babies. Others didn't move at all.

The babies kept crying.

In the stairwell, no footsteps echoed.

Outside, traffic began to hum.

No one knew where Amira had gone. But the ward did. The building did. The babies did. They cried in the absence like it was a shape they could feel — an outline of someone who once knew exactly how to hold them.

She didn't look back. Not once.

Because there was nothing left to see. No ritual. No farewell. Just a corridor she'd walked a thousand times, and this time, without return.

The silence she left behind wasn't empty.It was residual.

Like heat from a blown bulb.Like steam from a closed door.Like grief with no name.

In her absence, the ward whispered her story.

Not aloud.

But in the language of unmet eyes and unanswered cries.

Part 2: Critical Essay

The NHS in Crisis

In Britain, there is no symbol more mythologised than the NHS. It is the secular altar at which both left and right genuflect, the shorthand for compassion, and the last great project of national cohesion. And yet, inside its wards, something foundational is breaking.

The modern NHS is not collapsing from cruelty. It is collapsing from triage as ideology. Emergency has become permanent. Scarcity is now structure. And for professionals like Amira — a midwife in a central Birmingham maternity unit — care no longer means presence. It means *selective survival.*

On paper, the NHS still functions. Babies are delivered. Emergencies are treated. But behind those statistics lies an emotional and logistical battlefield. Migrant surges, asylum backlog, and reclassified refugee statuses have rerouted resources, often without clear policy guidance. The result is institutional improvisation: beds doubled up, interpreters unavailable, patients queued in corridors, risk assessments blurred into wishful thinking.

Maternity units have become ground zero for this crisis. They represent life at its most fragile and political tension at its most inescapable. When ten women arrive in labour and only four staff are on duty, who gets the attention? What languages are spoken? What cultural norms must be navigated or ignored? Amira delivers babies under fluorescent lights, praying she doesn't miss the signs of silent distress — signs she once knew by instinct, but now must interpret across translation gaps and unspoken fear.

Meanwhile, native-born patients — often older, poorer, and carrying years of untreated trauma — feel unseen. They notice that they wait longer. That their births are less attended. That they don't understand what's happening around them. They don't blame the new mothers beside them. But they begin to mistrust the system that no longer seems built for them.

And the staff? They crack. Quietly. A reprimand here. A breakdown there. Whispers about racism. Accusations of insensitivity. The pressure isn't just clinical — it's ideological. To question the structure is to risk moral exile. So they don't question it. They cope. Until they can't.

Amira's silence is not apathy. It is collapse. When she walks out of that ward, it is not because she doesn't care. It is because the system has demanded too much of her care, and returned nothing but risk.

The NHS, once a covenant, is now a crucible.And many of its best are burning out without noise.

Emotional Labour and Trauma

In the language of healthcare policy, there are metrics for everything: bed occupancy, wait times, staff-to-patient ratios, incident reports. But nowhere in the spreadsheet is there space for what breaks a person quietly — the accumulation of emotional labour, the repetitive trauma of showing up every day to scenes that should be exceptional but have become routine.

For midwives like Amira, trauma is not a rare event. It is embedded in the shift. Screaming mothers with no birth plans. Miscarriages announced through a translator.

Stillbirths delivered while another patient bleeds two beds away. A father filming her hands instead of holding his wife's. It is the violence of saturation, not aggression — the moral injury of being forced to prioritise life under impossible constraints.

What compounds this trauma is the expectation that it be managed with grace. Nurses and midwives are meant to be maternal, endlessly resilient, emotionally available. But the job now demands that they be counsellors, cultural interpreters, conflict mediators — all while charting notes, avoiding complaints, and covering the shifts of colleagues already broken.

There are no decompression chambers in these wards. No time between deaths and new life. The next cry begins before the last one fades. Amira learns to shut down instinct. She becomes procedural. Checks for breath, for pulse, for dilation. She does not process. She performs. And in doing so, she becomes a machine trained to forget each wound before the next arrives.

Burnout in the NHS is no longer episodic. It is cultural. It is endemic. It is an unspoken epidemic among women like Amira, especially those from working-class or minority backgrounds — those expected to be strong, adaptable, invisible. The trauma is medicalised in the paperwork: "Fatigue." "Stress leave." "Disciplinary review." But what it really is... is soul exhaustion. A kind of interior erosion that leaves the body upright and the spirit gone.

And when these women finally break — not with rage, but with quiet withdrawal — the system gaslights them. "She walked off the ward," the supervisor will say. "Abandoned her post." But they never ask what was done to her first. They never measure what it costs to care in a place that repays compassion with unrelenting exposure to pain.

Amira's silence is not neglect.

It is grief without oxygen.

Ethical Disjuncts

There was a time when medical ethics were anchored in universals: consent, clarity, patient autonomy. But in the modern NHS — and particularly in overstretched maternity wards with high migrant intake — ethics have become improvised, fractured across cultural expectations, language barriers, and institutional avoidance.

Amira knows what good care looks like. She was trained in it — the clear explanations, the gentle authority, the calming of panic through tone and touch. But when a patient arrives speaking no English, accompanied by a husband who insists on speaking for her, Amira faces a terrain she is unprepared for. The interpreter is delayed. The consent forms are unread. The woman screams, resists the exam, grabs Amira's wrist in confusion and fear. And the delivery proceeds not with understanding — but with containment.

This is not malpractice. It is systemic dislocation. The NHS now operates under pressure to provide culturally sensitive care in an environment that offers no time for cultural sensitivity. Staff are encouraged to defer, to adapt, to accommodate. But they are rarely empowered to make confident, clear ethical decisions when norms clash. Should the husband be allowed to film? Should female staff be prioritised regardless of availability? Should pain medication be withheld due to religious observance?

These are not abstract hypotheticals. They are real, daily dilemmas — and no one wants to answer them out loud. Because the risk is no longer just clinical — it's reputational. A single accusation of cultural insensitivity can trigger a review, a suspension, a public shaming. And so, staff like

Amira default to avoidance or appeasement, which creates not safer care, but timid care. Care that protects the institution more than the patient.

In this environment, trust corrodes. Not just between staff and patients, but within staff themselves. Whisper networks form. Resentments build. Some accuse others of being too soft. Others accuse them of being reckless. No one speaks openly — not in meetings, not in shift handovers, not in post-incident reviews. And so the ward becomes not just a site of birth, but of quiet ethical erosion.

Amira is not bigoted. She is not afraid of difference.She is afraid of being punished for misnaming a line she was never trained to see.

And in that fear, the moral core of her profession begins to fray.

Surveillance and Suspicion

Amira is watched more now than ever before — but not in ways that make her feel supported.

In the modern NHS ward, surveillance is everywhere, and none of it is neutral. Bodycams on security staff. Patient relatives filming on mobile phones. CCTVs in corridors. Colleagues logging minor infractions under the guise of "reflection." It is a theatre of oversight — not to ensure care, but to protect the institution. Everyone is accountable. No one is trusted.

For staff like Amira, the scrutiny is racialised, gendered, and classed. A moment of firmness with a patient becomes a tone complaint. A failed epidural becomes a whisper about training gaps. One misstep in a charged cultural context and the language shifts: "inappropriate," "unprofessional," "not in line with diversity expectations." And so she becomes guarded — not just in what she does, but in how she feels.

She notices the patterns. Which colleagues are allowed to raise their voices. Who gets the benefit of the doubt. Who is quietly pulled aside for "a quick word" and who gets written up. The official line is fairness, but the practice is triage by optics. To question something — anything — that intersects with culture, language, or status is to risk being seen not as concerned, but as problematic.

At the same time, Amira is also surveilled from below. Fathers film her with their phones while she examines their wives. Young men stand at the end of beds, arms folded, watching every move. If she objects, she's told to be understanding — "some families are protective." If she asks for help, she's told to de-escalate. She is expected to smile, to perform care like theatre, under a lens that captures everything except context.

The result is a culture of second-guessing. Amira no longer acts on instinct. She calculates. Who's watching? What's being recorded? How could this look in a report? Her movements grow hesitant. Her decisions slower. Not because she doesn't care — but because she cares too much about surviving the job.

Surveillance was meant to keep patients safe.But it has turned the carer into the observed.

And under that gaze, trust curdles.Not just between staff and patient — but within the self.

Policy vs. Practice

The NHS is built on policy. But it runs on improvisation.

Every shift begins with the fiction of readiness: staff rotas pinned to the wall, care protocols colour-coded, posters about dignity and respect laminated in staff rooms. Yet when the real work begins, the gap between what is mandated and what is possible becomes unbridgeable.

Amira walks into her shift knowing the ward is overbooked, the interpreter hasn't arrived, and the registrar hasn't slept. But the system insists on pretending that policy is practice. Officially, every patient has the right to informed consent, pain relief, cultural accommodation, language access, and privacy. Unofficially, there are three midwives for seventeen labouring women, and the ones who shout loudest get seen first.

She is expected to navigate a moral maze with no time, no tools, and no backup. One mother is sobbing through a translation app. Another is refusing a pelvic exam because her husband isn't in the room. Another is haemorrhaging, and no one has signed the consent form. These aren't just clinical dilemmas — they are structural failures dressed up as choices.

Management speaks in euphemism. "Dynamic risk assessments." "Fluid rostering." "Escalation pathways." These terms mask reality: Amira is carrying more than is safe, and everyone knows it. But if she raises the alarm, she becomes the problem. The system punishes those who name what can't be done.

So she doesn't speak. She adapts. She cuts corners she never thought she'd cut. Skips documentation. Makes calls she hopes she won't regret. She does her best — and it is not enough. It never is. But instead of questioning the policies, the system writes her up. A late entry. A missed signature. A patient's husband who complains about her "tone."

There is a cruelty in pretending that care is still what it used to be. That policies written in peacetime can survive a permanent emergency. The gap between ideal and reality becomes a source of guilt. Amira begins to feel like a liar

— not because she has done wrong, but because she must participate in the fantasy that everything is fine.

In the end, it is not one mistake that drives her out. It is the unspoken truth: she was never allowed to work honestly.

And honesty, in this ward, is a liability.

Institutional Shame and Silencing

Amira is not the first to leave.

Before her, there was Lauren — reprimanded for raising safety concerns during a night shift. Then Anita, who refused to sign a false incident report and found herself quietly rotated to bank shifts. Then Mariam, who cried during a disciplinary hearing and was told she might need resilience training.

The NHS doesn't fire its dissidents. It absorbs them. Discredits them gently. Wraps them in concern and redirection. But it does not listen.

The silencing is rarely direct. It comes in soft, bureaucratic tones: "That's not helpful right now." "Let's not catastrophise." "That kind of language could be misinterpreted." Staff are reminded to speak constructively, to channel concerns "through the proper forums." But those forums are black holes. Minutes are taken. Nothing changes.

The deeper shame is structural. Everyone knows the system is failing, but no one can admit it aloud. To name it would be to implicate not just management, but the entire political fiction that the NHS is coping — even thriving. And so institutions protect the illusion. Staff are praised for "going above and beyond," even as they unravel. When they collapse — emotionally, clinically, ethically — the shame is personalised. Burnout becomes their fault.

Amira felt it in her review meeting: the subtle suggestion that she was becoming "difficult," "overly emotional," "culturally insensitive." Not because she did something wrong — but because she asked why basic standards had vanished. Her questions were noted. Her attitude was flagged. Support was offered — counselling, coaching, a chance to "reset."

She declined.

Because what she needed was not therapy. It was truth. And the institution has no language for truth.

That is the final silence. Not just the quiet that descends in an exhausted ward at 3 a.m., but the institutional muting of those who see too clearly. Amira's silence is not weakness. It is resistance to a system that demands complicity, smiles, and euphemisms.

The shame is not hers. It belongs to the structure that asked her to sacrifice everything — time, sleep, certainty, safety — and then scolded her for noticing.

When she walked out, she took nothing. No badge. No apology. No note. Just her breath. And the decision not to give it away anymore.

Psychological Collapse

Amira does not fall apart in one day.

There is no breakdown. No dramatic sobbing in the sluice room. No panic attack in the corridor. What happens is slower — an internal erosion that moves like rot through the beams of a house. By the time it's visible, the structure has already failed.

The first sign is disconnection. A patient screams and Amira hears it like a radio in another room. She nods when colleagues speak but doesn't absorb the words. Her body performs — checks vitals, adjusts IVs, murmurs reassurance — but her mind drifts. Time bends. Days smear into one another. She begins to forget names. Then tasks. Then why she came here at all.

This isn't laziness. It's psychic triage. Her nervous system has been on high alert for too long. The adrenaline has dried up. She is no longer a responder. She is a witness. Trapped inside a carousel of suffering she can no longer enter or exit.

The second sign is fear — not of danger, but of herself. She no longer trusts her own judgement. She second-guesses every move. Did I check that baby's Apgar? Did I chart that haemorrhage? Did I imagine that tear? She rereads notes three times. Doubles back to rooms she just left. The fear isn't that she'll make a mistake — it's that she already has, and the system will pounce.

Then comes the dissociation. She stops dreaming. Stops listening to music. Eats standing up. The flat becomes a halfway house — just somewhere to sleep before the next shift. On days off, she doesn't leave bed. Not because she's resting. But because she can't face noise, or people, or daylight.

None of this is recognised by the institution. It looks like fatigue. Maybe stress. Something manageable. HR sends a link to a mindfulness webinar. Her supervisor suggests yoga. But what she needs is relief, not reflection. She doesn't need a mirror. She needs someone to say: *Yes. It is as bad as you think. And you're right to feel broken by it.*

Psychological collapse in healthcare doesn't always look like crisis.Sometimes it looks like competence with all the colour drained out.

When Amira finally walks out, it's not a scream for help .It's a quiet refusal to die on duty.

The Abandonment Frame

There's a particular kind of abandonment that happens in public service — when the state asks everything of a person, then quietly disappears the moment they can no longer give. It's not loud. It's not even personal. It's procedural.

When Amira leaves the ward that final shift, no one follows her. No one stops her in the corridor. No alarms go off. She simply vanishes between one shift and the next — logged out, unrostered, eventually archived under "Did Not Return."

The hospital doesn't ask why. It already knows.And it doesn't care. It can't afford to.

This is the abandonment frame: a systemic posture that appears caring but is functionally indifferent. It wraps itself in the language of support — wellbeing, resilience, flexibility — but beneath it is only attrition. The expectation is that if one leaves, another will step in. If not today, then soon. The body count is measured in rota gaps, not funerals.

Amira is not exceptional. She is typical. She is one of thousands of healthcare workers across Britain who disappear from the NHS each year — not because they were weak, but because they were abandoned while still standing. Asked to perform under impossible conditions, then labelled unprofessional for collapsing.

This abandonment is not just institutional. It is cultural. Society has developed a selective compassion — public applause for nurses during pandemics, but silence during staff shortages; documentaries about overstretched wards, but no votes for systemic change. The public mourns the NHS in theory but recoils from the truth of what it has become: a machine that eats its carers.

Amira's silence is not a failure of voice.It is the sound left behind when all explanations have been exhausted.

Her walkout is not a tantrum. It is a last act of agency.

And the ward she leaves behind? It won't collapse. It will absorb the loss. It will close one room, stretch one shift, ask one more student nurse to step up. The system survives. The soul does not.

The tragedy is not that Amira left.

It's that she was never truly there to begin with — not as a person.Just as a unit of care.

And when units break, they are replaced. Not remembered.

Part 3 : The Playground Divide

Alfie's World

Alfie held the badge in his hand like it might melt.

It was round, plastic, red and gold, with the words "WELL DONE!" in thick bubbly letters. He'd been given it during morning assembly by the deputy head — for reading out loud in class. Not because he'd wanted to, but because the teacher had picked him, and he hadn't said no fast enough.

The class had clapped. The teacher had smiled. The moment had passed.

Now, he walked home slowly, badge in his pocket, thumb rubbing the smooth surface as if trying to polish it away. His rucksack bumped against his back, too light for comfort. The pavement was cracked and uneven. He avoided the loose slabs by instinct.

His mum was on the sofa when he got in, one leg tucked under her, phone in hand, Jeremy Kyle murmuring on the telly behind her. She looked up when the door clicked.

"You're late," she said.

"Miss kept us behind."

"Did you eat?"

He shrugged.

She went back to her phone.

Alfie pulled the badge from his pocket and held it out. "Got this."

She looked at it, nodded once. "That's nice, love."

He waited for more. There was no more.

He placed it gently on the arm of the sofa, next to the empty mug and the rolled-up TV guide.

She didn't react. He picked it up and pocketed it.

In the kitchen, he opened the fridge. Bread, milk, half a cucumber in clingfilm. No ham. No butter. He poured himself a glass of water and drank it slowly, eyes fixed on the magnet stuck to the fridge door: "Every day is a new chance to shine."

It had been there since Year 2. He used to believe it.

Back in his room, he sat on the edge of the bed and turned the badge over in his palm. The back had a small plastic pin. It didn't work properly. The clip was loose.

He thought about wearing it tomorrow. Maybe.

But the thought sat heavy. Too visible. Too easy to mock.

He placed it on the windowsill, beside the pencil sharpener and the stone he'd found at the beach last summer. Things he didn't use, but didn't want to throw away.

Outside, the sun was already going down.

He pressed his forehead to the cold glass and stared at the playground behind the flats.

It was empty.But he still didn't feel alone.

Later that evening, he placed the badge back on the sofa.

She picked it up without thinking, and turned it over, squinting at the slip of paper taped to the back.

"Who's this from?" she asked, holding it out.

"Miss Patel," Alfie said.

"Is that the little one or the one with the scarf?"

He shrugged. "Both have scarves."

She laughed, but not at him. Just tired.

She held the paper closer. "What does this say?"

Alfie leant over. "It says I read in assembly. And... something about good pronunciation."

She nodded slowly. "Looks like it says... 'excellent clarity during shared text'? That it?"

He nodded. But he could see she wasn't sure.

"Handwriting's shite," she added, letting the badge fall back onto the cushion.

He picked it up and held it tight.

"Good job, anyway," she said, flicking the TV volume up. A judge show now. Americans shouting at each other.

He sat next to her and watched the colours on the screen blur into noise.

Something small curled up inside him — a feeling not quite disappointment, not quite shame. Just drift.

She didn't mean to make it nothing. She was just tired. Always tired. The kind of tired that made her squint at anything written, like it wasn't for her.

At school, the other parents sometimes helped with spelling homework. His didn't. She said it was *his job to know the difference between 'there' and 'their.'* He'd learned not to ask more than once.

He stared at the badge in his hand, the tape peeling now. The ink was smudged.

He could still make out the last line: "Alfie spoke with real confidence."

It was true. For once, he had.

But saying the words aloud in class had been different from saying them at home. At school, he had to speak slowly, clearly, because no one around him did. The kids shouted in other languages. The classroom buzzed with accents and half-said things. When he spoke, it felt like stepping off a cliff.

He always wondered what it sounded like to them.

To her, the badge was a scrap of plastic and biro.

To him, it was a map. A fragile one. Half unreadable, even at home.

Lost in Class

Alfie sat at the back of the room, near the radiator that only worked when the weather didn't need it.

Miss Patel was reading from the whiteboard, slowly, clearly, with pauses between each phrase. It was about Roman roads — how they were straight and strong, and how people still walked them today.

Alfie listened, but no one else did.

The classroom hummed with low chatter in a dozen dialects. At the front, two girls whispered in Arabic, giggling behind their sleeves. A boy near the window flicked through a Polish-English dictionary, mouthing words silently. In the corner, the TA was translating in Urdu for a boy who never made eye contact.

Miss Patel didn't raise her voice. She never did. She just spoke louder into the void, as though if she said the words slowly enough, they might become real.

Alfie wrote "straight roads" in his book, then stopped. He didn't know what came next.

He looked around. No one else was writing. One boy was drawing a dragon. Another had his head down on the table. No one was listening. Not really.

When Miss Patel asked a question — *"Why did the Romans build straight roads?"* — no one answered.

Alfie raised his hand.

She smiled, relieved. "Go on, Alfie."

"Because it was faster?" he said, unsure.

"Exactly. Direct routes. Very good."

No one clapped. No one even looked at him.

He glanced at the boy beside him, who was carving something into the desk with a compass. The letters were in Cyrillic.

Alfie didn't know what they meant.

At break, he didn't go outside. He stayed in the library, between the shelves, tracing his fingers along the spines of books he'd already read. The librarian smiled at him, but didn't speak.

He liked it there — the stillness, the English. The paper didn't talk back in foreign sounds.

He sat on the floor with a book about whales. Read the same sentence three times.

The blue whale's heart is the size of a small car.

He imagined being that big. That strong. That steady.

He imagined what it would sound like to speak, and be heard, all the way across the sea.

It happened during PE.

They were meant to be playing dodgeball, but the balls were half-flat and the lines on the hall floor were faded. Miss Farrow tried to explain the rules, but most of the class were already shouting, pushing, arguing in their own languages. She blew the whistle, gave up, and told them to "just play."

Alfie didn't want to. He stood near the edge of the court, arms crossed, eyes on the fire exit. The games never made sense anymore. No one passed. No one played fair. It was all noise and chaos and someone always ended up crying.

He tried to move out of the way as one of the balls bounced toward him, but a boy — tall, older, with sleeves too long — shoved past him to grab it. Alfie stepped back.

"Watch it," he muttered.

The boy turned. Said something sharp in another language. Alfie didn't understand.

"I said watch it."

The boy narrowed his eyes. Stepped closer. Then — fast, casual — punched him in the shoulder. Not a hard punch. Not a proper fight. Just enough to sting.

Alfie stumbled, caught his breath.

Miss Farrow saw. She had to have seen. She was standing right there.

But she only blew her whistle and called, "Keep it friendly, boys."

Alfie stared at her. Waited for something more.

Nothing.

He didn't retaliate. Just rubbed his arm and walked to the edge of the hall.

The boy laughed — not cruelly, just like it didn't matter. Because it didn't.

At the end of the session, Miss Farrow called Alfie over.

"You okay?" she asked, like she already knew the answer.

He nodded.

"Sometimes there's a bit of misunderstanding. Don't take it to heart."

He nodded again.

"Try not to provoke, yeah?"

"I didn't."

"I know. It's just— things get heated."

She meant well. He could tell. But she looked tired. Worn down. Like she'd said the same thing a hundred times.

Alfie walked back to the classroom without saying another word.

That night, when his mum asked how school was, he said, "Fine."

Because it was easier than explaining that getting punched didn't matter —not when you couldn't prove anyone cared.

Fence Line

It started on a Tuesday, just before the bell.

The playground was noisy — always was — full of bouncing footballs, screeching swings, kids yelling across languages. Alfie stood by the far edge, near the wire fence where the grass turned to mud and the trees pressed in from the estate beyond.

He liked the corner. It was quiet. No one played there.

That day, he saw someone standing by the far end — just beyond the bins, near the broken gate. A figure. Not a teacher. Not a kid either, or not exactly. Just... still.

Alfie squinted. The sun was low behind them. He couldn't see the face. Just the shape — long coat, pale hands, hair the colour of old wood.

The figure was watching him.Not the others. Just him.

He looked away. Looked back.

Still there.

Then the bell rang, sharp and metallic, and the figure was gone.

No footsteps. No gate creak. Just vanished.

He didn't say anything at lunch. Didn't draw it. Didn't write it down.

The next day, it happened again. Same spot. Same stillness.

The third time, he walked closer. Slowly. Pretending not to look. But when he glanced up — it was already watching him. Eyes dark, unreadable. Mouth moving.

Not speaking. Mouthing.

No more games.

That's what it said. He was sure of it.

He didn't tell Miss. She wouldn't listen. Would say it was imagination. Would log it on some sheet. Call it "a safe-guarding concern" and smile too much.

He didn't tell his mum either. She'd just say he needed more sleep.

That night, he lay awake, staring at the ceiling. The sentence looped in his head. Not scary. Not even sad. Just... final.

No more games.

He didn't know what it meant. Not exactly. But something inside him — something quiet and old — did.

And the next day, he didn't go to the fence.

Not because he was afraid.

But because he was sure the figure would be there.

And he wasn't ready to hear what it would say next.

The figure came every day after that.

Always in the same spot — half-shadowed behind the broken fence, just where the trees met the edge of the tarmac. Never moving. Never closer. Just there.

Alfie tried to ignore it. Focused on his lunch. Laughed too loudly at nothing. But his eyes always drifted to the corner. And it was always there.

Watching.

On Thursday, he stood still and watched it back.

The world around him blurred — the clatter of the climbing frame, the screech of laughter in three different tongues, the football thudding against walls. None of it mattered.

Only the figure.

It lifted a hand — slowly, deliberately — and pointed at him.

Then again: the mouth moving.

Three words. Slow. Measured.

No. More. Games.

Alfie didn't move.

He didn't feel scared. He felt known.

He mouthed the words back.

The figure smiled. Not kindly. Not cruelly. Just… in reco gnition.Like it had been waiting for him to understand.

Then the bell rang.

And just like always, the figure was gone.

He didn't rush inside. He walked slowly, deliberately, every step placed like punctuation.

In the classroom, Miss Patel was explaining fractions. The words landed on him like rain on dry concrete — soaking through, slow and useless.

Someone passed him a worksheet. He stared at it. Didn't lift his pencil.

Outside the window, he could just make out the top of the fence.And beyond that — nothing.

He thought about the words again.*No more games.*

He didn't know who the figure was. Or what it wanted.

But he knew it wasn't lying.

There were no games left.

Not here.Not for him.

Red Card

It was during circle time.

Miss Patel had written a question on the board:"What makes someone feel welcome?"

The class sat cross-legged, restless, picking at sleeves, whispering in hushed tones. Some of the kids understood. Some didn't. A few nodded because others did. One boy picked his nose and wiped it on his jumper.

Alfie sat between Leila and Pavel. He didn't speak unless he had to.

Miss Patel pointed to the question. "Let's share. Who wants to start?"

Hands rose. Safe answers followed.

"Smiling."

"Sharing lunch."

"Saying hello in their language."

Miss Patel beamed. "Lovely."

Then she called on Alfie. He hadn't raised his hand.

"Alfie, what do you think makes someone feel welcome?"

He hesitated.

"I dunno."

"That's okay. Just try."

He shrugged. "Maybe if they spoke English?"

The room went still. Not loud — *still*.

Miss Patel blinked. "Pardon?"

Alfie shifted. "Just... it's hard when no one talks to you. Not in English, anyway."

Leila made a face. Pavel snorted.

Miss Patel's smile tightened. "That's not a very kind thing to say, Alfie."

He froze. "I didn't mean it unkind."

"Language is important. We mustn't make others feel excluded."

He looked around. No one was looking at him.

"I feel excluded," he said, but it came out too quiet.

"What was that?"

"Nothing."

Miss Patel moved on, but her tone had changed — a stiffness in her voice, a slight frown behind her eyes.

At break, he stayed inside. Pretended to be tired. Pretended not to care.

He sat by the radiator and picked at the Velcro on his shoes until it frayed.

Later, when his mum asked why he looked miserable, he said, "Got told off."

"For what?"

"Saying something wrong."

"Was it rude?"

"No."

She shrugged. "Then don't worry about it."

But he did.

Because he hadn't meant to be rude. He'd only told the truth. And the truth — in that room, on that day — had been punished.

He lay in bed that night and tried to imagine what he should have said. Smiling? Sharing? Speaking in their language?

But he didn't know how.

He only knew his own.

And it wasn't welcome anymore.

By the end of the week, Alfie couldn't even remember what he'd said.

It had become a story passed between classrooms — that Alfie had said something *"unkind," "insensitive," "not inclusive."* No one used the word racist, but the shadow of it hung in the air, heavy and implied.

He hadn't been sent home. There was no official sanction. Just the look from Miss Patel, the whispered meeting with the teaching assistant, the note scribbled in his planner: *"Needs to reflect on word choice."*

He read that line five times. It didn't sound like him.

At lunch, the other boys moved to another table. Slowly. Not cruelly. Just... without him.

By Tuesday, even the TA seemed distant. She corrected his tone when he asked for a new pencil. Told him to "think about how that might come across." He didn't know what she meant.

Everything he said now felt dangerous.

So he stopped saying much at all.

At home, he stared at the mirror in the hallway and practised sentences. *Can I go to the toilet? That's not fair. Please stop doing that.* They all sounded wrong in his mouth. Flat. Accused.

He felt like he'd slipped out of the script, and no one would hand him the next page.

In his workbook, he drew a small figure standing in a field with no sky. Just a blank space above it. He didn't label it. Didn't colour it in. Just left it there, ungrounded.

Miss Patel didn't comment.

She didn't say much to him at all anymore.

On Friday, he got a red card for "attitude." It stayed in his tray all day, folded neatly.

When he showed his mum, she frowned.

"What did you do?"

"I don't know."

"Well, they don't give these out for nothing."

He didn't answer.

He didn't know how to explain that he wasn't being punished for doing something wrong — but for no longer knowing what was right.

That night, he dreamed of the figure at the fence.

It said nothing this time.

Just stood there, waiting.

Speech Delay

The speech therapist's office smelt like lemon wipes and dust.

Alfie sat on a small blue chair, knees too high, hands in his lap. Across from him, the therapist — Miss Hughes — flicked through laminated cards with pictures on them. She smiled too much.

"This one?" she asked, holding up a drawing of a ladder.

"Ladder," Alfie said.

She nodded. "And this?"

"Bus."

"And this?"

He paused. It was a hedgehog, but it had been drawn strangely — all curve and spike and no face. He hesitated.

"Hedgehog," he said quietly.

Miss Hughes made a note. "Good, good."

She didn't say what wasn't good.

Back in the staffroom, she spoke to Miss Patel in low tones.

"His expressive range has narrowed. He's not using prepositions consistently. Vocabulary's thinner than expected for his age. I think we're seeing signs of regression."

Miss Patel frowned. "He was doing fine in September."

Miss Hughes nodded. "Well. Something's shifted."

They filled out a form. The word *referral* appeared three times. *Monitoring* twice.

No one asked Alfie how he felt.

At lunch, he sat by the bin shed, picking at the laces of his shoes. The playground felt louder than usual — voices in Hindi, Arabic, Polish, something else he couldn't place.

He watched two boys argue, neither using words he understood.

He didn't try to join in. He'd stopped trying.

He opened his lunchbox. Cheese sandwich. Apple slices going brown. He ate one, slowly.

From the corner of his eye, he saw a shape at the edge of the fence.

Not the figure this time.

Just a shadow. A gap in the hedge that hadn't been there before.

He stared at it until the bell rang.

That night, he told his mum they'd taken him to see someone about his talking.

"What for?" she asked.

"Said I don't use words right."

She frowned. "What words?"

"I don't know."

"Did you say something you shouldn't have again?"

"I don't think so."

"Well, you must've."

He nodded, because it was easier.

In bed, he whispered the word *hedgehog* over and over until it stopped sounding like anything.

It came in the quiet, after the fridge had stopped humming and the telly downstairs had clicked off.

Alfie lay in bed, the covers pulled up to his chin, eyes fixed on the ceiling. He didn't move, didn't blink. He'd learned that stillness made the dark feel smaller.

The shadow in the corner formed slowly — not sudden, not sharp, just... there.

Same shape as before. Tall. Thin. Still.

It stood by the wardrobe, just beside the cracked bit of wallpaper where the cartoon rocket used to be. Its arms hung by its sides. Its head tilted slightly, like it was listening.

Alfie's throat tightened, but not with fear. Not exactly.

He sat up slowly, not taking his eyes off it.

"Why're you here?" he whispered.

The figure said nothing. Didn't move.

Then, softly, it mouthed something. Not the words from the playground.

This time, just one:

"Gone."

Alfie blinked. "Who's gone?"

The figure tilted its head the other way. Mouth moved again.

"You."

Alfie didn't speak.

Outside, a car door slammed. Somewhere far off, a dog barked once, then stopped.

He looked again. The figure hadn't moved. But it felt closer now.

Not in distance — in meaning.

He whispered, "I didn't go anywhere."

But he wasn't sure that was true.

He hadn't spoken in class all week. Hadn't played football at break. Hadn't drawn maps. Hadn't told his mum about the second red card. Hadn't looked anyone in the eye except Miss Hughes, and even then, only once.

Maybe he had gone.

Not all at once. Just... piece by piece.

He lay back down, facing the wall. Pulled the covers over his head.

Didn't say goodnight.

When he looked again, the figure was gone.

But the room didn't feel empty.

It felt like something had taken root there. Quiet and slow.

Not to scare him.

Just to remind him.

Withdrawal

On Monday morning, Alfie didn't get out of bed.

His mum shouted up the stairs twice. No response. On the third go, she stomped up, phone in one hand, toast in the other.

"What's this?" she said, pulling the curtains open. "You're not sick."

Alfie pulled the covers tighter.

"I'm not going."

"Like hell you're not. Get dressed. Bus is in twenty minutes."

He didn't move.

She stood in the doorway, waiting for something — a tantrum, a sniffle, an excuse. But he just lay there, eyes fixed on the ceiling.

"I don't want to," he said.

"That's not a reason."

"I can't."

She lowered the toast to her side. "What do you mean, you can't?"

He didn't answer.

She stared at him, then sighed. Sat on the edge of the bed. "Is someone bothering you?"

"No."

"Then what is it?"

He shook his head. "It's loud. And no one talks to me. Or they do, and I don't get it. And Miss thinks I'm rude."

His voice cracked a little on that last word, and he hated it.

She exhaled, long and slow.

"You've got to go, Alfie. That's just life. We all do things we don't like."

He said nothing.

She stood. "Right. I'll call the office. One day. But that's it."

He nodded, not because he agreed, but because the conversation was over.

When she left, he lay there in the half-light, the window throwing long stripes across the carpet. He stared at the ceiling and imagined the map again — his map. The one with no labels. No colour. Just outlines and space.

He wondered if the figure would be at the fence today. If anyone else had ever seen it. If it was waiting.

He didn't want to find out.

Downstairs, the toaster popped.

He closed his eyes and listened to the sounds of the house — the familiar rhythm of his mother's slippers, the clink of a spoon, the radio murmuring through static.

All of it so known.

So safe.

So far from the hallways he no longer understood.

The map started as a circle.

Just a rough outline in pencil, smudged at the edges. Then a few lines — roads, maybe. Rivers. Boundaries that didn't quite connect. He drew slowly, carefully, erasing often. Not to fix mistakes, but to blur things. To make the edges less certain.

He didn't label anything. No country names. No cities. No compass rose. Just lines crossing other lines, floating shapes, clusters of dots like constellations. It looked like a place — but a place half-remembered, not learned.

He worked in silence. The telly was on downstairs, but it sounded far away.

In one corner, he drew a house. Not his house. Not anyone's, really. Just four walls and a triangle roof, a door with no knob.

In the middle, he drew a fence. It cut through the page, long and jagged.

On the other side, a figure. Thin, alone. Watching.

He coloured everything in grey.

No green grass. No blue rivers. Just graphite.

He didn't think about what it meant. He just drew. Letting his hand move without asking questions.

When his mum came in later with a sandwich, she saw the map and paused.

"What's that, love?"

He shrugged. "Nowhere."

She looked at it, nodded slowly. "Looks cold."

He didn't reply.

She set the plate down and left the room.

He stared at the drawing for a long time.

Then, with the side of his palm, he smudged it all. One big sweep across the paper. Blurred the house. Wiped the fence. Erased the figure.

He left only the circle.

A shape with no contents.A place with no name.A boy with no map.

Part 3: Critical Essay

Language as Access and Alienation

Language is not just communication. It is access — to identity, to instruction, to belonging. In the context of a British primary school, it is the gateway through which children learn not only facts, but how to exist in a shared cultural space. And when that language collapses under the weight of multilingual saturation, the school becomes not a community, but a cacophony.

Alfie, the central figure in *"The Playground Divide,"* is not unusual. He is a native English speaker in a classroom where English is no longer dominant. His learning environment is filled with sounds he cannot parse, codes he cannot crack, peers he cannot understand. The playground, once a place of imagination and social play, becomes a frontier — full of mouths he cannot read and games he is no longer invited to join.

This phenomenon is not anecdotal. Across inner-city schools and even smaller towns, the rise in English as an Additional Language (EAL) students has transformed classroom dynamics. In some areas, more than 50% of pupils do not speak English at home. That in itself is not a failure — bilingualism is not a threat. But the infrastructure to support it is absent, and the speed of demographic change has far outpaced the pedagogical response.

Teachers are overwhelmed. Lesson time bleeds into translation sessions. Behavioural corrections are missed because verbal cues don't land. Group work breaks down because shared vocabulary is missing. Alfie doesn't just fall behind academically — he loses social footing. Humour doesn't translate. Sarcasm fails. He cannot read the unspoken rules of new peer hierarchies.

Language has become tribal. It clusters — Polish with Polish, Arabic with Arabic, Somali with Somali — and the English speaker, ironically, becomes the linguistic outsider in his own land. He is not marginalised by design, but by omission. And as teachers are told to prioritise inclusion, his silence is misread as confidence or disinterest.

But it is something else: disinheritance. He begins to speak less. Think less. Retreat inward.

The tragedy is not that other children speak different languages. The tragedy is that no one has the courage to name the consequences. In trying to welcome all, the system has left some children functionally stranded in their own country.

Alfie cannot say what he feels.And soon, he may not feel able to say anything at all.

Behavioural Disparities

In a classroom fractured by linguistic and cultural divides, behaviour management ceases to be consistent. It becomes calculated risk — for both the teachers enforcing rules and the students navigating them. What was once straightforward discipline now demands translation, caution, and political sensitivity. The result is an uneven system in which some children are quietly excused and others are quietly punished.

Teachers know this, even if they rarely say it aloud.

In Alfie's case, he sees injustice but doesn't have the language or status to name it. A classmate throws a chair and is calmed down with soft words in another language. Alfie kicks a bin and is sent out of the room. A new boy shouts during assembly — the staff call it trauma. Alfie sighs when his book goes missing — he's told not to be disruptive.

These moments add up. Children understand fairness better than adults do. They recognise double standards instinctively. And when they see that the same action draws different responses depending on language background or cultural expectations, trust collapses. Discipline loses credibility. Resentment festers.

This isn't about racial prejudice. It's about institutional paralysis. Teachers are terrified of complaint. A raised voice might be misunderstood. A referral could be mislabelled. A standard punishment risks being reframed as bias. So they adapt. They soften. They reclassify behaviour as "expression." They lower expectations for some — and tighten the grip on others.

This creates a silent hierarchy of accountability. Children like Alfie — native-born, quiet, unexceptional — become the bearers of disproportionate scrutiny, because they are seen as safe to correct. They're the ones who "should know better." The ones who don't have a social worker or a translator in the room. The ones whose parents aren't expected to lodge a complaint.

But Alfie does not feel seen. He feels cornered. When he lashes out, it isn't rebellion — it's a plea for equal footing. But it's read as defiance, or entitlement. He is punished, but not understood.

In schools that claim to be inclusive, the true privilege is this:To misbehave and still be protected.Alfie doesn't have that privilege.

He must behave perfectly in a system that has already decided he doesn't matter quite as much.

Curriculum Collapse

The curriculum was once Britain's great equaliser — a shared canon through which children, regardless of class or background, were inducted into the cultural architecture of the country. It offered continuity. Identity. A sense that everyone was learning from the same map.

That map is now torn.

Alfie sits in a classroom where the content of the lesson no longer anchors him. The texts have changed. The history is diluted. The stories are chosen less for their meaning than for their perceived neutrality. Shakespeare is optional. The Tudors are shortened. Religious education avoids specifics. Cultural references are flattened into generalities. Even phonics is adjusted to accommodate pronunciation patterns unfamiliar to English.

This isn't malice. It's accommodation. But the effect is the same: Alfie senses that the curriculum is being edited in real time — that what once felt firm is now fluid. What's removed is not just knowledge, but confidence.

Teachers are under pressure. To diversify. To decolonise. To avoid offence. What began as an effort to broaden horizons has — in places — become an avoidance of anchor points altogether. The Britishness of the curriculum has become embarrassing, something to tiptoe around. And so Alfie is taught stories that mean less and less to him, and are only marginally more meaningful to his classmates.

Meanwhile, his parents — themselves products of a firmer educational era — struggle to help. Homework now includes culturally curated reading lists they don't recognise. Mathematics is taught in methods they were never shown. Even the calendar of the school year has shifted — new holidays, new sensitivities, new avoidance zones.

This fragmentation undermines the very idea of shared education. The classroom becomes not a place of cohesion, but of parallel learning, where some children grasp the subtext while others translate the surface. The curriculum becomes a diplomatic document — careful, diluted, and fragile.

For Alfie, the result is subtle but corrosive. He is not angry. He is lost. He cannot articulate why nothing sticks. Why the stories he's told feel rootless. Why school now feels like a waiting room, not a place of discovery.

When a curriculum no longer reflects the society it's meant to sustain, the child stops looking outward.

He looks down. Or worse — he stops looking at all.

Mental Health in Children

Alfie doesn't know he's slipping. No child does — not at first.

He isn't diagnosed. He isn't disruptive enough for referrals. He isn't violent, or withdrawn in the way that raises alarms. He's just... quiet. A little slower to answer. A little more tired in the morning. Less eager to speak up. More prone to staring at corners.

This is how mental health decline looks in children like him — gradual, muted, invisible against a backdrop of louder needs.

In overstretched, linguistically fragmented classrooms, teachers can't catch every flicker. The focus is on those in crisis. Alfie is not in crisis — he is in erosion. A daily dulling of curiosity and confidence, compounded by isolation he cannot name. His friends don't play with him anymore. He can't follow the jokes. The rules of the playground have changed, and he was never told the new ones.

When the speech and language therapist finally sees him, they note "regression in expressive language". It's framed clinically. Neutral. But the truth is brutal: Alfie is losing his words.

Not because of any disorder. But because he is learning not to speak. He has discovered — faster than any adult intended — that silence is safer than error. Better to stay quiet than misstep in a space where every word might be misunderstood, mocked, or missed entirely.

Children need feedback. Need eye contact, response, mirroring. When those vanish — when half the class doesn't share your vocabulary, and the teacher is over-whelmed — speech becomes futile. Alfie internalises that futility. He doesn't know how to say "I feel excluded," so he says nothing. Doesn't know how to explain that he's frightened of a world with no fixed rules, so he shrinks.

He is not mentally ill. He is mentally unmoored.

And in an institution that prides itself on inclusion, there is no protocol for this kind of loss. No intervention for the child who fades, rather than breaks. The system waits for him to crack — by then it will be too late.

Language is not just a skill.It is a tether to the self.

And when that tether snaps, children don't always fall.S ometimes they drift. Quietly. Out of reach.

Institutional Abdication

Schools have always done more than teach. For genera-tions, they have been frontline institutions of social order — feeding the hungry, identifying abuse, stabilising frac-tured families. But in recent years, that quiet heroism has collapsed under the weight of demands they were never meant to carry.

What remains is institutional abdication — a slow, sys-temic retreat from the responsibilities that once made schools civic anchors.

For children like Alfie, the signs are everywhere. His school no longer has a permanent headteacher — just a "transitional leadership team." The pastoral officer is shared across three sites. The Special Educational Needs Coordinator (SENCO) is off sick. Assemblies are infrequent. There's no school play this year. No library hours. No one left to supervise lunch unless a volunteer shows up.

These are not isolated gaps. They are structural symptoms of a system in retreat. Where once schools were buffers against social breakdown, now they are repositories of that breakdown — expected to absorb it, manage it, and conceal it from public view.

Multilingualism has accelerated this collapse. With dozens of first languages spoken among pupils and only one or two trained support staff, the school can no longer communicate effectively with many of its parents. Letters go untranslated. Behavioural notes are misunderstood. Cultural tensions are suppressed, not resolved. Teachers learn to avoid confrontation, to tolerate breaches of conduct they would once have addressed.

No one is trained for this. There is no roadmap for a school where half the class cannot understand the fire drill. Where safeguarding forms are mistranslated. Where complaints are filed in languages that must be subcontracted for interpretation.

So the school responds the only way it can: by doing less.

Fewer detentions. Fewer interventions. Fewer honest conversations. The safest path is passivity masked as inclusivity — to smile, de-escalate, defer.

But the children notice. They know when adults are overwhelmed. They see which rules bend, and for whom. They absorb the message: nothing is fixed. No one is in charge. If things get bad, no one will help.

And in that realisation, a deeper injury is inflicted — not physical, not academic, but moral.

Alfie's school is not failing because its staff are bad.It is failing because the institution itself has surrendered.

And the children are left to teach themselves how to survive.

Class, Race, and Fear

There is a quiet fear running through British classrooms — not of children, but of adults. Teachers, especially those in multicultural schools, are no longer just educators. They are navigators of race, class, politics, and perception. And in this landscape, fear of being misunderstood outweighs the duty to act.

In Alfie's school, discipline is no longer a neutral act. It is a performance fraught with risk. Teachers must ask themselves: Will this be misread? Will this parent escalate? Will this decision be framed as bias? The effect is not balance — it is paralysis.

The result is unequal enforcement. White working-class boys like Alfie often receive harsher correction for smaller infractions. They are easier to discipline because they are seen as less volatile, less protected, less likely to escalate. There is no cultural complexity in Alfie's behaviour, no social worker attached to his file. He is not "at risk" — so he is punished by default.

Meanwhile, when a child from a more sensitive category acts out, staff hesitate. They soften their tone. Delay action. Frame it as trauma or miscommunication. This is not compassion — it is professional survival.

Teachers are not racist. They are frightened.

Frightened of being recorded. Reported. Suspended. Cancelled. One mistake, one poorly chosen phrase, one confrontation in the wrong context — and their career is over.

So they tread carefully. But careful teaching is not the same as honest teaching. And it is certainly not the same as leadership. It creates an imbalance in the classroom: Alfie sees others push boundaries that would crush him. He doesn't hate them — but he begins to feel something worse than hate: irrelevance.

Class intersects with this fear in brutal ways. White working-class children are not seen as vulnerable. They are seen as resilient, even when they're failing. Their frustration is read as aggression. Their silence as indifference. Their anger as entitlement. No margin for context. No allowance for grief.

So Alfie learns to internalise. To comply. To say nothing.

He learns the most dangerous lesson of all:That fairness isn't real — and that speaking out won't change a thing.

This is not equity.

It is quiet discrimination — polite, unspoken, and policy-proof.

The Invisible Friend Archetype

When institutions fail children, imagination steps in to fill the void. For some, this manifests as escape — stories, fantasy, invention. For others, it becomes a surrogate for companionship. And in Alfie's case, it emerges as something both tender and disturbing: a figure glimpsed at the fence line, mouthing silent warnings — a presence only he sees.

The invisible friend is not new. It is a known mechanism of child psychology — a way to externalise fear, to test boundaries, to cope with isolation. But in Alfie's world, this figure isn't playful. It doesn't invite mischief or offer comfort. It is spectral, repetitive, silent. It mouths one phrase: *"No more games."*

This is not fantasy. It is cognitive protest.

Alfie creates the figure because he cannot trust the adults around him. The teachers are overwhelmed. His mother is tired. The rules keep changing. No one explains why he's punished more harshly, why he can't understand the other kids, why he feels alone even in a crowd. So the mind supplies what the world will not: a witness. Someone who sees, who echoes his confusion, who reflects back the chaos in a language only Alfie understands.

Psychologists call it displacement. But in this case, it's something deeper — a kind of haunting. A child's unconscious recognition that something has gone missing: fairness, security, predictability. The ghost isn't of a dead person. It's of a dead structure. A vanished order.

The figure Alfie sees doesn't hurt him. It doesn't comfort him either. It simply watches. Just like he does — at lunch, in the classroom, on the walk home. Always observing. Never participating. The invisible friend is his mirror — not of who he is, but of what he is becoming.

And this is the true cost of institutional failure in childhood:When systems fail to nurture, the imagination doesn't grow wild.It turns inward. It ossifies. It builds silent witnesses instead of dreams.

Alfie's ghost is not a symptom of illness.It is his only honest companion in a dishonest environment.

The adults around him do not see it.But it sees them. And it remembers.

Futureless Maps
Alfie draws maps.

Not of the world — but of a world. His own. Crayon lines curve and stop abruptly. Streets without names. Houses without windows. Trees with no leaves. There are no flags. No labels. Just outlines. Borders that bleed into nothing.

When asked what the map shows, he shrugs. "I don't know," he says. "It's just where I go sometimes."

In the classroom, it's easy to mistake this for play. But in truth, Alfie's map is a diagram of disorientation — a child's attempt to sketch meaning in a place where meaning no longer holds. He doesn't understand the social geography around him. He doesn't see where he fits. So he draws what he does know: absence, edges, the empty space where belonging should be.

This is not uncommon. In classrooms where language has fragmented, where discipline is uneven, and where identity is politicised before it is understood, children retreat from coherence. They stop building futures. They stop imagining stability. Instead, they reproduce what they see: systems without clarity, places without direction, stories without endings.

These aren't the chaotic scribbles of creative abandon. They are the soft blueprints of grief.

In Alfie's world, no one talks about the future. There are no long-term projects, no plans beyond next term. His mother is too tired. The school is too busy. The authorities are too remote. He's not encouraged to imagine who he'll be — only how to behave until then.

This absence of projected self is devastating. Childhood should be about narrative expansion — the joyful stretching toward what could be. But when the present feels alien and the past is discredited, the future becomes a blank space too painful to colour in.

Alfie draws maps with no destination because no one has shown him where he's going.

He is not rebelling. He is responding. To a society that no longer speaks in continuity. To a school that speaks in caution. To adults who speak in scripts. He responds with silence and lines — and in those lines, the contours of a country that once offered direction, and now only offers delay.

The map is not incomplete.

It is accurate.

Part 4: Freezer Vans

The List

Malik stared at the sheet in his hand. A4, double-spaced, clipped to a clipboard that smelt faintly of bleach.

Collection Route 3 – Environmental Health (Special Duties)Six addresses. All marked with codes: *OD, ND, Undiscovered*. No names. Just postcodes and case numbers. One had an asterisk. He didn't ask why.

The man issuing the sheet — Gareth, bald, ex-Army, all wrists — gave a brief nod. "New rota's been merged. Low-capacity mortuaries up north, so you'll be doing pickups direct. Most'll be domestic. A few... less clear."

"Less clear?" Malik asked.

"Found in hostels. Some canal pulls. No ID yet." He tapped the sheet. "Follow the route. Log the time. No extras unless authorised."

Malik folded the paper once, then again. Slid it into the dashboard slot beside a half-used bottle of sanitiser.

The van was waiting — white, nondescript, the rear fitted with a chilled compartment and heavy-duty straps. The doors hissed when they opened. The cold wrapped around his ankles as he stepped up.

This wasn't what he'd signed up for. His last contract was for fly-tip clearance and biohazard removal. Needles, mattresses, rats. Bad, but impersonal.

This was different.

"You're covered under Section B," Gareth added, handing over gloves. "No next-of-kin contact. No media interaction. Keep it civil, keep it quiet."

Malik nodded.

He started the engine. The van rumbled, thick with its own breath.

As he pulled out of the depot, the city blinked awake around him — grey streets, flashing traffic lights, bin bags split open like broken promises. A man in a hoodie pushed a trolley full of metal down the pavement, whistling.

He removed the folded paper from the dashboard. The first address was ten minutes away. A stairwell flat above a betting shop. He glanced at the clipboard again. *Male. Approx 30. OD suspected.*

He didn't know the name. He wouldn't be told the name.

The radio played quietly — a talk show, someone complaining about fuel prices, laughter in the background.

Malik turned it off.

The city moved past him — not fast, not slow, just *onward.*

He tightened his grip on the wheel.

The list sat beside him now, like a passenger.And for the first time, he wondered who would be on the next one.

The building smelt like wet socks and burnt oil.

Malik climbed the stairs slowly, gloves already on, body bag folded under one arm. The fluorescent lights above flickered, buzzing faintly like dying insects. On the third landing, a police officer stood with arms crossed, trying not to look bored.

"Environmental?" the officer asked.

Malik nodded. "Collection."

The officer pointed to the alcove beside the lift. "There."

The boy couldn't have been more than seventeen. Slumped against the wall, legs splayed awkwardly, one trainer off. His hoodie was zipped up to the chin. His eyes were open but unseeing.

Next to him lay a foil wrap, scorched and torn. A lighter. A mobile phone with a cracked screen, still lit up with missed calls.

Malik crouched, careful not to let the bag brush the wall. He checked the tags — pre-logged, correct postcode, correct case number. No ID.

The boy's hand was curled into a loose fist. Malik hesitated a second before gently straightening the fingers.

No pulse. No warmth.

He lifted him with slow efficiency — cradling the back, supporting the legs — and guided him into the bag. The zip caught once. Then closed with a sound too final for how young he looked.

The officer spoke again. "Family not notified. No match yet."

Malik didn't reply.

He carried the bag down the stairs alone. No gurney. No assistance. Just the weight of someone who hadn't made it past whatever line he'd been trying to cross.

Outside, the van door yawned open. Malik slid the stretcher in and fixed the straps. The refrigeration unit hissed softly as it kicked into gear.

He stood by the open door for a moment.

The city moved around him — cars passing, phones ringing, someone laughing down the street. A busker played a tinny cover of a love song around the corner.

No one noticed the bag.

No one asked who it was.

Malik got back into the van, started the engine, and checked the list again.

Five more.

One with an asterisk.

He pulled out, joining the flow of traffic like he was just another delivery driver on a Tuesday.

And maybe he was.

Canal Watch

The canal ran slow that morning — slick and green under a sky like brushed steel.

Malik parked at the towpath, hazard lights blinking against the fog. Two police vans were already there. A rope cordoned off the embankment. A man in hi-vis stood knee-deep in the water, guiding the stretcher toward the concrete edge.

Malik stepped out of the van, nodded at the constable, and walked to the tape."Male," the officer said. "No ID. Clothes suggest recent arrival. Possibly crossed the previous night."Malik didn't ask for more.

The body had already been zipped, water pooling at the seams of the bag. The feet poked out slightly — bare, pale, swollen.

By the time Malik returned with the stretcher, a small group had gathered by the railings. Three older women in fleece jackets. A teenager with headphones around his neck. A man in paint-spattered trousers sipping from a takeaway cup. They weren't shouting. Weren't asking questions. Just standing — still, quiet, watching.

The police tape fluttered lazily. The water rippled like it had secrets it no longer cared to hide.

Malik avoided eye contact as he opened the rear doors. He slid the stretcher out and locked the wheels. The body bag was damp, the black vinyl streaked with silt and canal scum. He covered it with a tarp, more out of habit than necessity.

No one said a word.

The man with the coffee muttered something to the teenager, who didn't reply. One of the women crossed herself, slowly.

Malik lifted the stretcher. As he did, the tarp shifted slightly. A corner of the man's face became visible — just the curve of a cheek, one swollen eyelid, waterlogged skin pale as wax.

No one gasped. No one turned away. This was not the first body pulled from the canal.

The officer helped him load the stretcher into the van. It slid into place beside the boy from the stairwell. Malik closed the door gently, as if sound might disturb something.

"Anyone coming to identify him?" he asked.The officer shook his head. "Doubt it. Might get a call from Border Force. Or not."

Malik nodded, returned to the driver's seat. As he turned the ignition, he glanced up.The group was still there. Staring at the van like it carried something they couldn't name but already knew.Not horror. Not outrage.Just recognition.

A boy had drowned last winter. A woman the summer before. No one put flowers down anymore. The canal had become what it always threatened to be — a grave no one blessed.

Before pulling away, Malik looked in the rearview mirror. Not at the road, but at the quiet shape in the back.

It had taken hours, probably, to drift into that bend of the canal. Maybe longer. The body had been caught on a submerged trolley — the officer said it like it was normal.

The group remained in the mirror for a few seconds.Then the van turned the corner, and they disappeared.

The radio came on — a newsreader talking about housing pressures and emergency intake. Malik turned it off.

As he drove, he glanced at the clipboard. 'Unknown male. Non-UK national. Approx. 20.' Nothing else. Not even a guess at a name.

The canal ran parallel to the road for a while, silent and watchful. Malik imagined the body floating there before dawn — face to the sky, the water holding him like a second skin. He wondered if the man had known where he was. If anyone had told him.

He blinked and looked away.

Next address: a hostel. Suspected overdose. Basement level.

He tightened his grip on the wheel. Behind him, the refrigeration unit hummed. Steady. Cold. Unconcerned.

By the time he reached the next stop, he'd forgotten the group's faces.

But not the way they'd looked at him.

Like he was driving something sacred.

Or something they'd all been waiting to see.

The Names

The hostel was tucked behind a shuttered café, its windows barred and grey with condensation. Malik knocked once, then pushed the door open.

Inside, the air was thick with bleach and cheap air freshener. The manager — a tall woman with red eyes and no makeup — gestured toward the back staircase without speaking.

"Second floor. Room 12."

Malik nodded.

Room 12 smelt of instant noodles and mould. The bed was unmade. A TV flickered blue in the corner. The man lay on the floor, half in shadow, his hand still gripping a torn paper bag.

There was no sign of violence. No sign of care, either.

Malik crouched, unzipped the body bag, and opened it out across the floor. The man had already begun to stiffen. Malik worked quickly, carefully, as he always did. Right arm. Left arm. Legs bent, lifted. One motion at a time.

As he reached for the zip, something shifted.

A whisper.

Low. Dry. Barely sound at all.

He froze.

The whisper came again — a breath of syllables, not language. Just the shape of speech, as if the body had saved its last word for the moment it was being packed away.

It was a name. Maybe.

"Eli... shah..."

Malik's throat went dry. He looked at the man's face. Eyes closed. Lips parted. No movement. No breath.

Just silence.

He zipped the bag slowly.

Tighter this time. Careful not to pull it too fast.

Downstairs, the manager was filling in a form. She didn't ask if it was done. Just passed him the pen. Her hands shook slightly.

Malik loaded the stretcher without speaking.

Back in the van, he wrote the name on a scrap of paper. Not official. Just his own.

Elisha.

He folded the paper and slid it into the dashboard.

Not for records.

Just so someone had said it.

The van was full now. Bodies. Stories. Exits no one would notice.

Malik drove toward the depot, the city stretching ahead like a question.

He didn't turn on the radio.

He listened instead.

Just in case someone else had something left to say.

The next day, he told himself it had been nothing.

A sound. A breath. A shift in the air. Not a name. Not a voice. Not real.

He told himself that as he shaved. As he buttoned his shirt. As he clicked the van doors open and slid into the seat.

The slip of paper was still in the dashboard: Elisha.He didn't throw it away.

The first call was from a care home. Elderly male, natural causes. No family. No assets. Just a life signed off by an administrator.

Malik arrived mid-morning. The nurse on duty didn't look up from her clipboard. "He was in Room 3C. Quiet one. Didn't talk much."

The room was small — bed neatly made, books on the shelf. The man lay curled, arms across his chest, face sunken but calm. He looked asleep, almost thoughtful.

Malik opened the bag, checked the tags, and moved methodically.

Halfway through the zip, it happened again.

A whisper.Dry. Crackling like heat on plastic.

This time: "Ray."

He froze, heart knocking once — hard.

The room was silent.

He looked at the man's face. The lips were closed. The chest unmoving.

But the air held something — a pressure, as if a word had just been spoken and was still hanging between surfaces.

Malik finished the zip.

Back in the van, he reached over to the dashboard. Placed a second slip of paper beside the first.

Ray.

He didn't tell anyone.

At the depot, Gareth asked how the run went. Malik shrugged. "Standard." No one asked more.

That night, at home, he sat by the kitchen window long after dark. The house was quiet — his daughter at a friend's, his phone face down. He stared at the notes on the table. Two names. No proof.

He wasn't afraid.

But he wasn't at ease either.

It wasn't superstition. It wasn't delusion.

It was something else.

Recognition.

Not of the voices — but of their insistence.

As if the bodies didn't want to be remembered.They just didn't want to be filed.

The Supervisor

The third name went on a napkin.

It came from a man found in a shopping centre stairwell — no ID, no phone, just a bus ticket in his pocket and the faint smell of antiseptic. Malik zipped the bag slowly, as always, and heard it clearly this time.

"David."

No one else in the stairwell. Just flickering lights and CCTV no one would watch.

At the depot, Gareth was waiting by the van.

"Need to talk," he said, folding his arms.

Malik stepped out, the back doors still ajar. "What about?"

Gareth gestured toward the dashboard. "Been flagged you're keeping personal notes."

Malik blinked. "What?"

"In the van. Handwritten entries. Not part of the log."

"I'm just writing down—"

Gareth raised a hand. "Doesn't matter what. Just don't. Looks unprofessional if the wrong person checks."

"They're names."

"Unconfirmed names. From unverified sources."

Malik didn't speak.

Gareth stepped closer. "Look, I get it. You see a lot. You hear things. But this isn't a diary service. It's public contract work. Our job is process, not memory."

"They matter."

Gareth sighed. "Mate, none of it matters. That's why we're the ones doing it."

He clapped a hand on Malik's shoulder, turned and walked away.

The van door swung shut on its own.

Inside, the napkin sat folded beside the other notes.

Malik stared at them for a moment, then slid them all into his coat pocket.

Not out of defiance.

Out of respect.

Later that day, he didn't write down the fourth name. He heard it — barely — from a girl pulled from behind the bins behind a petrol station. Young. No paperwork. Just a hospital bracelet with a barcode.

The name came just as he pulled the zip closed: "Mina."

He didn't reach for a pen.

He just whispered it once under his breath, barely louder than the van's hum.

Mina.

The name landed in the air like a feather.

Not official. Not filed.

But said.

The list was left on the break room table — six pages, double-sided, stapled in the corner. Malik noticed it because of the red ink. Gareth never used red.

At the top:

Q3 Response Unit – Rota Allocation & Exposure Logs

Printed three days ago.

He flipped through it idly at first, skimming the columns — van numbers, route codes, pickup types, "biohazard class," "external contact risk." Then he saw the names. Not of the deceased — of the drivers. Staff IDs. Exposure tallies. Tick boxes.

Each name followed by a string of codes, then a percentage.

Malik stopped when he reached his own.

Khan, M.Driver ID 311-AVExposure Index: 88.2%

Next to it: a note.

"Pending fatigue referral. Monitor for signs of burnout/noncompliance."

He stared at the words for a long time.

No one had spoken to him. No meeting. No welfare check. Just a number on a sheet. He was being tracked like a cracked pipe or a faulty van tyre.

He read it again.

Noncompliance.

He knew what it meant. The notes. The slowness. The quiet refusals.

He folded the page and slid it under his coat.

Gareth walked in moments later, chewing on a protein bar.

"Heading out again?" he asked.

Malik nodded.

Gareth didn't look at him. "Good lad."

In the van, Malik didn't start the engine right away. He sat with the door open, the breeze touching his face like a question.

He reached into his pocket and pulled out the slip with Mina's name on it.Looked at it. Folded it again. Put it back.

Then he took the exposure sheet from his coat.

Read his name one more time.Like it belonged to someone else.

He didn't throw it away.

He drove with it sitting on the passenger seat — crisp and weightless, like it wasn't tracking the slow vanishing of a man still doing the job.

Return to Sender

The canal looked different at night.

Darker, yes — but also calmer. Less like a forgotten place and more like something waiting. The water moved just enough to break reflections, distorting the streetlights above into rippling question marks.

Malik stood by the railings, hands in his coat pockets, the cold seeping through slowly. The van was parked just out of sight. Empty. For now.

He hadn't meant to come here. Not really. The route was done. The paperwork was filed. But his hands had turned the wheel this way without asking his permission.

The towpath was empty. No police tape. No crowd. Just the smell of algae and something metallic underneath.

He looked down into the dark.

It was the same stretch where they'd pulled the migrant boy — the one with no name, no papers, no weight in the system except the physical kind.

He leant against the railing and closed his eyes.

The hum of the refrigeration unit echoed in his memory. The sound of zippers. The voice — or imagined voice — whispering names he never asked for but couldn't forget.

He said them now, under his breath. "Ray. Elisha. Mina."

The words vanished into the air like steam.

And then he heard another name.

Not from the canal. Not from the past.

From behind his teeth. His own voice.

"Malik."

It didn't feel like a whisper.

It felt like a confirmation.

He opened his eyes.

The water looked the same.

But now it felt like it was watching him too.

He turned to leave.

One last glance at the canal, at the black ribbon of water coiled beneath the footbridge, and then he stepped back onto the path. Gravel shifted underfoot. The van's headlights blinked through the trees, waiting like they always did.

Then he heard it.

Soft. Distant. Impossible.

"Layla…"

He stopped.

The sound wasn't sharp. It didn't echo. It settled.

Like breath against his ear.

He turned, scanning the path behind him. No one. Just branches. Fence. A cigarette butt glowing faintly in the dark near the bins — unattended.

"Layla…"

This time, the voice wasn't even trying to be loud.

Just sure.

His heart thudded, slow but deep. He walked back toward the railing. Looked again at the canal.

Empty.

No ripples. No figure. No one leaning over the edge.

But he knew what he'd heard.

His daughter's name — said the way he said it. Not shouted. Not frightened. Just spoken. Familiar. Too familiar.

He reached for his phone. Checked the time. Checked for messages.

Nothing.

Layla was with her friend. Movie night. Pizza. A room full of thirteen-year-old girls and Instagram laughter. She was fine. He knew she was fine.

Still, he called. Let it ring once. Twice.

"Dad?" she answered. Slightly annoyed.

"You good?"

"Yeah. Why?"

"No reason. Just checking."

"Okay. I'm with Mia. Can I go?"

"Yeah. Sorry."

She hung up.

He stood there for a long time.

The night was colder now. The wind tugged at the corner of his coat. But the sweat on his palms had already cooled.

It wasn't about fear. Not really.

It was about proximity. How close the names were getting. How thin the membrane had become between what was real and what was logged. Between the voices he heard and the ones he hoped to never hear.

He returned to the van.

Didn't start it right away.

Just sat in the cab, staring into the mirror.Not at the road.

At the empty stretch behind him.

Final Route

The depot was quiet when he arrived.

End of shift. Late. Too late for anyone to be clocking in, too early for the cleaners. The floodlights buzzed above the loading bays, casting long shadows across the yard.

Malik parked beside Bay 4. Killed the engine. Sat there for a moment, hands still on the wheel.

Then he climbed out and walked to the back.

The van was colder than usual. He could feel it through the steel before he even opened the doors.

He clicked the latch. Swung the doors wide.

Empty.

No stretcher. No straps. No bags. No forms.

Nothing.

He stood there, staring at the space that should have been full.

He checked the log. He'd marked a collection for 17:40. Pickup confirmed by phone. Flat in Leyton. A woman. No name yet.

He remembered the call. The address. The lift not working.

He remembered the door being open.

He remembered her face.

But there was no body.

Not here. Not anywhere.

He checked again.

Still nothing.

He ran a hand over the interior wall, fingers brushing the hooks where the belts usually hung. Bare. Clean.

Like it had never held anything at all.

He stepped back and looked into the dark space — into the cold, hollow cube that had become his second home.

And for the first time in weeks, he felt something he hadn't expected.

Not fear.

Relief.

A moment of stillness that didn't ask for logging. A breath that didn't demand paperwork. A silence that didn't need to be processed.

He closed the doors gently.

Stood in the yard for a long time, looking at the other vans lined up like teeth.

He got back in the van and started the engine.

He drove to the edge of the yard. Past the bins. Past the barrier gate left raised. Past the sign that read *"Council Property — Authorised Vehicles Only."*

The air felt clearer beyond it.

Lighter.

He didn't look back.

Not once.

He just drove until the only sound above the engine was his own breath and the faint hum of traffic, far ahead, calling.

The motorway was empty at that hour — just a long, grey ribbon disappearing into the mist.

Malik didn't know where he was going. He hadn't turned the satnav on. He hadn't touched the clipboard since Leyton. The van moved by muscle memory, drifting past service stations and exit signs he didn't read.

The fog began about twenty miles out — low at first, then thick, swallowing the hedgerows, the lay-bys, the blue motorway signs.

He didn't slow down.

The world outside the windscreen turned to blur. White lines. Brake lights. Shapes dissolving.

Inside, the van was quiet. The hum of the refrigeration unit had stopped hours ago.

He glanced at the rearview mirror, even though he knew it would show nothing.

Still, he looked.

Just empty space.

No body. No bags.No name waiting to be written down.

He could have turned around.

Pulled into the next junction. Found a café. Called it in.

Instead, he kept driving.

Through the fog. Through the quiet. Through the weight that had stopped feeling like weight and started feeling like truth.

This wasn't escape.

It was refusal.

To log. To carry. To pretend.

He passed a sign: Services — 2 miles.

Didn't turn.

The fog thickened. The headlights caught it in cones of dull silver.

And in that moment, Malik thought he heard something.

Not a whisper.

Not a voice.

Just... his name.

Said gently. Not behind him. Not in his head.

Beside him.

He didn't check the seat.

He didn't need to.

He kept driving.

The road disappeared into the mist, endless and unresisting.

And Malik, for once, didn't feel like the one delivering the forgotten.

He felt like he'd finally joined them.

Part 4: Critical Essay

Who Counts the Dead?

There is no ceremony for the dead in Britain's neglected quarters — just collection. A body is logged, zipped, loaded. Paperwork is filed. If the name is known, a line goes to next of kin. If it isn't, it disappears into the system with a time stamp and a freezer slot number.

This is the world Malik inhabits in *"Freezer Vans"* — not as a mourner or investigator, but as a driver. A council worker. A quiet cog in the unspoken industry of death. He collects the bodies no one talks about: overdose victims, rough sleepers, migrants found in canals, pensioners dead for days before anyone noticed.

In the era of civic withdrawal, the question is no longer *how do we grieve?* but who gets counted at all?

There is an emerging division in death — not moral, but procedural. Migrant fatalities often trigger a cascade of re-action: press releases, diplomatic calls, NGO mobilisation. They become data points in national conversations. But the local dead — particularly the white working-class poor — vanish quietly. Their deaths are chalked up to lifestyle, mental health, "existing conditions." No vigils. No press. No outrage.

This isn't about competing tragedies. It's about visibility.

Malik doesn't differentiate between the bodies. They weigh the same in his van. But the system does. He sees which names trigger paperwork, which ones get whispers in town halls, and which are dropped off and forgotten before the bag even cools.

And he feels it — the hierarchy of worth. The invisible triage that outlives people.

The state used to bury its citizens with dignity. Now it barely notices when they disappear. This isn't a failure of empathy. It's a logistical philosophy: stretch services, tighten criteria, bury discretion under budget lines.

Malik is not political. He is tired. He is practical. But every time he loads another stretcher, he sees what no spreadsheet will show: that some deaths echo, and some are absorbed in silence.

The morgue doesn't ask questions.The van doesn't protest.

But the road remembers.

Bureaucratic Sanitisation

Malik does not see tragedy.

He sees fields in a spreadsheet. Case numbers. Body temperatures. "Pick-up confirmed at 07:14." "Delivered to Site B." Death has been flattened into function — not to dehumanise deliberately, but to manage discomfort. It's not denial. It's formatting.

This is the process of bureaucratic sanitisation — the quiet, procedural dissociation from what is being handled. In local government systems, the language of death has been replaced by euphemism: "decedent," "unclaimed remains," "end-of-life logistics." Each phrase is a soft glove around the truth.

Malik has been trained not to react. The protocol is clinical: verify ID (if available), tag toe or wrist, zip carefully, lift with a second person, if necessary, record time, maintain dignity. The last phrase — *maintain dignity* — appears on every form, but nowhere in the action. What does dignity mean, anyway, in a van that smells of disinfectant and rubber? In a cold room lined with shelves of people no one claimed?

Sanitisation is not inherently cruel. It began with good intentions — to protect workers, to shield the public, to prevent emotional collapse. But over time, the layers of process became barriers to meaning. What was once solemn has become sterile. Death is now an administrative task — no different from refuse collection or meter reading. You don't have to feel it. You just have to log it.

For Malik, this creates a slow interior rupture. He knows he should care more. That he used to care more. But the system has trained him otherwise. The more clinical he becomes, the more efficient he is. And efficiency is what's rewarded.

The horror, then, is not what he sees. It's what he no longer sees. The girl in the stairwell. The man in the underpass. The bloated figure pulled from the canal. They are not mourned. They are processed.

The form doesn't ask about last words. It asks about postcode, time of collection, ethnicity if known.

That's how meaning disappears.Not with violence — but with drop-down menus.

Frontline Grief

Grief used to belong to the family. Now it belongs to the workers.

Not because they claim it — but because there's no one else left to carry it.

Malik doesn't cry. He doesn't light candles. He doesn't know the names of half the people he collects. But he feels it, piece by piece — the grief of routine exposure, the quiet toll of seeing too much and being asked to say nothing.

There are no chaplains for drivers. No therapists for contractors. No commemorative plaques for the dead whose names aren't verified. Malik isn't part of a trauma response unit. He's a council employee with gloves, boots, and a clipboard. But he's also the last person to see these bodies in their original context — a stairwell, a bus stop, a hostel mattress. The place where they stopped being alive.

And there is no protocol for that.

Frontline grief is different from personal loss. It isn't sharp. It's grit in the system — building up in the joints, the breath, the space behind the eyes. It becomes fatigue, detachment, a slight pause before sleep. A dull resistance to lightness.

When Malik goes home, he doesn't talk about his work. No one wants to hear it. His daughter asks why he smells like bleach. His neighbour asks if he's still doing "the body job." He says yes. They say nothing else.

This kind of work creates internal silence. Because to speak of it would require breaking open a space that no one has made safe. Malik isn't angry. He's wearied. And the longer he does it, the harder it is to feel anything specific. The grief becomes *ambient* — a fog you forget you're breathing.

The system depends on this. On the unspoken endurance of people like Malik. They are not paid to care. But they must not break. Their grief is a private matter. Their discomfort is their own problem.

And yet: without them, the system would collapse. The deaths would pile up. The paperwork would clog. The headlines would come.

So they keep going.

They carry what the public cannot bear to see.

And their grief is buried long before the bodies are.

The New Poor

In Britain today, poverty has been reframed — not erased, but reclassified. The old poor, the domestic poor, are no longer headline material. Their deaths, their overdoses, their slow exits from dignity aren't considered evidence of a failing system. They are seen as natural casualties of a changing world.

Malik sees this firsthand. He collects two kinds of bodies: the *new poor* and the *invisible poor*. One gets mourned in public; the other disappears in silence.

When a migrant is found dead in temporary housing, it triggers outreach. When an asylum seeker overdoses, charities speak. When a refugee drowns in the canal, the story circulates — as tragedy, as indictment, as evidence of state cruelty. And rightly so.

But when a local boy dies behind a pub, it's "substance abuse." When a middle-aged woman freezes in her flat, it's "neglect." When an ex-serviceman collapses under a bridge, it's "complex needs."

These terms aren't lies. But they are absolutions.

They suggest that British poverty is the result of bad luck or bad choices — not policy. Not abandonment.

And so, in a perverse twist, the newly arrived poor are treated with more urgency than the poor who have always been here.

It's not that one group is more deserving. It's that one group has advocates. Legal status. Oversight. Human rights lawyers. Foreign governments. Media sympathy.

The other group — Malik's own — has none of that.

Their poverty is domestic, unphotogenic, and politically complicated. To speak of them is to court discomfort. To admit they exist in their thousands is to reopen a class wound this country has never learned to bandage.

Malik doesn't blame anyone. But he notices the imbalance.

He picks up bodies from estates where people live on Pot Noodles and forgotten promises. Where third-generation council tenants no longer believe in help. Where no one protests when a body goes undiscovered for a week. No headlines. No questions. Just another line on a borough report.

The dead don't complain.

And the living have stopped expecting fairness.

So Malik lifts them all — migrant or native, old or young — with the same tired care. But he knows, deep down, only some of them will be missed.

And none of them will be counted the same.

Canal as Metaphor

The canal winds through Malik's route like a quiet witness. Not wide, not fast, but always there — a thread of still water running past housing blocks, industrial ruins, shopping trolleys rusting beneath the surface. It's not a landmark. It's a backdrop. And yet, over time, it becomes the story itself.

Bodies turn up there. Not often, but often enough. A migrant boy with no ID. A local addict who lost his footing. A teenager no one looked for. The canal doesn't discriminate. It simply receives.

But in *"Freezer Vans,"* the canal is more than a setting. It is a metaphor for the state itself — slow-moving, silty, neglected. Once vital, now incidental. Once engineered to connect people, now avoided by them.

Canals were built for transport. For goods, trade, purpose. They were channels of economic life. But now, they serve as corridors of unseen loss. No sirens. No press. Just occasional splashes followed by the quiet churn of response teams.

To Malik, the canal is the final resting place of lives the state cannot categorise. The drowned are often undocumented — not just in immigration status, but in meaning. They fall between systems. Too new to be protected. Too disconnected to be remembered. Too complex to be explained without awkward truths.

And yet the canal remembers them. Not as names, but as interruptions: the sudden discovery, the blocked lock, the news that doesn't reach the news.

In a nation obsessed with boundaries — territorial, legal, social — the canal is a border that no one guards. It marks not a line of defence, but a line of failure. A fluid space where people slip not through gaps in fences, but through gaps in care.

Malik pulls them out. Zip. Lift. Log. No headlines. No vigils. Just weight.

And every time he drives past the canal, he wonders who will be next. Not in fear. Not in blame. Just in resignation.

Because the canal, like the system, just keeps flowing. Sl uggish. Silent. Unchanged.

Naming and the Erasure of Identity

The dead arrive without names.

Sometimes there are papers — damp, faded, inconsistent. Sometimes there are tattoos, guesses, language fragments. But more often, there is just a body and a number. Malik records them as instructed: "Male, approx. 30–35, medium build, unknown ethnicity." The forms allow for that now — unknown is a legitimate category.

This is not neglect. It is procedure. But procedure has its own violence. Because what is erased through omission is not just the individual — it is the idea that they were ever part of anything larger.

In *"Freezer Vans,"* Malik begins to hear the names spoken back to him — whispered, hallucinated, imagined. They echo from the bags, rise from the stretchers, cling to the back of the van. These aren't ghosts in the traditional sense. They are corrections. They exist because the silence cannot hold.

In death, naming is everything. It is how we honour. How we mourn. How we place someone in the world they've left. Without a name, a person is data. A line on a spreadsheet. A cost. A burden. A logistical inconvenience.

The system isn't cruel. It is overwhelmed. But in its overwhelm, it has abandoned the symbolic rituals that distinguish a body from a person. Malik does his best. He writes down first names when he hears them, even if they're uncertain. He speaks them aloud in the van. He remembers their shoes, their hair, their weight.

It is not enough. But it is something.

The wider culture contributes to this erasure. Media outlets hesitate to publish names that might complicate a narrative. Obituaries focus on the dramatic dead — the politically useful dead. The others? Quietly processed, quietly buried.

Even in life, many of these people were nameless to the state — "asylum seeker," "client," "resident," "case." In death, they vanish entirely. And so Malik becomes, unknowingly, their final witness. Not because he has the power to remember them, but because no one else will.

This is not sentiment. It is a quiet act of resistance.

To say a name — even in private — is to insist that
someone was here.

And that they should not have left without being known.

Ghost Bureaucracy

The paperwork never ends.

Each collection generates forms, logs, digital entries,
confirmation emails. Malik types the same codes over and
over: *DOA, No NOK, Unattended Death.* The forms give the
illusion of closure, but in reality they are echo chambers —
records of loss that no one reads, stored in systems no one
checks.

This is what *ghost bureaucracy* looks like: a structure that
survives in documentation, long after it has ceased to function in substance.

The council department Malik works for has layers of
protocols — many written by people who haven't touched
a body in years. There are folders of revised guidance,
audit trails, and escalation chains. But when Malik calls for
clarification — on identification, on delays, on conflicting
instructions — no one answers. Phones ring out. Inboxes
auto-reply. The decision-makers are "working from home"
or "between roles."

He is left carrying the weight. Not just physically, but
morally.

The system pretends it is precise. But the precision is cos-
metic. Beneath the surface, there is rot: misfiled deaths, repeated mistakes, bodies mislabelled and quietly corrected.
No scandal. No foul play. Just decay disguised as procedure.

This ghost bureaucracy isn't malicious. It's exhausted. Its
goal is no longer care — it is deflection. Keep the records
tight, the processes clean, and the moral burden is trans-

ferred. The system hasn't failed — Malik has. Or the family has. Or the decedent. Or the timing. Or the funding.

Everyone is responsible.Which means no one is.

And so Malik continues. Logging the dead. Uploading their details. Following the manual that no longer matches the world he works in. He knows that once the body leaves his van, it enters another system — another corridor of refrigeration and filing and delay. The person becomes metadata. The story ends in archive.

He has seen bodies come back. Misdelivered. Wrong borough. Wrong name. Wrong everything.

And each time, he fixes it quietly. No escalation. Just deletion and re-entry.

Because if the system is a ghost, then he is its medium.He keeps it moving. Keeps it fed. Keeps it polite.

But he knows the truth:

You can bury a body.But you cannot bury a bureaucracy.

Vanishing Points

Malik's route ends where the road does — at the back of the mortuary, where the van doors open and the stretcher wheels clatter over concrete. He delivers the body. He signs the form. He turns around.

But the dead do not always vanish when logged. Some linger — not as ghosts in the supernatural sense, but as imprints, unanswered questions, names unspoken. They haunt not homes, but systems. And Malik begins to feel that it's not the bodies that are disappearing.

It's him.

In *"Freezer Vans,"* the final act is a metaphorical disappearance — Malik opens the last van and finds it empty. No body. No form. Nothing to log. And so he drives, not toward a destination, but away — into the fog, into silence.

This is the vanishing point — the moment when a person doing unbearable work under unbearable conditions becomes unseen even by the system they serve.

It begins gradually. Fewer check-ins. Less eye contact from supervisors. A sense that his role is mechanical. Disposable. He is not thanked. Not consulted. Not remembered. Only useful until broken.

He has seen this before in others. Drivers who walked away mid-shift. Council workers who stopped showing up. No one chased them. Their names disappeared from the rota like chalk in the rain.

This is not rebellion. It is administrative death — the quiet falling away of those who have nothing left to give and no language left to explain why.

Malik feels it coming. Not as crisis, but as stillness. A kind of resignation that wraps around him like the cold of the van. He starts driving slower. Stops logging his thoughts. Feels less real each day.

And the system? It does what it always does. Absorbs the absence. Shuffles duties. Adjusts targets. The machine stutters, then resumes.

Malik's final journey is not a suicide. It's not a breakdown. It's a refusal to participate in a system that forgets the living as quickly as the dead.

He doesn't need to be found.

Because he was lost long before he disappeared.

Part 5: The Housing List

Expecting

Jake kept the letter in his wallet like a promise.

Folded twice, edges frayed, the council crest smudged from handling. It wasn't a guarantee, not exactly — "subject to availability," "provisional allocation pending final review" — but it was something. A step. A beginning.

He took it out sometimes when Ruby couldn't sleep, rubbing her belly with one hand and squinting at the lines with the other.

"Two bedrooms," he whispered once. "Corner unit. White goods included."

She laughed. "What the hell are white goods?"

"Fridge. Cooker. Washing machine, I think."

She turned onto her side, wincing slightly. "Just hope the boiler works."

Jake smiled, but didn't answer.

They were living in his brother's flat for now. One bedroom. Damp patch above the window. A mattress on the floor. It wasn't home. It wasn't anything. Just a place to wait.

The baby was due in four weeks. Maybe sooner. Ruby's belly rose and fell like a tide, her breathing shallow in the early mornings. He sometimes watched her sleep — her face drawn, the bags under her eyes deeper each day.

She didn't complain. She rarely did. But she looked at the door differently now, like she was measuring what came next and wondering if it would ever arrive.

Jake checked his email twice a day. Called once a week. The housing office always said the same thing: "You're on the list. No update yet."

Still, he believed it would come.The flat. The keys. The quiet room with space for a cot.

They'd walked past the building once — low-rise, red brick, three storeys, a patch of grass out front. A man with a dog sat on the steps. He didn't look up. Ruby squeezed Jake's hand tight as they passed.

"I could live there," she said.

He nodded. "You will."

She paused. "We will."

He kissed her forehead.

Now, lying beside her in the soft dark, he rested his hand on her stomach and whispered to the baby.

"We're ready," he said.

No reply, of course.

But he believed it anyway.

Because sometimes a promise is the only thing you can hold onto when everything else is still waiting to arrive.

The neighbour's name was Sheila. Lived two doors down in the same estate Jake's brother was squatting. Sixty-something, chain smoker, always wearing slippers no matter the time of day.

She caught them on the stairs one morning — Ruby holding her back, Jake carrying two bags of frozen veg and a tin of formula his brother had scrounged from somewhere.

"Any news on the flat?" Sheila asked, eyes darting to Ruby's belly.

Jake nodded. "Should be soon. Council said we're top of the list."

Sheila exhaled through her nose, sharp. "They say that to everyone, love. I've been waiting six years for my bathroom to get tiled. Still pissing in a plastic pan."

Ruby gave a polite smile, tired around the edges.

Sheila lit a cigarette, waving the smoke away with her hand. "You'd best be realistic, that's all. These days, they give first dibs to anyone with a foreign name and a good story."

Jake bristled. "It's not like that."

Sheila shrugged. "You say that now."

He shifted the bags in his hand. "We've got a letter. Allocation pending."

"They gave a letter to the fella in 3B last month. He's still waiting. Meanwhile, they've moved in a family of eight upstairs. No English, four kids, none in school. Got brand-new carpets, though."

Ruby pressed her hand against the wall to steady herself. "We just want somewhere clean."

Sheila nodded, not unkindly. "So did we all."

She stubbed the cigarette out on the railing, ground it under her slipper.

"Just don't pin your heart to it, love," she added as she turned to go. "Hope makes fools out of good people in places like this."

Jake didn't answer. He looked at Ruby instead. She didn't meet his gaze.

Back in the flat, she lay on the sofa, one hand on her belly.

"Do you believe her?" she asked.

"No."

He placed the bags down, stared at the letter taped to the fridge.

"She's wrong," he said.

Ruby didn't respond.

Outside, someone was shouting. A baby cried. A door slammed hard enough to shake the floor.

Jake stood in the kitchen for a long time, the cold from the floor creeping up his legs.

Reassigned

Jake found out through the post.

A brown envelope, same as the last one, same council stamp. But this time, the language was different.

"We regret to inform you that due to a reassessment of priority needs, your provisional allocation has been withdrawn. Your application remains active and under review."

He read it twice. Then again. The letter was polite. Neutral. Cold.

He didn't show Ruby at first.

She was in the bath, feet swollen, eyes closed. He stood in the hallway, letter in hand, unsure if reading it aloud would make it more real.

When she came out, towel wrapped high, he was still staring at it.

"What's that?"

He handed it over without speaking.

She read it once. Then folded it slowly and placed it on the table.

"So who got it?"

Jake shrugged. "Don't know. Letter doesn't say."

She stared at him. "Did you call?"

"Not yet."

"Call."

He did, that afternoon. Waited on hold for seventeen minutes. When the voice finally answered, it was cheerful. Unconcerned.

"Ah, yes. Your case has been reclassified. The flat at Willow Court has been allocated to an emergency intake household."

"Emergency?"

"Yes, a refugee family. Sudanese. Four children. High-need status."

Jake tried to speak but only managed, "We were—"

"Yes, you were high on the list, but this was a reallocation under regional dispersal obligations. It's a Home Office directive, not a council one."

"But what about us?"

The voice softened. "Your application remains active."

He hung up before she could say *thank you for your patience*.

He told Ruby. She didn't cry. Just nodded, slow and hollow.

"They gave it to someone else," she said, as if it were a maths problem.

Jake sat down at the kitchen table. The chair wobbled under him.

"They have four kids," he said. "We don't even have one yet."

Ruby laughed. It wasn't kind.

"No. We don't."

She didn't speak again that night.

The letter stayed on the table, unfolded, a soft crease down the middle.

Jake stared at it until the words blurred.

And for the first time since they'd found out about the baby, he wondered if they were going to make it.

She left the next morning.

No fight. No shouting. Just silence and a bag packed while the kettle boiled.

Jake heard the zip from the kitchen. Thought it was her coat. Then saw the rucksack over her shoulder, the phone charger wound around her fingers like wire.

"Where are you going?" he asked.

She didn't look at him.

"Mia's. Just for a bit."

He nodded slowly. "Okay. I'll come with—"

"No." Her voice was sharp, then softened. "Just me."

He stepped back, hands at his sides. "You're not serious."

"I can't do this here, Jake."

"Do what?"

"This. All of it. Waiting. Hoping. Being told 'not yet.'"

He opened his mouth to answer but had nothing that wouldn't sound like a repeat of something he'd already said.

"The flat's gone," she continued. "We're not next anymore. Maybe we never were."

"We can appeal."

She laughed — tired, hollow. "Appeal to who?"

Jake stared at her, trying to hold something steady between them. Her eyes were already somewhere else.

"I need space," she said, softer now. "Somewhere that isn't falling apart. Someone that doesn't look at me like I'm the one breaking."

He felt something sharp rise in his throat but swallowed it down.

"When are you coming back?"

She adjusted the strap on her shoulder. "When there's something to come back to."

Then she walked to the door. Opened it.

Paused.

"If you get a call from the housing office, tell them I left because I was tired. Not angry. Just tired."

He didn't move.

The door closed behind her with the softest click.

Jake stood in the middle of the flat. The silence felt like it had weight now. A presence. He sat down on the edge of the sofa and stared at the wall.

The cot box was still in the corner. Unopened. Half-covered by a blanket.

He reached for the letter on the table. Read it one more time.

Then folded it once, twice, again, until it was small enough to lose.

Telegram

He found the link on a forum buried deep in a thread about council backlogs.

The title was vague: "Reclaim Local — Private Channel". Just a few hundred members. Most of the posts were images — crumbling estates, headlines about new arrivals, screenshots of social media arguments. Anger disguised as conversation. Frustration polished into clarity.

Jake didn't post. Not at first. He read.

One man shared a photo of a family moving into a refurbished flat. Captioned it *"fast-tracked again."*

Another shared a spreadsheet — anonymous, supposedly from inside a council office. *"This is what 'emergency reallocation' looks like."*

Someone else posted a voice note: a gruff accent saying, *"They want us to be quiet. Not stupid. Just quiet. Like we're lucky to have what's left."*

Jake scrolled late into the night.

The channel was full of people like him — not violent, not cartoon villains, just exhausted. Their profiles were vague: initials, old football crests, cartoon avatars. Some claimed to be ex-military. Others said they'd worked in housing before "it changed."

He saw a message that stopped him:

"If your place is given away, give them something back. Even if it's just a crack in the wall."

No one commented.

But it stayed pinned for hours.

He didn't share his story. He didn't mention Ruby. Or the letter. Or the look on her face when she left. But he felt something settle in his chest as he read. Like the tension that had been building for months finally had a name.

Later, a notification popped up.

"You've been added to Reclaim Local – Tier 2."

A private message followed. From someone named "GS13."

"Tell us where you are. What they took. We'll show you what to do next."

Jake didn't respond.

He just stared at the message. Then turned his phone face down on the table.

Outside, the estate was quiet — a kind of quiet that used to mean safety.

Now it felt like surrender.

The channel changed after that.

Less talk. More footage.

Jake sat in the dark with his phone screen lighting his face, scrolling through videos he never would've searched for on his own. A bin fire outside a council office. A man in a balaclava spray-painting *WE WERE HERE FIRST* across a shuttered block. A group gathered at night, filming the empty shell of a former pub converted into housing.

He watched one video three times:A phone camera sweeping across a burnt-out stairwell.The caption read: *"New intake cancelled. Message sent."*

No one in the comments named the place. But it looked like somewhere familiar. Brick the colour of rust. Balcony rails Jake had seen before.

One voice note played while he made tea — deep voice, calm:

"They won't hear you till you make noise. Not online. Real. They forgot us, so we remind them."

He stirred his tea twice. Let it go cold.

That night, he dreamed of the cot in a room with no windows. Smoke curling under the door. A woman outside, walking away without looking back.

He woke with the sheets tangled and his heart racing.

The next day, he opened the channel again.

A new post. Anonymous.

"Sabotage isn't violence. It's a signal. They burn your name off the list. Burn it back on."

Jake didn't repost. Didn't reply.

But he didn't close the app either.

He scrolled past photos of tower blocks. Redacted memos. Maps with dots on them — red for "occupied," blue for "reclaimed."

A private message appeared from GS13.

"You in?"

Jake didn't type. Just watched the blinking cursor.

It disappeared.Then reappeared.

"You've already started. Just finish it."

He looked out the window.

The sky was low and grey. Across the way, another flat had fresh curtains. Pale blue. Clean. The lights were on inside, but the windows were shut.

He wondered what their list had looked like.

Or if they ever had to wait at all.

Initiation

They met just after dusk, near the bandstand at Grange Park. The benches were wet, the air cold, the kind of evening that made the world feel smaller.

Jake recognised the man by his jacket — army surplus, one sleeve patched with black tape. He was sitting on the far bench, facing away from the path, hood up.

Jake approached slowly. "GS13?"

The man nodded but didn't look up. "Sit."

Jake obeyed.

For a moment, there was only the sound of distant traffic and the rustle of wind through bare branches.

"You know why you're here?" the man asked.

Jake hesitated. "I think so."

The man lit a cigarette, cupping the flame. His face flickered — early forties, hard-lined, eyes that didn't flinch.

"You've been watching long enough," he said. "You know what's happening."

Jake nodded.

"They've taken the flats. They've taken the rules. They've taken the right to even say it out loud." He turned to Jake. "And they laugh when we ask what happened."

Jake said nothing.

The man took a drag. "It's not about hate. Don't let them paint it that way. This is about fairness. Return. They burned your name. You burn the file."

Jake looked down at his hands.

"You ready?" the man asked.

Jake swallowed. "What do you want me to do?"

The man reached into his coat, pulled out a folded map — photocopied, faded. A circle drawn in red ink over a housing office on Worsley Street.

"Paper records are stored in the back unit. Security light's broken. One camera. You go in, you leave a mark. Smoke. Smashed glass. Nothing big. Just enough."

Jake stared at the map.

"Why me?"

"Because you're not angry," the man said. "You're empty. That's the right kind. Anger fades. Emptiness stays."

He stood, stubbed the cigarette out against the bench.

"You'll know what to do when you get there."

Then he walked away.

Jake sat for a long time after.

The map stayed in his hand. Damp at the corners now. Ink smudging where his thumb pressed too hard.

In the distance, a dog barked. A child laughed.

But the park felt silent.

Like a stage waiting for the next act to begin.

Jake didn't sleep that night.

He sat on the edge of the mattress, the map unfolded on the floor in front of him, the red circle glowing faintly in the light from the phone screen. The messages kept coming — not many, just a few from GS13.

"Tomorrow.""Windowed side.""Bring your own mark."

He read them twice, then turned off the screen.

The next day, he walked past Worsley Street twice. Low brick building, metal shutters, two council logos peeling at the edges. A cracked window on the side, taped over but not replaced. The bin shed out back was full of broken office chairs and rusting mop buckets.

It didn't look important. That made it worse.Like all the weight of his failure had come from somewhere so empty.

That evening, another message arrived.

"We all start somewhere. You're not burning it down. Just saying you were here."

Attached was a photo — someone else's mark. A fire alarm smashed with a hammer. Graffiti scrawled across a door in thick black letters: *"YOU FORGOT US."*

Jake felt something tighten in his chest.

He didn't want to destroy anything.

He wanted someone to explain why they hadn't chosen him. Why he wasn't enough.

That night, he packed a can of spray paint in a Tesco bag. Red. The only colour left on the shelf. He brought gloves too — not because anyone told him to, but because it felt right. Like there was a line he wasn't ready to cross.

He waited until past midnight. The streets were slick with rain. Worsley Street was dark, one lamp buzzing overhead.

He stood across from it, heart thudding, fists clenched.

No one was watching.

No one cared.

And for the first time in months, he felt visible.

He stepped into the alley, past the bins, to the blank wall.

He shook the can.Pressed the nozzle.

But the paint didn't come.

The pressure was gone. The can was dead.

He stared at the metal in his hand like it had betrayed him.

Then he laughed — short, breathless, nothing like joy.

He left the can on the ground.

And walked home.

Still empty.

But not invisible anymore.

Misfire

He saw the woman by accident.

Late afternoon, queueing outside the pharmacy — clipboard in hand, council lanyard swinging from her coat. She was talking to someone in a high-vis jacket, nodding too much, laughing too brightly. Jake stood behind them with a prescription bag in his hand and the same pit in his stomach he'd carried since Ruby left.

He recognised her name from the letter. Housing Liaison — Priority Allocations.

He didn't decide to follow her. He just didn't turn the other way when she walked off. Past the Tesco. Down the high street. Into the estate by the new builds where the gardens had fences and the front doors were painted.

She walked slowly, unaware. He stayed back. Ten paces. Then fifteen.

She paused at a zebra crossing. Checked her phone. Turned into a cul-de-sac. Detached houses, white stone, fresh gravel crunching beneath her shoes.

Jake stood at the corner, just out of sight. His fingers were tight around the prescription bag.

The house she entered had a green front door. A string of fairy lights around the porch. Through the window, he could see a hallway lined with coats, shoes in neat rows. A warm yellow light spilling into the hallway.

He stood there for a long time.

Nothing dramatic pulsed in his chest. No urge to smash anything. Just a dull ache. Why her? Why did she get a hallway like that?

He thought about walking up the drive. Saying something. Asking a question.Not about policy. About fairness.

But he didn't.

He turned around. Walked back the way he came.

Past the shops. Past the chippy with the flickering neon
sign. Past the corner where Ruby once kissed him just because.

When he got home, he sat in the dark for an hour.

Then picked up a brick from the yard. Walked to the side
of the building.And smashed his own kitchen window.

Glass shattered inward. But some caught his hand.

The sound echoed across the empty courtyard.

He stood there, breathing hard, staring at the jagged
frame.

Then he smiled — not because it felt good, but because
something finally broke on his terms.

The sound startled the pigeons on the roof. One flew off in
a panic. The others didn't bother.

Jake stood there, the brick still in his hand, shards of glass
at his feet. Cold air spilled out of the kitchen like a warning.
Somewhere in the estate, a dog barked once, then fell silent.

No lights came on. No neighbours peeked through
blinds. It was late enough for people to pretend they didn't
hear, and early enough for no one to care.

He dropped the brick.

It thudded into the grass.

The broken pane looked like a mouth left open in surprise.

Inside, the flat was quiet. The glass had scattered across
the worktop, into the sink, onto the tiled floor. A photo
of Ruby, still stuck to the fridge, fluttered slightly in the
breeze.

He stepped inside. The crunch of glass under his shoes felt deliberate.

He didn't sweep it.

He sat on the floor, back against the cabinet, and let the cold settle into his bones. The wind rattled the torn edge of the curtain. His breath fogged faintly in the air.

There was no satisfaction. No fear of consequences. Just a strange, steady calm.

No one would come. There was nothing to report. He'd vandalised his own home — if it could still be called that.

He thought of Ruby. Wondered if she'd hear about it. If she'd think he was unravelling.

Maybe he was.

But in that moment, sitting on cracked lino with blood beading faintly at his knuckles, he felt more present than he had in weeks.

No form. No phone call. No explanation.

Just action.

He looked around the kitchen. The cot box was still there, unopened. A layer of dust on the top now. He reached out, pulled it toward him, and laid a hand on the cardboard.

It was heavier than he remembered.

He didn't open it.

Not yet.

But he knew he would.

And not for the baby anymore.

For something else. To build something. Anything.

Even if it was just to prove the future still had room for his hands.

The Cot

The cot took three hours to assemble.

Not because it was complicated — it wasn't — but because Jake worked slowly. Carefully. As if each bolt, each slat, each instruction step was a kind of ritual. Something to prove the day still had shape.

He cleared the centre of the room first. Moved the table, kicked glass into the corners, swept the floor without really seeing it. Then he opened the box, laid out the pieces, and began.

It was quiet work. The only sound was the occasional click of wood into place, the metallic turn of the screwdriver. The wind still came through the broken window, but he barely felt it now. His breath fogged less.

He didn't rush.

He hadn't touched the cot since Ruby bought it. They'd chosen it together. Simple white wood, rounded edges, a soft mattress that came vacuum-packed in plastic. It had arrived a week after the promise of the flat. She'd wept when she saw it.

Now, she wasn't here.

But the cot was. The last thing left from a future that had been taken in parts.

When he finished, he stood back and looked at it.It didn't look out of place.

It looked sacred.

There were no sheets. No toys. No mobile hanging from the top. Just the frame, clean and empty, in the centre of a room with cracked tiles and one shattered pane.

He didn't decorate. Didn't pretend.

He just stared at it.

Then, slowly, sat beside it on the floor.

The cot wasn't a beginning now. It was a witness.

To what he'd lost. To what he might still be. To what no one had answered for.

He ran his fingers along the rail.

The flat was cold.

The room was still.

And for the first time in days, he felt like something had been built — not imagined, not postponed, but built.

Even if it held nothing.

Jake climbed into the cot just after midnight.

He didn't plan to — just sat beside it until his body gave up pretending it had anywhere else to go. The floor was too cold. The sofa too far. The mattress, still wrapped in its protective film, let out a soft crackle as he lay down.

It was a tight fit. His knees bent double, one shoulder pressed against the railing. The cot creaked once under the shift of weight, then held.

It smelt faintly of cardboard and dust.

He rested his head on his arm and stared up at the ceiling. The patch above the lightbulb had started to brown — water damage from the flat above. He made a mental note to report it.

He wouldn't.

The wind whispered through the broken window. The curtain moved like a slow breath. Somewhere in the estate, a siren rose and fell. Then silence again.

He closed his eyes.

The cot was meant to be Ruby's idea. Her gesture of readiness. Her quiet resistance to a world that gave nothing for free. She'd measured the room for it. Cleared space. Asked if they should get a mobile — something with stars.

Jake had nodded then, thinking he'd have time. A room. A key. A future.

Now he had none of those things.

Just this cradle for a child who hadn't come, and a version of himself who never arrived either.

He pulled the spare blanket over his chest. It didn't cover his feet.

Still, it felt like shelter.

Not from the cold.From the noise. The waiting. The shame.

He imagined someone opening the door and seeing him there — full-grown, curled inside a symbol. They'd laugh. Or stare. Or ask what he thought he was doing.

But he wouldn't answer.

Because this was the only place left that hadn't rejected him.

He breathed slowly.

Not asleep.

Not awake.

Just present.

Cradled by a promise that had outlived the system that made it.

Part 5: Critical Essay

Housing Prioritisation and Resentment

Britain's council housing system was never perfect, but it once operated under a rough code of fairness: time served mattered, need was visible, and the queue — however long — was knowable. That moral framework has collapsed. In its place stands a system governed by triage, exception, and invisible mechanisms that few understand and even fewer trust.

"The Housing List" captures this collapse through one couple, Jake and Ruby, who represent a demographic long eclipsed by policy: the native-born working poor who play by the rules and are met with silence. Promised a flat with the impending birth of their child, they find it reassigned at the last minute to a newly arrived family under emergency provisions. No one explains. No one apologises. No one seems accountable. The message is simple: your place has been repurposed.

This isn't fiction for many. Across Britain, families are being bypassed on housing lists not because they lack need, but because their need is no longer considered exceptional. Instead, policy now prioritises "statutory emergency"— often defined through asylum, resettlement, or homelessness status. These categories aren't illegitimate, but their acceleration has created a two-tier system: one visible and empathetic, the other buried under backlogs and resentment.

The problem isn't just material. It's moral. The old housing queue at least offered dignity through structure. People waited, but they waited with the belief that time and contribution counted for something. Now, that belief is eroded. Jake doesn't riot when he's displaced — he internalises the insult. His partner leaves, not because they are poor, but because they are powerless. They cannot compete in a system that has redefined urgency without communicating the rules.

This is the soil in which quiet fury grows. Not hatred — despair. Not bigotry — betrayal. Jake doesn't blame the Sudanese family. He blames the council. The state. The voice on the phone that told him "we appreciate your situation" while handing his future to someone else.

And the most dangerous resentment is the kind that cannot be spoken without moral consequence. To question the allocation logic is to invite accusations of prejudice. So people stay silent. And the silence grows thicker. Louder.

Housing was once about shelter.

Now it's about symbolism — of who matters, who's heard, and who has a right to call this place home.

Family Breakdown under Policy Pressure

Housing instability doesn't just affect bricks and mortar — it corrodes relationships. Couples built on shared struggle begin to fracture when the future becomes illegible. Promises postponed become plans abandoned. Hope becomes burden.

In *"The Housing List,"* Jake and Ruby are not dysfunctional. They are young, broke, and expecting their first child. What they lack in resources, they make up for in belief: that if they wait their turn, do what's asked, stay on the list, the system will reward them with security. A home. A place to begin.

But when the promised flat is reassigned, that belief dies — and something else dies with it.

Ruby doesn't leave Jake because she doesn't love him. She leaves because she no longer trusts that their life together can begin at all. Their future was tied to a room with a working boiler and enough space for a cot. When that's taken — arbitrarily, without explanation — she sees only dead ends. She leaves to escape stagnation, not affection.

This is how policy becomes personal. The state never tells Jake "You're not a priority." But the reallocation speaks louder than any letter. The subtext is clear: your need is not urgent enough, your patience not important enough, your contribution not recent enough.

Young working-class couples like Jake and Ruby occupy a policy blind spot. They are not affluent enough to rent privately. Not unstable enough to qualify for emergency accommodation. Not politically fashionable enough to attract NGO advocacy. They are simply... waiting. But waiting, under pressure, is corrosive. It breeds doubt. Frustration. Resentment not just toward institutions, but toward each other.

Statistically, housing insecurity is a key driver of relationship breakdown. The stress fractures are invisible at first — short tempers, quiet disappointments, missed appointments. Then the split comes. One partner moves out. The child is raised in instability. Another family atomised by a spreadsheet.

And what does the system do? It resets the file. Jake becomes a single applicant. Lower priority. Another delay. Another intake cycle. The family unit, once strong enough to endure low income, collapses under structural indifference.

The cost isn't just a flat.

It's futures unmade. Lives diverted. A generation asked to begin on foundations already cracked.

Jake and Ruby aren't failed parents.

They're the product of a system that rewards survival over continuity.

And eventually, even the patient stop waiting.

Radicalisation and Despair

Radicalisation in Britain is often discussed in terms of ideology — online grooming, echo chambers, foreign influence. But for men like Jake, it begins somewhere far more mundane: disappointment.

Not anger. Not hate. Not even politics.

Just the slow erosion of belief that anything will change — and the realisation that the system will never speak for people like him.

"The Housing List" does not portray Jake as a monster. He isn't a thug. He isn't militant. He is bereaved — not of a person, but of a future. When Ruby leaves, when the flat goes to someone else, when the council gives him scripted apologies instead of answers, Jake doesn't riot. He scrolls. He listens. He finds a Telegram group that speaks in a tone he recognises: plain, blunt, angry.

This is how it begins. Not with ideology, but with recognition.

The group gives language to what Jake has been told he isn't allowed to say. That fairness is dead. That locals are invisible. That quiet men who play by the rules get nothing. It offers not nuance, but clarity. A villain. A reason. A call to matter again.

For working-class men in post-industrial Britain, radicalisation is rarely about doctrine. It's about dignity. The language of grievance hardens into the language of resistance because the system gives no other outlet. No politician speaks for Jake. No NGO campaigns for his disappointment. No institution lets him express resentment without branding it bigotry.

So he turns inward. Then online.

Despair is fertile ground for radical thinking. It doesn't require conversion — only fatigue. And the far right understands this. They don't have to convince Jake that he's right. They only have to convince him that everyone else is lying.

Jake isn't drawn to extremism because he hates. He's drawn to it because he feels hated — or worse, ignored. He doesn't want chaos. He wants a reason to believe that his life isn't a clerical oversight.

And when the mainstream offers only silence, the margins offer noise.

Dangerous noise.

But, to Jake, it sounds like truth.

The Telegram Effect

The internet was meant to democratise information. But for people like Jake, it has done something far more intimate: it has made their disillusionment feel communal.

He doesn't attend rallies. He doesn't write letters. He doesn't vote anymore. But he joins a Telegram group. Why? Because it doesn't ask him to perform. It asks him to *witness*. To read. To scroll. To feel seen by strangers who, like him, feel like they've been left behind and laughed at.

This is the Telegram Effect — not a formal recruitment pipeline, but a distributed system of grievance amplification. The platform is encrypted, fast, and anonymous. But more than that, it's *familiar*. Its tone mirrors the pub talk that has been slowly purged from polite society. It offers voice notes, videos, memes — quick jolts of rage and clarity.

Jake finds what the council could not offer him: explanation. The flats are going elsewhere because of quotas. The welfare is stretched because of fraud. The culture is shifting because "they" don't care about "us." It's all reductionist, but it's emotionally legible. It doesn't ask Jake to justify his pain — it validates it.

More importantly, it turns that pain into actionable identity.

In the group, Jake isn't just a man who lost his flat. He's a local. A patriot. A truth-teller. The algorithms feed him images of burned estates, headlines stripped of context, footage of council meetings where nothing is said. He doesn't see nuance. He sees proof.

The Telegram world doesn't radicalise by argument. It radicalises by accumulation. Every image, every post, every story compounds the feeling of betrayal. And it's all served without filter, without counterpoint, without pause.

It is not Jake's politics that shift — it's his threshold for consequence. The more he absorbs, the more normal it feels to contemplate direct action. Not mass violence — but something small. Symbolic. A gesture of anger to mark his place.

In the digital wilderness, recognition becomes affirmation. And affirmation without structure becomes risk.

This is how a quiet man ends up walking into the night with a purpose no one saw coming.

Not because he changed.

Because no one offered him an alternative story to believe in.

Fragile Masculinity and Parenthood

Jake's breakdown is not ideological. It is intimate. At its core lies a deeper, older pain: the loss of his ability to provide.

In *"The Housing List,"* the failed promise of a council flat is more than a housing issue — it is a blow to Jake's masculine identity. Not the chest-puffing stereotype, but the quieter, generational model of manhood passed down in working-class Britain: provide. Protect. Prove your worth through work and shelter.

When that collapses, what's left?

Jake's father rented. His grandfather probably built half the estate he's now being shut out of. That lineage — however humble — held pride. It said: "I made something stable." But Jake has nothing to show Ruby. No keys. No plan. No home for their child. His role as partner and parent unravels before it begins.

Modern discourse mocks this. Fragile masculinity. Male ego. Patriarchal nostalgia.

But what Jake experiences isn't ego. It's dislocation. He is a man told that his worth lies in contribution — and then told his contribution no longer counts.

He cannot provide financially. The job centre offers retraining in things he doesn't understand. He cannot provide space. The flat is gone. He cannot even provide clarity — Ruby asks him *what happens next*, and he has no answer.

And so he folds inward. Watches videos of other men who feel what he feels. Joins chats where his failure is reframed not as weakness, but as injustice. Where fatherhood is no longer about raising a child, but reclaiming ground.

This is the danger of unmet masculinity — when the desire to protect becomes the instinct to defend. Not violently, necessarily. But with suspicion. With withdrawal. With anger rebranded as principle.

Jake doesn't want to dominate. He wants to feel useful. Needed. Heard.

When the system fails to give him a role in building the future, the internet gives him a role in avenging the past.

And in doing so, it replaces the potential of fatherhood with the ritual of resistance.

Not because Jake rejected his child.

But because the state rejected his right to welcome that child with dignity.

Bureaucratic Ghosting

Jake's descent doesn't begin with a confrontation. It begins with silence.

No call. No warning. Just a missed appointment, a new name on the tenant list, and a polite voicemail telling him to "contact housing services for further clarification." When he does, he's put on hold. Redirected. Spoken to with sympathy that masks administrative indifference.

This is bureaucratic ghosting — the process by which the state withdraws without owning its withdrawal. Not through denial, but through omission. Not cruelty. Just cold procedural drift.

Jake had a file. It had a note: "Expecting — priority pending." Then the note was replaced by a reassignment flag. No one explained. No one thought they needed to. The emergency override had been activated. "Unavoidable." "High need." "Complex criteria." The language of modern social housing — vague, technical, and bulletproof.

The message is never spoken plainly: *You don't count anymore.*

Instead, it's translated into protocol.

Jake calls. Waits on hold. Gets referred to someone else. That someone else is "on leave." The system doesn't shut him out — it erases him gradually. Not with denial, but delay. Not with confrontation, but inertia.

This is more than bad customer service. It's existential negation. A slow unwriting of the citizen. Jake wasn't asking for charity. He was responding to an offer — a promise. A promise now withdrawn by a system that has trained itself never to apologise, only to escalate.

In place of answers, Jake is given slogans: "Housing stress is a complex picture." "We're doing all we can." "Resources are being allocated according to guidance."

What he hears is: go away quietly.

This is how modern institutions avoid accountability — by hiding behind process. No one is malicious. No one is rude. But no one, anywhere, can help.

And in the void where accountability should be, suspicion grows. Not because Jake is paranoid, but because the silence feels intentional. Strategic. Designed to exhaust.

He stops calling. Stops emailing. Starts scrolling instead. Because the internet, unlike the council, answers back.

Even if what it says is dangerous.

Rebellion without Clarity

When Jake joins the Telegram group, he isn't looking for revolution. He's looking for recognition. What he finds instead is momentum — a rising current of images, slogans, clips, statistics stripped of context and injected with fury.

And soon, without ever deciding to, he starts to move with it.

This is rebellion without clarity — the kind that emerges not from doctrine but from drift. Jake doesn't read manifestos. He doesn't chant. He doesn't even know the names of the men he's messaging. But the cause begins to shape

itself around his loss. It gives his eviction a narrative. His
breakup a reason. His silence a reply.

It doesn't matter that the posts contradict each other.
That the targets shift — the council, the state, "immigration," "globalism," "elites." What matters is that the anger
makes sense in a way nothing else does. It's not coherent,
but it's felt. And Jake feels something, finally.

He begins with watching. Then reposting. Then messaging.

Then meeting.

A man in a park. A conversation in code. A gesture of
solidarity — or is it surveillance? He's not sure. But he says
yes when asked to prove he means it.

What does he mean?

That's the danger. He can't articulate it. He only knows
that something has been taken — and that no one in power
has acknowledged it. Not the housing officer. Not the MP.
Not the charity leaflets shoved through his door. No one.

So he acts.

Not with violence. Not yet. But with gesture. He smashes
a window. Follows someone home. Leaves a mark. Nothing
that will make the news — just a moment of assertion in a
life that has offered him none.

And afterward? Regret? Shame?

Not exactly.

Just clarity.

Because for the first time in months, he did something
that the system couldn't ignore. He left a mark. A noise. A
message.

Even if he doesn't know what it said.

This is the rebellion we rarely talk about — the one without slogans or certainty. The one that lives in the cracks
between form letters and waiting lists.

It's not organised.

It's not noble.

But it is real.

Symbol of the Crib

In the final scene of *"The Housing List,"* Jake returns to the flat. Not the one he was promised, but the one he still inhabits — alone, broken, stripped of the future he tried to build. In the centre of the room, he assembles the baby's cot. Not as a gesture of hope, but as a funeral for what was supposed to be.

The cot is not furniture. It is symbol — of arrival, of intention, of continuity. In a country where inheritance has become a myth for the working class, the cot is a declaration: something is beginning. We are ready.

But Jake's cot holds nothing. No baby. No bedding. No future. Just air.

It becomes a monument. A silent indictment of a system that promised support but delivered silence. Jake doesn't burn it. He doesn't smash it. He assembles it with care. He centres it in the room like an altar. Then he sleeps in it, alone — not as a parent, but as a ghost of one.

In that moment, the story is no longer about housing. It's about disinheritance. Not just of property, but of meaning. The cot is what he should have passed on. Instead, it becomes the last thing he holds onto.

Modern Britain is full of cots like this. Unused. Half-built. Packed away in hall cupboards. They belong to families who waited for the system to respond and were met with bureaucratic vagueness. To parents who didn't leave, didn't riot, didn't scream — just waited too long.

The state does not remove these cots.

It makes them irrelevant.

And in doing so, it turns preparation into grief.

Jake doesn't leave a note. He doesn't post about it. He doesn't speak to anyone. He simply lies down inside the structure of a life he no longer believes in.

And the cot stands there — empty, perfect, accusing.

This is what loss looks like in an age without conflict: not fire, but stillness.

Not theft, but redirection.

Not death, but disappearance.

A man. A child. A home.

All present.All missing.All recorded as "unverified need."

Part 6: The Knife in the Mosque

The News

The morning came soft and grey. Rain slicked the pavement outside Khalid's shop, pooling in the cracks of the kerb. He unlocked the metal shutter with practiced rhythm, his fingers stiff from sleep and age. A sparrow darted from the awning as he ducked beneath it, balancing the day's newspaper under one arm.

Inside, the strip lights hummed faintly as they warmed up. He moved through the aisles, adjusting crisp packets, straightening bread. His shop was clean, quiet, small — four aisles and a till. Just enough to keep the days in order.

At 8:11, his phone vibrated. A message from his niece: "Have you seen the news?" No punctuation. Just the question, dense with something unsaid. He wiped his hands on his apron before opening the app.

There it was. His nephew's face — blurry, pulled from some grainy social media post — beside a headline: *Arrest Made in Local Mosque Incident*. Below, a second line: *Sources suggest terror link not ruled out.*

Khalid read it twice. Then again. His breath slowed. He sat on the stool behind the till, elbows on knees, the phone resting in his palm. The boy's face looked younger than he remembered. Or maybe it was just that he hadn't seen him in months. University. Work. Distance.

He thought of the last time they'd spoken — Eid, maybe the one before last. Polite, distracted conversation. Khalid had asked about grades. The boy had nodded, eyes on his shoes. It hadn't meant anything then. It didn't mean anything now. Did it?

Outside, a van rolled by. A man paused at the window, looked in, then kept walking.

Khalid didn't move. The screen dimmed, then blacked out in his hand. A familiar voice on the radio mentioned congestion on the ring road, rain expected through mid-day. He reached out, switched it off. The silence deepened.

There would be more messages. More questions. Maybe the police. Maybe worse.

But in that moment, all Khalid could hear was the door chime from last night — the soft ding as a woman left with milk, her child trailing behind her, waving. She'd said thank you. He remembered that clearly.

He stood, slowly. The day had to begin. Bread to restock. A crate of eggs still in the back.

They arrived just after noon. Two officers — plainclothes, polite, the kind of calm that meant they were already recording. Khalid had just finished stacking soft drinks when the bell above the door rang. The woman smiled first.

"Mr. Hanif?" she asked.He nodded. "Yes.""I'm Detective Rowe, this is Detective Mason. Could we have a word?"

She gestured toward the back of the shop. He hesitated, wiped his hands on a cloth, then led them to the stockroom. Boxes of cereal leant precariously along one wall. The smell of cardboard and bleach hung in the air. He didn't offer chairs. There weren't any.

"It's about your nephew," Rowe began. "Tariq Hanif. You've seen the news?"

Khalid nodded once. His eyes stayed on the floor.

Rowe continued. "We're speaking to family, trying to build a picture. Just routine."

Mason said nothing, just stood there, arms folded. Watching.

Khalid looked up. "I haven't seen him. Not for a while. He's at university, I think.""You think?""He doesn't come round much."

Rowe softened her voice. "Has he ever spoken about political matters? Religious grievances? Any change in behaviour?"

Khalid frowned. "He was quiet. Studious. Spoke less, maybe, the last couple years. But that's... normal."

Rowe nodded. "Any unusual visitors to your home or shop? Has he ever mentioned travelling abroad?"

"No."

A pause. Mason shifted. "What about the mosque?"Khalid blinked. "What about it?""Is he active there? You? Any recent tensions?"

Khalid's mouth felt dry. "We go to pray. That's all."

Rowe studied him. The hum of the fridge buzzed behind them. "We're not accusing you of anything, Mr. Hanif. We're just looking for context."

Khalid wanted to ask what Tariq had done. What they thought he had planned. But he didn't. He nodded again. "If I remember anything, I'll let you know."

"Good," Rowe said. She handed him a card. "If he contacts you, let us know immediately."

They left without browsing. Without buying. Just a nod, a thank you, and the chime of the door again.

Khalid stood in the doorway, watching them walk to the unmarked car. Mason glanced back once, expression unreadable.

Then the engine started, and they were gone. He folded the card in half without reading it and slid it into his pocket. The stockroom smelt too clean. Too quiet.

He returned to the till. Two teenagers had come in and left without speaking.

Reputation

The headline sat beneath the fold, but the word was unmistakable.

TERROR ARREST: Local Links Investigated

And there it was, four paragraphs down — "Sources confirm the individual, believed to be Tariq Hanif, is the nephew of well-known shop owner Khalid Hanif, who declined to comment."

He hadn't declined. He hadn't been asked.

The copy was thin, padded with conjecture and unnamed "community concerns." No quotes. No clarifications. Just a cluster of sentences that blurred fact and innuendo into something combustible.

The paper had been left on the shop counter — not delivered, not paid for. Someone had placed it there. Deliberately.

Khalid stood behind the till, rereading the article. His name in print, nestled next to "radical," "mosque," "concerns." He traced the letters with his eyes, not fingers. It felt like touching fire.

At 10:07, his first customer walked in — an elderly man who usually asked after Khalid's health, who always paid in coins. Today, he nodded, wordless, and left without his usual mint lozenges. A second customer, a young mum with a buggy, turned around before reaching the milk.

By noon, footfall had dropped by half.

Khalid didn't speak. He didn't call anyone. He just re-stocked the same shelf twice, wiped down surfaces already clean, opened the back door for air he didn't want.

At one, he stepped outside and leant against the brick wall. Across the street, a boy stared, then was tugged away by his father. Behind the glass, his reflection looked older, smaller. Like someone watching himself be erased in real time.

A woman passed and clutched her handbag closer. He said nothing.

Back inside, he folded the newspaper neatly and placed it beneath the till. Not out of denial, but preservation. Proof, perhaps. That it had begun here — not with a crime, not with a trial, but with a name, printed beside the wrong word.

He tried to recall the last time he'd laughed in this shop. A joke from a customer, something about lemons and losing teeth. The memory came half-formed, like a face in fog.

At 3:12, no one had come in for over an hour. He sat, back straight, hands in lap, waiting for the next ding of the door.

It did not come.

The receipts told the story first. The till counted the numbers without emotion: £37.40. That was Monday. By Friday, it was £11.65.

Milk curdled in the fridge. Fruit softened in crates. Bread went hard in its plastic skin. Khalid threw out more than he sold.

He adjusted the hours without telling anyone. Opened later. Closed early. It made no difference. The chime of the door came maybe five times a day now — and even then, they didn't linger. No small talk. No nods. Just coins and silence.

A supplier left a voicemail: "Need to confirm next week's order — or we'll assume cancellation." He didn't call back.

He swept the floor twice a day, even when it was clean. Wiped the windows. Polished the till. The ritual mattered more than the result. If he stopped moving, the weight might settle.

On Wednesday, a regular — white, middle-aged, red coat — came in and hovered by the crisps. She picked up a packet, held it, then put it back. She glanced at him. Not a glare. Something worse. Hesitation with fear behind it.

She left without buying anything.

He watched her walk down the street, pause at the corner shop near the bus stop, and step inside. That shop had fluorescent lighting and sticky floors. But it didn't have his name printed in the paper.

At prayer that week, the imam mentioned patience. "Sometimes, we are tested not with pain, but with silence," he said. Khalid nodded, but felt nothing.

He stopped restocking the chocolate bars. The fridge buzzed loudly in the quiet. He found himself muting the radio, then unplugging it altogether.

On Friday evening, he counted the cash and found coins he didn't remember taking. He re-counted. Same result. It didn't matter.

That night, he dreamed the shop was full again — voices, footsteps, a line at the till. But when he looked up, their faces were blurred, mouths moving without sound. He tried to speak, but the till drawer wouldn't open. His hands were covered in ink.

He woke up before dawn and opened early, out of habit. At 7:03, the first bus passed, and no one looked in.

The Meeting

The mosque smelt of carpet shampoo and old books. Khalid removed his shoes and walked the narrow hallway toward the office, the soles of his socks whispering against the floor. It was early evening; Maghrib had passed. Only a few boys lingered in the prayer hall, their laughter echoing faintly before the doors closed behind him.

The council met on Thursdays — four men, seated around a laminate table in the back room. A whiteboard with faded marker lines stood behind them. Tea had been poured, untouched. Someone had brought biscuits.

Khalid stood in the doorway. "I just want a few minutes," he said.

They looked up, surprised. Then nodded. The eldest gestured to the empty seat.

He sat, hands folded.

"I need help," he said. "The papers printed my name. Business is dying. People avoid me. It wasn't me. It wasn't even proven." He paused. "I just... I thought you should know."

The room fell still. One man tapped his pen against a closed notebook. Another sipped tea without tasting it.

After a moment, the chairman — a soft-spoken man with an accountant's face — leant forward. "Brother Khalid, we understand your distress. This is a difficult time. For you... for all of us."

Khalid looked at him. "Then say something. To the community. Just a sentence. That I'm not involved. That I'm not—" He stopped.

The chairman's voice gentled. "You know how things are. Even addressing it makes it louder."

Another man added, "We're trying to protect the mosque. If the media think we're taking sides..."

"I'm not a side," Khalid said. "I'm one of you."

Silence again. The heater clicked as it shut off.

One councilman cleared his throat. "We suggest patience. Lay low. Things pass."

"Do they?" Khalid asked. No one answered.

He stood. His chair made a soft scrape. "I've been coming here since '94. I helped fix the roof when it leaked. Ran the Eid food drive three years running. I'm not asking for favours. I'm asking for the truth."

The chairman lowered his eyes. "We'll make du'a for you."

Khalid nodded once. Then left.

The hallway was empty. His shoes waited quietly by the door. Outside, the street was dark, the shopfronts asleep. He walked home without looking up, the sound of the mosque door closing behind him echoing longer than it should have.

It was after Isha when the message came.

A text. No greeting. No name. Just:*Better not speak publicly. Not now. Too much at stake.*

Khalid read it twice, thumb hovering over reply. He recognised the tone more than the number — the smoothness of warning wrapped as advice. It was always phrased like this, when they wanted you to disappear gently.

He didn't reply.

The next day, a younger council member caught him near the wudu area. They spoke in low tones, beside the boiler room, where the walls absorbed sound.

"Uncle," the man said, too casually. "I know things are heavy right now. But you should leave it."

Khalid met his eyes. "Leave what?"

"The noise. Papers. Police. People are unsettled. It's not a good time for... statements."

"I didn't make a statement."

The man hesitated. "Even being seen talking to media — it reflects back. On us. You understand."

Khalid smiled without humour. "I've said nothing. And still I'm mentioned."

"That's why silence is safer."

"For who?"

The younger man had no answer. He reached for a sip of water he didn't need. "The chairman said we'd support you. Quietly. With prayer."

Khalid nodded. "Quiet support. Public silence."

He turned to leave, but paused at the door. "Do you think I did something wrong?" he asked, not turning back.

The man said nothing. But that nothing stretched long enough to become an answer.

That evening, Khalid stood in the back of the prayer hall. The rows were full. Recitation filled the space, gentle and rhythmic. He mouthed the words but could not feel them.

Afterward, he lingered in the courtyard. Conversations bloomed around him but did not reach him. He was greeted with nods, not warmth. A boy handed out dates. Khalid took one, held it in his palm until it softened.

He walked home past his darkened shop. The shutters were half-lowered, the windows fogged from within. It looked like a place already closing.

In bed, he stared at the ceiling. Not angry. Not afraid. Just weightless. The kind of silence that doesn't ask for comfort — only space.

He understood now. They didn't think he was guilty. They thought he was inconvenient.

And in the quiet, that hurt more.

Tip-Off

It was a Tuesday morning. The kind where the sky forgot to turn blue. Khalid sat behind the till, the shop still unopened, his coat still on. He hadn't swept. He hadn't stocked the milk.

His phone sat on the counter. The Prevent card — creased, faded — was tucked beneath it. He took it out, flattened it on the glass, and dialed.

A recorded voice answered first. Then a beep. Then a pause that felt like a decision.

"Hello," he said, quietly. "My name is Khalid Hanif. I... I spoke to officers last week. About my nephew."

He paused. The shop hummed around him, lifeless.

"There's something else. I don't know what it means, but—someone has been speaking after prayers. Not on the mic. Just... with the younger ones. I saw him last Friday. I've never seen him before."

He swallowed. "They listen to him. I can't hear what's being said, but the boys—one of them I know, he's only sixteen—he's different now. Quieter. Absorbed."

A silence passed.

"I'm not saying it's dangerous. I'm saying it might become."

He looked up. A pigeon landed outside, pecked at nothing.

"I'm not calling out of fear. I'm calling because no one else will. And if something happens..." He exhaled. "I want it known that someone tried."

He hung up.

No dramatic moment followed. The shop remained still. The bread remained stale.

He opened the shutters late that day. Three customers came. One spoke. The other two left coins without eye contact.

At maghrib, he noticed two of the boys from the mosque walking down his street. One of them glanced into the shop but didn't wave. They moved past like shadows, drifting into corners.

That night, he couldn't sleep. He kept replaying the message he left, line by line. Was it too vague? Too soon? Too much?

He imagined the voice on the other end, unknown, hearing his words with narrowed suspicion: a shopkeeper, a Muslim, reporting on his own. It would not sound brave. It would sound rehearsed. Maybe calculated.

He lay in bed, staring at the window, the light from the streetlamp carving lines across his wall.

No knock came. No reply. Just the same silence as before, now thickened by exposure.

He had spoken. That much was true.

What that meant — he did not know yet.

They came just after fajr.

Not in sirens or boots — just two cars, idling in the dawn mist. The knock was soft but insistent. Khalid had just finished praying. He opened the door in his socks.

"Mr. Hanif," said the man in front, "we need to ask you some questions. You'll need to come with us."

Khalid blinked. "Is this about my call?"

They didn't answer. The street was still asleep. A fox darted between bins. He looked at his slippers by the door but didn't reach for them.

Inside the car, the windows fogged quickly. No one spoke. The seats smelt like dust and plastic. He kept his hands folded in his lap.

At the station, they took his phone, his coat, his watch. Asked him to remove his shoes again. He was led to a room with white walls and no clock.

A man he didn't recognise sat across from him. He had a laptop open but didn't type. "You made a call yesterday."

Khalid nodded.

"Why?"

"I told you. I saw something. Someone."

"Who?"

"I don't know his name. I told the person on the line. I described him."

The man nodded. "Yes. Vague. You mentioned young people being influenced. But you didn't mention that your own nephew is already under investigation."

Khalid inhaled slowly. "That's why I called. I thought—maybe they're connected."

The officer tilted his head. "Or maybe you're distancing yourself. Establishing a cover. Reporting just enough to appear helpful."

Khalid stared. "I've run a shop for twenty years. I've never—"

"We're not accusing you," the man said, gently. "We're clarifying context."

Two hours passed. Then three. They brought him water in a paper cup. He didn't drink it. A second officer entered, asked the same questions in different words.

"Why now?""Why him?""Why you?"

No charges were made. No lawyer called. Just the suggestion — subtle but clear — that his concern made him interesting.

By dusk, they released him. No apology. No eye contact.

Outside, the city moved as if nothing had happened. Buses groaned. Teenagers laughed. The world did not stop for the accused.

Khalid walked home in borrowed shoes, the paper soles whispering shame. A man on his street crossed to the other side without looking.

Later, in the stillness of night, the memory of the cell returned.

Lock-Up

He hadn't spoken about it. Not even to himself. But the memory returned in full, uninvited.

The cell was beige. A pale, artificial shade that swallowed time. One bench. One toilet. One fixed light that never dimmed. Khalid sat cross-legged on the floor, coat bundled behind his back, trying not to feel the cold.

He had asked for his watch. They said no. Asked for the time. No one answered.

It was somewhere between dusk and nothing when he heard it — soft, distant, and unmistakable.

The call to prayer.

Not from the corridor. Not from a speaker. It came as if through the wall itself — as if the bricks remembered.

Allahu akbar, Allahu akbar...

He closed his eyes. The voice was clear, resonant. Male, young, unfamiliar. It didn't matter. The words moved through him like warmth.

He hadn't prayed since the arrest. There had been no space for it — not in the holding room, not under suspicion. But now, in this square of silence, something inside him leant toward it.

He stood slowly. Faced the corner away from the door. Raised his hands.

He forgot how stiff his knees had become.

Each movement was careful, deliberate. The room didn't echo. But it held him. He whispered the surah, kept his eyes low. When he bowed, the ache in his back reminded him of age. When he rose, the ache in his chest reminded him of something else.

He thought of his father's hands — broad, calloused, steady in sujood. He thought of the prayer mat they used to share during blackouts. One lightbulb, one recitation, the world stilled.

The sound in the cell faded before he finished. But the rhythm remained.

When he sat back down, it was not peace he felt. It was something older — memory without comfort. A tether.

A slot in the door opened. A face appeared briefly, then vanished.

He drank the water they'd left him, finally. Lukewarm. It tasted of metal.

There were no answers. No timelines. No explanations.

But for the first time since it began, he felt solid. Not because he knew what would come — but because he remembered who he was when no one was watching.

He lay on the bench with his coat over his chest, eyes open, breath steady.

And waited.

Khalid had drifted into sleep as though stepping into water — slowly, without resistance. The light above him never dimmed, but his eyes gave in.

The dream was not vivid, but full.

He stood in white. Simple cloth, draped across his body. His feet were bare, pressed into warm stone. All around him, the hum of voices, the rhythm of movement. He knew this place. Not from memory, but from repetition —

images, stories, prayers. The Kaaba rose before him like a mountain turned inward.

And then he saw his father.

Not younger. Not older. Just... whole. The way he looked on Eid mornings — shirt ironed, beard combed, face lit from within. He turned to Khalid and smiled, the kind of smile that asked nothing, proved nothing. Just love, unstated.

They stood together in the crowd, but it was as if they were alone. His father raised a hand, fingers brushing Khalid's cheek. No words passed. None were needed.

Then the crowd moved — tidal, immense — and his father walked forward, barefoot, shoulders squared. Khalid followed, but the distance between them widened with every step.

He called out — once, then again. But the sound made no echo. His father never turned.

Still, Khalid wasn't afraid. There was no panic in the separation. Only ache. The ache of things unfinished, unspoken. The way sons never quite say what they mean.

He stopped walking. Let the crowd carry his father onward. The cloth at his shoulder slipped slightly, but he didn't adjust it.

The sky above Mecca shimmered gold.

Then the dream had begun to crumble — the stone flickered, the light dimmed. The hum of prayer was replaced by a buzz — artificial, sharp. The cell light. The cold bench. His coat slipped from his chest.

He sat up, heart steady. The floor beneath him was concrete, not stone. His father was gone. But something had lingered.

He placed his hand on his chest, just over the ribs. Closed his eyes again, just for a moment.

Not to sleep. But to remember.

Closed Shop

The street smelt of smoke before he saw it.

Khalid had turned the corner just after dawn, his borrowed shoes soft against the pavement. The air was grey, not from fog but from ash, still hanging low. A tape fluttered across the shop's entrance — police-issued, sagging.

The windows were blackened. The shutter had melted inward, like paper touched by flame. One corner of the doorframe was still smouldering. The sign — "Hanif & Sons" — was gone. Charred remnants clung to the frame like dead leaves.

He stopped a few steps short. There was no crowd. Just one officer, yawning into a clipboard, who looked up and then away.

"Was anyone inside?" Khalid asked.

The officer blinked, unsure if he should answer. "No reports of injury. Fire started overnight. Accelerant, likely. We're looking into it."

Khalid nodded once.

He didn't move closer. Didn't ask to go in.

The glass crunched under the officer's boot as he shifted. "Do you need someone to talk to? We have support services—"

Khalid raised a hand, palm open. The man stopped speaking.

The shop had burned clean. No flour bags, no crates, no shelves. All the years — the slow accumulation of trust, of habit — gone in a night of heat and silence.

He imagined the fire. Quick, private. No explosion. Just light — sudden and total. The till bursting, the walls darkening, the roof sighing as it gave way.

There had been no warning.

No symbol scrawled in paint. No threats. Just erasure.

A neighbour peered out from a window across the street, then drew the curtain.

Khalid turned away.

He walked home slowly, the soles of his feet feeling every stone. The birds were awake. A bus passed. Life continued with indifference.

When he reached his door, he didn't go inside. He stood on the step, eyes closed, smoke still in his nostrils.

No rage came. No tears. Just a hollowing — deep and precise. As if someone had scooped out the centre of him, and left the outline standing.

The street behind him brightened with the rising sun.

The next day, a reporter came.

She knocked gently, a canvas bag slung over one shoulder, press badge visible but not flashing. Khalid opened the door partway, still in his prayer clothes, the tint of ash clinging faintly to the hallway.

"Mr. Hanif," she said. "I'm very sorry. I was hoping you might speak to us. Off the record, if needed."

He looked at her. Not coldly. Not kindly. Just looked.

"We're doing a wider piece," she added. "About Islamophobia. Arson. Prevent. We can help set the record right."

Khalid paused. "Which record?"

She shifted. "The article from before... it mentioned you. We could clarify things. Tell your side."

He stepped back slightly, still holding the door.

"Did you print my name when I hadn't spoken?" he asked.

She hesitated. "I wasn't part of that piece."

He nodded. "But you work for the paper."

"Yes."

He almost smiled.

"I have no side," he said, softly. "Not anymore."

She opened her mouth, then closed it. After a beat, she offered a card. He didn't take it.

"Thank you," he said. Then shut the door.

Inside, the hallway was dim, quiet. He walked to the kitchen. Made tea. No sugar.

At Dhuhr, he prayed alone. The carpet was threadbare beneath his knees. The light from the window touched the floor in stripes. His hands trembled slightly during sujood.

Later, he walked past the shop again. The tape was gone. Someone had sprayed a cleaner over the charred door. A few teens were laughing at something on their phones nearby. One of them glanced at him. Said nothing.

He didn't stop.

That evening, the mosque's WhatsApp group sent out a generic statement: *"We condemn all acts of hate and violence. We continue to pray for unity."*

He muted the thread. Deleted the Prevent number. Threw out the coat he'd worn in the cell.

Night came soft and early. He sat in the dark for a while, TV off, curtains half-drawn.

Someone passed outside. A dog barked once.

Khalid didn't move. Didn't speak.

He just sat there.

Breathing.

Whole, and emptied.

Not broken. Just... left behind.

Part 6: Critical Essay

Community Surveillance and Misjudgement

In a time of heightened suspicion, the gaze turns inward. For Britain's Muslim communities, this surveillance is not only state-imposed but self-inflicted. The architecture of mistrust forms from both the outside and within. Khalid, the shopkeeper at the heart of this story, finds himself enmeshed in a web of double exposure: watched by the authorities and monitored by his own community, yet trusted by neither.

The term "community" implies safety, shared values, mutual defence. But when the mosque council urges silence rather than support, that promise erodes. They are not malicious — they are afraid. Fear of association, fear of guilt by proximity, fear that one mistake will brand them all. So, the logic goes: better to disavow than to defend. The cost is borne by those who do speak, who raise their heads above the parapet. Khalid does so and is promptly abandoned.

Surveillance here does not serve security. It amplifies suspicion. The moment Khalid's name is printed alongside the word "terror," his years of quiet service — running the shop, giving to charity, advising the young — are erased. A name alone suffices. In that instant, he is rebranded, not as a person but a risk. The irony is almost unbearable: the very act of warning is what condemns him.

There is a tragic circularity at work. The state demands vigilance from Muslim citizens; when that vigilance is exercised, it is misread. The local community, meanwhile, knows that attention brings heat, so they choose opacity. In this standoff, sincerity has no place. Only quietism, performance, or ruin.

The breakdown is not one of culture, but of trust. Between state and citizen. Between mosque and individual. Between faith and public life. And when trust collapses, surveillance is no longer a tool — it becomes a condition. A state of being watched and watching back, endlessly, until nothing remains but reflexive silence. Khalid's story reveals the cost of this collapse: reputations lost, livelihoods destroyed, warnings ignored — all in the name of prevention.

And yet, this is not a story of innocence wronged. It is more precise, more painful. It is a story of integrity punished.

Prevent and Perception

The Prevent programme was built on the premise that danger could be pre-empted — that radicalisation has signs, steps, precursors. It offered a policy of vigilance masquerading as care. Yet within many Muslim communities, Prevent is not perceived as a shield but as a net — one cast wide, indiscriminately, and often without recourse.

Khalid's story highlights the paradox. He engages the system in good faith, submitting a warning through the proper channel. His action is not impulsive, nor vindictive — it is cautious, even reluctant. He seeks to protect his community. But his intervention is met not with gratitude, nor even scrutiny, but with accusation. He becomes suspect by association, then by proximity, and finally by the sheer act of speaking. Prevent, in this rendering, does not prevent — it punishes.

The deeper tragedy is epistemic. Who is permitted to know? Who is believed when they speak? Khalid is not listened to as a concerned citizen; he is heard only as a Muslim man, already tethered to the frame of threat. The institutional lens distorts intention: a warning becomes self-incrimination. Perception supersedes content. His truth — factual, anxious, civic — is filtered through a system primed to detect shadows rather than light.

Trust, once again, is the casualty. Prevent presumes a cooperative relationship between the state and the surveilled. But the programme's very structure erodes that possibility. When suspicion is formalised into policy, when cultural identity itself becomes diagnostic, what space remains for dialogue? Khalid's mosque, wary of becoming a target, chooses silence. The police, conditioned by false positives and reputational risk, default to scepticism. The result: a loop of mutual disbelief.

The broader failure is not just strategic, but symbolic. Prevent claims to safeguard society from extremism, but in practice it fractures society further. It teaches communities to fear openness and institutions to fear context. It positions the whistleblower as a likely threat. What then is the citizen to do?

In Khalid's case, the cost of speaking is indistinguishable from the cost of staying silent. That is the final misjudgment — that suspicion can be managed without corroding the very civic participation it depends upon.

｡｡*｡*

Family Guilt

Guilt, when tethered to blood, becomes unshakable. It clings to the innocent, not as a stain of action but as a shadow of proximity. Khalid's ordeal is not only legal or economic — it is moral. His nephew's alleged crime, abstract in detail and undefined in evidence, becomes his burden to carry. In this, family becomes both the wound and the indictment.

The British justice system is not built to assign guilt by relation. Yet the cultural climate into which Khalid is cast does just that. His shop is avoided not because he has done anything wrong, but because he might be "connected." The newspapers do not need to state it plainly — adjacency suffices. One headline, one phrase — "uncle of suspect" — and he is marked. Here, guilt is not a verdict, but a vapour. It lingers in the aisle, at the till, on the surfaces of goods untouched.

For many migrant families, the collective reputation functions like a membrane — thin, delicate, constantly tested. One rupture, even accidental, puts the entire family on display. The young man's alleged act becomes a referendum not just on him, but on his upbringing, his religion, his community. It is an unspoken collectivism imposed from outside — a reversal of the individualist ethos. Where others are judged on personal behaviour, Khalid is judged on his bloodline.

This dynamic breeds internal distortion. It drives wedges between generations. Elders become silent enforcers of respectability; the young grow restless under the weight of inherited surveillance. In Khalid's world, the older men at the mosque council fear further scrutiny, but they also fear moral responsibility. The impulse to protect the community mutates into the instinct to suppress — not for justice, but for survival.

And within Khalid himself, the guilt metastasises. Not because he condoned anything, but because he didn't see it coming. Because in the eyes of others, he should have known. This, too, is its own form of collapse: not a crisis of conscience, but a crisis of memory. Every shared meal, every conversation with his nephew is retrospectively re-read for signs. It is a grief with no clear loss, a shame with no clear cause.

To be family in such a frame is not to be close — it is to be watched together.

Economic Fallout

There is a particular cruelty in how suspicion translates into economics. It is quiet, legal, deniable — and devastating. Khalid's livelihood, built over decades, unravels in a week. No official sanction, no formal closure, just a slow, collective turning away. Customers stop coming. Suppliers delay responses. A reputation, once a community cornerstone, becomes its own liability.

The shop is more than income. It is standing, memory, routine. It is where children once came for sweets, where neighbours exchanged greetings, where the rhythms of British Muslim life — modest, unremarkable — quietly persisted. Its decline is not merely commercial; it is existential. When the door stops chiming, when the shelves remain full at closing time, what disappears is not just trade, but place.

Suspicion functions here like rot: invisible at first, then irreversible. No vandalism. No boycotts. Just the erosion of trust, automated by fear. This is economic violence without spectacle. Its efficiency lies in its plausibility. Who can prove why someone doesn't enter a shop? Who records absence?

Khalid is left with the debris of two systems collapsing at once. One is institutional: a state structure that labels him a threat. The other is social: a local economy that once anchored him, now voids him. His name is printed

— wrongly, carelessly — in a headline, and that's enough. Apologies, if they come, arrive too late, with no restitution. The damage is structural, not sentimental.

What is striking is how quickly the community recalibrates. Where once Khalid was trusted, he is now tolerated at best. His attempts to explain — to contextualise, to defend — only deepen the discomfort. In a culture allergic to complexity, nuance sounds suspicious. So he stops talking. Stops asking. The tills stay silent.

The shop's destruction is a parable of modern collapse: no flames, no chains on the door, just a man alone behind a counter, watching his days hollow out. The "war on terror" often conjures images of raids and rhetoric. But here, its frontline is economic. A small business becomes collateral, not from bombs or protests, but from insinuation.

What burns is not the shop — not yet — but everything it stood for: belonging, continuity, trust. And when it finally does go up in flames, no one is there to witness it but him.

Speechlessness in Faith

Faith communities are often imagined as places of refuge — havens from the chaos outside, sanctuaries for those cast adrift. But what happens when the sanctuary itself demands silence? Khalid turns to the mosque not only as a place of worship but as a site of belonging, of guidance. Instead, he is met with evasion. Not denial of his struggle, but a cold calculus: your suffering is real, but your speech is dangerous.

This silence is not born of apathy, but of fear layered over time. Years of being scrutinised, misquoted, made responsible for acts committed far away or by strangers who happen to share a name or a prayer. The mosque council has seen what public visibility costs. It has learned that to speak out is to invite headlines, surveillance, visits from plainclothes officers. And so the strategy becomes one of internal containment. Keep it quiet. Manage it ourselves. Don't escalate.

What's lost in this equation is precisely what faith should provide: witness. Not solution, not verdict, but presence. A place where suffering is seen, not edited. But Khalid's story is processed through reputational anxiety. He is not offered counsel, only caution. Not solidarity, but risk assessment.

The result is a subtle form of excommunication — not from prayer, but from voice. He may still kneel, still recite, still share the room. But he is not to speak of what has happened. His pain must not leave the threshold. The mosque becomes less a house of God and more a bunker — fortified against intrusion, even if it means keeping its own wounded outside.

This speechlessness is distinct from dignity. It does not arise from reflection or transcendence, but from suppression. It hollows the spiritual core. Prayer is reduced to repetition; communion becomes choreography. Faith, stripped of its moral imperative, becomes ritual without reckoning.

And so Khalid begins to pray alone. Even in a shared space, he is isolated. The sacred language no longer brings comfort. Not because the words have changed, but because the space around them no longer permits honesty.

This is not an attack on religion — it is a mourning for what fear has done to it. When the faithful can no longer speak their grief, the silence becomes its own kind of desecration.

Mistrust and Misdirection

The machinery of counterterrorism is built on the assumption of risk detection — that patterns can be spotted, intentions parsed, interventions timed. But in practice, it often operates more like a mirror maze: each step forward distorts rather than clarifies. In Khalid's case, mistrust governs every interaction. The authorities distrust him because of where he comes from; the mosque distrusts him because of what he might say. Trapped between institutions allergic to nuance, his warning becomes lost in translation — not linguistically, but morally.

He makes contact with Prevent not to harm but to help. He does what every government pamphlet suggests: "If you see something, say something." Yet the act of saying something redirects suspicion back onto him. The message he delivers is uncomfortable, politically sensitive, inconvenient. Rather than address its content, the system interrogates its source. Why is he bringing this up? What's his angle? Is this an attempt to deflect blame?

This is misdirection as defence — a refusal to see the subject, so the focus shifts to the speaker. It is the institutional equivalent of looking past someone. There is no clear accusation, just a mounting sense that his very presence is a problem. The system does not respond to his warning with urgency, but with caution. Not the good kind — the self-protective kind.

Mistrust becomes the ambient condition. Everyone is shielding themselves: the police, the mosque, the public. And in that mutual shielding, clarity is sacrificed. The question — Is there a threat? — gets buried under another: Can we afford to believe him?

The danger here is not only that real threats go undetected. It is that trust, once broken, corrodes the civic ground entirely. If those closest to potential harm cannot speak without penalty, the whole idea of prevention collapses. The system begins to eat its own logic.

Khalid's case is not an outlier; it is a diagram. A man with no prior suspicion raises a legitimate concern and becomes the target of that concern. The institutions meant to protect him reflexively defend themselves instead. His truth is not denied but diverted. His sincerity is filed under "possible risk." And so, the real threat — whatever it was — walks on, unseen.

Who is the Informant?

In a culture saturated with suspicion, the figure of the informant becomes spectral. Everyone could be one; no one admits to being one. Information itself becomes a pollutant — its source always under question, its purpose always doubted. In Khalid's case, the tragedy lies not only in being misread, but in being reclassified. His moral act — alerting authorities — is absorbed by a system that no longer distinguishes between witness and threat.

The informant is traditionally imagined as duplicitous: embedded, hidden, serving power through betrayal. But Khalid is none of these things. He is open, hesitant, even vulnerable. He does not trade information; he offers concern. Yet the role is thrust upon him, not by the community — who would shun him as a traitor — but by the state, who redefine him as a subject of interest.

This double bind is uniquely cruel. To the authorities, he is suspect for knowing too much; to his peers, he is tainted for having spoken at all. Both lenses distort him. The question "Who is the informant?" morphs into a darker one: "Who decides what an informant is?"

At root, this is about narrative control. The state imagines itself as the arbiter of truth, yet it cannot bear truths that disrupt its bureaucratic expectations. So it twists them into procedural anomalies, or risks. Communities, meanwhile, have learned that even the appearance of cooperation with such structures can mark someone for social exile. The moral terrain is reversed: to keep silent is to survive; to speak is to fall.

Khalid's transformation from citizen to suspect happens without process. No charges, no accusations, no defence. Just a shift in posture, in gaze. The officers no longer hear what he says — they study why he's saying it. Paranoia, once projected outward, now turns inward.

This confusion corrodes both civic trust and ethical clarity. When warning and betrayal become indistinguishable, all speech curdles. What remains is silence — not born of cowardice, but of learned futility. Khalid tries to serve justice, and is instead rebranded by the very system he hoped to aid.

In the end, he becomes what the system cannot tolerate: a man who tells the truth without agenda. And for that, he is punished.

Quiet Collapse

Some endings do not arrive with noise, but with absence. Khalid returns home to find his shop — his life's anchor — reduced to ash. There are no protests, no arrests, no slogans. Just a quiet char. A silence where commerce, community, and meaning once stood. This is not collapse as spectacle; it is collapse as drift. Slow, unnoticed, irreversible.

Throughout his ordeal, Khalid follows the rules. He cooperates, warns, endures. And yet at each stage, the institutions around him choose self-preservation over justice. The mosque closes ranks. The police divert suspicion. The press invokes his name with strategic vagueness. Every structure that should have upheld him instead retreats. What remains is the lone figure — not radical, not vengeful — simply hollowed.

He does not speak at the end. Not out of guilt or fear, but because the structures of voice — institutional, communal, spiritual — have failed him. His silence is not submission; it is the residue of clarity. He has seen the cost of speaking, and the void it leaves when no one listens. In this, his story mirrors the wider erosion of civic life in contemporary Britain: the slow substitution of procedure for principle, of scrutiny for solidarity.

This is the quiet collapse — not of buildings or banks, but of bonds. Between neighbour and neighbour, between citizen and state. Trust no longer breaks in crisis; it leaks. Until one day, nothing is left but suspicion and ash. Khalid's silence, in the final scene, is less a retreat than a verdict. Not on himself, but on the system that mistook his loyalty for danger.

There is no redemption offered. No restitution. The shop is gone, the nephew remains a shadow, and Khalid — once a fixture of the street — is now a man moving without witness. This is not an isolated tale. It is the anatomy of a wider disinheritance: of meaning, of place, of the right to speak and be believed.

What he leaves behind is not a legacy, but a question — unspoken, unresolved: If even the faithful are forsaken, what future remains for those still trying to belong?

Part 7: Teacher's Exit

Year 10

The knife wasn't large. Folding. Black handle. Not serrated. It sat at the bottom of the boy's bag, beside a flattened sandwich and two pens without lids. Rachel saw it when the zip snagged halfway, when the boy turned to the window, sulking.

"Empty it, please," she'd said.

His fingers froze. Then moved slowly. One book, then another. Then the sandwich. Then silence.

She leant forward. Reached in. Her hand found the plastic casing first, then metal. She drew it out carefully. No theatrics. Just weight and shape and silence. The classroom had stilled behind her.

She didn't raise her voice. "Whose is this?"

The boy said nothing. He was thin, wiry. Brown hoodie too big for him. His name was Ahmed. Year 10. Recently placed. New enough that the register still hesitated.

"It's not mine," he said finally.

"Where did it come from?"

Shrug.

She looked at him. Not harshly. Just long enough to be clear. "You can't bring this into school."

He stared past her, toward the radiator.

She walked to her desk and placed the knife gently in a drawer. Locked it. Wrote the time in the corner of a scrap paper. The class was watching, silent. No jokes. No whispering. Just held breath.

Rachel turned back. "Everyone take out your books. Page 94."

No one moved at first. Then slowly, the shuffle resumed. Chairs creaked. Pages turned.

Ahmed didn't speak for the rest of the lesson. She didn't push. Didn't call him out. She taught as if it were a normal day, as if a blade hadn't been folded beside a sandwich. But her voice felt thinner. Like a thread stretched too tight.

After the bell, she waited until the room cleared.

He lingered by the door.

"Did you mean to bring it?" she asked.

He shrugged again. "In case."

"In case of what?"

He didn't answer. Then, softly: "In Syria, we keep one."

She nodded. "But here, it's different. This—" she tapped the drawer "—it gets reported."

He looked down. "Will they send me away?"

"No," she said. Then, "Not for this."

He left without a sound.

Rachel sat alone for a moment. The drawer still locked. Her fingers resting on it.

The knife hadn't been brandished. Just carried.

But that didn't matter anymore.

The email came before lunch.

"Please report to the Head's office at 12:45. Immediate."

No subject line. No greeting. Just that.

Rachel walked the corridor with her staff badge swinging against her chest, past the Year 8s who always left lunch trailing crisps and noise. She knocked once, then entered.

Three people were waiting. The Head. A governor she barely knew. And someone from HR — clipboard already open.

"Rachel," the Head said. "Take a seat."

She sat.

"This is about an incident reported this morning. With a Year 10 student — Ahmed."

She nodded. "Yes. He had a knife. I secured it. Locked it in the desk. Followed safeguarding protocol."

The governor leant forward. "There's a concern the response may have lacked... cultural awareness."

Rachel stared at him.

"Sorry?"

"We've spoken with the student. He felt targeted. He says the knife wasn't intended as a threat."

"It was in his bag," she said, evenly. "I didn't accuse him. I removed it, calmly."

"There's also a claim that you raised your voice."

"I didn't."

"We'll be conducting a full review," the HR woman said. "In the meantime, we're placing you on precautionary suspension. Effective immediately."

Rachel blinked. "You're suspending me. For confiscating a weapon."

The Head shifted in his chair. "We're not drawing conclusions. But we have to be seen to respond proportionately."

"To whom?"

"To the context," he said. "To the sensitivities involved."

Rachel looked at them, one by one. Their faces were calm. Sympathetic. Distant.

"I want the statement I gave. And a copy of the complaint."

"Of course," HR said. "In due course."

She stood. "What happens to the boy?"

The governor smiled, small. "That's a separate conversation."

She left the room without shaking hands. Her classroom door was already being unlocked by a cover supervisor when she returned. A clipboard in her hand. Averted eyes.

In the staffroom, her mug had already been moved. Desk half-cleared. Phone badge revoked.

By 1:15, she was in her car, keys shaking slightly in the ignition.

She didn't cry.

She didn't call anyone.

She drove home in silence, the blade of the morning now replaced by something sharper: the knowledge that doing the right thing had become the wrong shape.

Review

The room was neutral. Beige walls, soft chairs, a tray of untouched water glasses. A projector screen in sleep mode blinked quietly behind the panel.

Rachel sat at one end of the table. Notepad unopened. Hands folded in her lap.

Across from her: the Head, the HR rep, a governor with laminated policies fanned in front of him, and a cultural liaison officer she'd never seen before. Introduced simply as "Imran."

"We're here to conclude the investigation," the Head began. His tone was clipped, practiced. "This is not a disciplinary panel. It's a restorative review."

Rachel said nothing.

The HR rep continued. "The focus is on impact, not intention. We understand you followed certain procedures. However—"

She paused. Looked up, as if the word itself required permission.

"—there have been concerns raised that your approach lacked cultural sensitivity."

Rachel blinked. "Removing a knife?"

The governor stepped in. "It's about how. The perception. There are trauma considerations. Refugee experience. Symbolism."

Rachel leant forward slightly. "He brought a weapon into school. I acted to prevent harm. I didn't raise my voice. I didn't accuse him."

"We're not disputing the presence of the item," said Imran, softly. "But in some cultures, carrying a blade has protective meaning. Not aggression. You might have asked before assuming."

"I didn't assume. I saw a knife. I removed it."

The room paused. The HR officer cleared her throat.

"We've concluded that while your actions were procedurally sound, the tone and manner created distress. Especially in a cross-cultural setting."

Rachel laughed, once. Quietly. "So the knife is real. The threat is real. But I'm the harm."

"We're asking all staff to undergo a short cultural competency refresher," said the Head. "To ensure these situations are handled with more nuance."

Rachel looked at the water glasses. None had fingerprints.

"Will that be all?" she asked.

The Head nodded. "There's one further matter. We'd like to propose a nondisclosure agreement. Not disciplinary — just closure. For everyone."

A document slid across the table.

She didn't pick it up.

She stood. "You've made your decision. I won't be back."

They didn't stop her.

At the door, Imran offered a polite nod. As if they'd spoken the same language.

Outside, the sky had turned to drizzle. Her car looked smaller than she remembered.

She didn't cry.

She just drove somewhere she hadn't planned to go. Anywhere but back.

The envelope came by courier.

Plain. No letterhead. Just her name, spelled correctly for once. Inside: a printed agreement, two copies, a prepaid return envelope. Paperweight law. Soft language, sharp edges.

Rachel read it at the kitchen table. Mug of tea gone cold. The house was quiet except for the fridge humming, indifferent.

This agreement confirms mutual closure and prevents further reputational harm to all parties. No admission of wrongdoing is made. The employee agrees to refrain from discussing the incident with media, staff, or external persons. A modest severance will be issued upon signature.

She turned the page. Nothing about the knife. Nothing about the child. Nothing about the panic she'd buried behind protocol.

Only clauses.

The school wanted clean hands. No noise. Just a line drawn and filed. She could almost hear the phrasing if she refused: "We tried to be generous. She chose otherwise."

She placed the paper back in the envelope. Did not seal it.

That evening, a former colleague messaged: *Heard you're taking time off. Hope you're okay x*

Rachel typed nothing in return. She deleted the message.

At night, she took the agreement out again. Left it on the sofa. Stared at it from across the room.

It wasn't the money. It was the silence. The price of her voice, calculated and stapled.

The next morning, she took the envelope to the post box.

She stood there for a long time, arm raised, flap open.

Then slowly, she tore the agreement in half. Once. Then again. Folded the pieces neatly and slid them into her coat pocket.

Not defiance. Not theatre.

Just refusal.

She walked to the river instead. Sat on a bench, watched the water move past, fast and directionless.

When she came home, she filed nothing. Told no one.

The school would write their version. The file would remain. Her name, recorded next to "incident." A scar in the database.

But she had spoken the truth. Even if no one kept a copy.

Last Class

The board still held the smudged outlines of last week's lesson — metaphors and motifs, half-erased. Rachel didn't wipe them. Just picked up the marker and wrote one word beneath them:

Doublespeak.

Year 10 filtered in slowly, reluctant and half-alert. A few muttered greetings. Most kept their heads down. Ahmed was absent. No one mentioned him.

She waited until they were seated.

"Today's our last session on Orwell," she said. "We're looking at the difference between what is said, and what is meant."

A few eyes lifted. One girl opened her notebook.

Rachel circled the word on the board. "Doublespeak is when institutions change language to hide meaning. They don't say *torture* — they say *enhanced interrogation.* They don't say *war* — they say *operation.* Why?"

A boy in the back shrugged. "Makes it sound better."

"Exactly," Rachel said. "Language shapes memory. If we forget the word, we forget what happened."

She turned to the novel. Held it up. *1984,* worn spine, dog-eared.

"In the story, the Party controls everything by controlling language. No words = no rebellion. No record = no truth."

A hand went up. Cautious. From a girl near the window.

"Miss... is that real? Can that really happen?"

Rachel looked at her. Not gently. Not unkindly.

"It already does," she said.

The room shifted, just slightly. A silence crept in — not heavy, just alert.

She placed the book down. "One day, you'll be told something didn't happen. Even though you remember it. Even though you were there. They'll say you misread. Misunderstood. Overreacted."

No one moved.

"That's when you'll need language. To say: *No. I saw it. I know what it was.*"

A few students looked at each other. One boy began tapping his pen. The spell broke.

The bell rang.

Chairs scraped back. Bags zipped. Voices rose. The class emptied in minutes.

Rachel remained. Erased the board slowly. Left the word *Doublespeak* untouched.

The cover teacher arrived early. She didn't look Rachel in the eye.

"You're done, then?" the woman asked.

"Yes," Rachel said. "I'm done."

She handed her key over. Walked out with nothing but her bag. Past the staffroom, past the copier, past the hallway where the motivational posters peeled at the corners.

No one stopped her. No one called out.

The corridor swallowed her footsteps. She didn't look back.

She tried once.

Not formally. Not through grievance channels or press. Just a quiet conversation in the staffroom.

It was the day before she left. The kettle was humming. The clock above the sink ticked with that loud, institutional click. Rachel sat across from Mark — English, ten years in, the kind who called students "mate" and meant it.

"I'm not coming back next term," she said.

He looked up, surprised. "Oh?"

"They're calling it a mutual parting. After the review."

Mark hesitated. "The knife thing?"

She nodded.

He scratched his chin. "Bit of a storm, that one."

"I followed policy. They said I made the boy feel unsafe."

"Did you?"

"No. I made the room safe."

He nodded. Slowly. Neutral.

She waited. For outrage. For sympathy. For anything resembling care.

Nothing came.

"We all have to be careful now," he said finally. "These days... things get political fast."

Rachel laughed once. "Since when was safety political?"

Mark sipped his tea. "Since always, really."

The silence between them stretched.

"Anyway," he said, standing, "sorry it ended like this. You were good. The kids liked you."

She didn't say thank you.

He left his mug on the table and walked out.

Alone in the room, Rachel looked around. The peeling laminate. The stack of untouched CPD manuals. A poster that read *Every Child Matters*.

She stood, walked to the noticeboard. Pulled down a flyer for an anti-bullying week no one had attended.

There had been a moment to speak louder. To write something. To demand clarity. She hadn't taken it.

Because no one had listened the first time.

Because the room had been full, and still she'd been alone.

Now, she understood.

It wasn't that they disagreed.

It was that they were tired. Afraid. And used to watching the door close on people like her.

She picked up her bag and walked out, the fluorescent lights buzzing overhead like static.

In the corridor, a cleaner passed with a trolley.

Rachel smiled. The woman didn't look up.

Farewell

It was left on her desk. Folded neatly. A supermarket card — sunflowers, pale yellow. Inside: blue ink, slanted hand, a short message.

Thank you for caring. For trying. Some of us noticed.

No name.

No clue.

She stared at it for a long time. Not touched by the sentiment — but by its anonymity. Even gratitude, now, required caution.

She placed the card into her bag without folding it again. No sense creasing what had barely survived.

Her desk was already half-cleared. The drawers empty except for a broken stapler and one paperclip. The poster of Orwell she'd kept taped to the cupboard had curled at the corners. She left it.

A few students passed the room. None stopped. One glanced in. Rachel gave a small nod. The girl looked away.

The silence of endings is different than other kinds. Not hostile. Just final. A kind of vanishing made polite.

She walked through the building slowly. One last round — the library still missing books, the IT room always locked, the mural near reception painted over after some incident last year no one now discussed.

Near the lockers, someone had scrawled *LIAR* in marker. She didn't stop to wonder who it was meant for.

Back at reception, the clerk handed her a brown envelope. Final paperwork. Nothing to say.

She signed where indicated.

"Best of luck," the clerk offered.

Rachel nodded.

Outside, the sky was pale. The wind was picking up. Leaves skittered across the pavement like small, unsure things.

She walked to her car, unlocked the door, sat for a moment before starting the engine.

The card sat on the passenger seat, unopened again. She didn't look at it.

The building behind her remained exactly as she'd left it.

No one ran out.

No one waved.

Just another gap to be filled by someone else, quickly.

It was a Monday morning, three days after her last day.

Rachel was heading to the supermarket — small list, no rush. The car had sat untouched over the weekend, dusted with rain and leaves.

She noticed it before she reached the driver's side. A long, jagged line carved into the paint. Deep. Shiny beneath. Fresh.

The word spanned both doors.

Racist.

No punctuation. No doubt.

She stood there for a moment, keys in hand, the cold wind tugging at her coat. A neighbour across the road was watering plants. She didn't look up.

Rachel crouched to run a finger along the edge. The metal was raw. The line wasn't shaky — it had been done with purpose. Someone had taken their time.

She didn't call anyone.

Didn't report it.

Didn't photograph it.

She unlocked the door, sat inside, turned the key. The engine stuttered once, then caught.

For a moment, she stared through the windscreen at the street. Nothing moved. No faces in windows. Just bins and stone and the smell of damp.

She drove to the supermarket, parked at the far end of the lot. When she returned, groceries in hand, the word was still there. Of course it was.

She drove home, reversed into the driveway, and left the keys in the ignition longer than she needed to.

Inside, she placed the groceries quietly. One apple bruised. Milk slightly warm.

Later that evening, she searched for quotes from body-repair shops. Then closed the tabs.

She sat on the sofa, coat still on, and looked at the card again — the unsigned one.

She opened it.

Reread the same line.

Some of us noticed.

But not enough to name themselves.

Not enough to speak.

Outside, the wind picked up again. Something scraped against the window — a branch, or maybe just the cold.

She didn't move.

The word was still out there, carved into metal. A sentence no one had said to her. But one someone wanted her to carry.

And she did.

Not with shame.

Just weight.

New Work

The warehouse smelt of cardboard and dust. Long aisles, fluorescent buzz, metal shelves stretching toward a ceiling she couldn't touch. No windows. Just strip lighting and the low whine of conveyor belts.

Her badge said *RAE HAN*, clipped to a blue lanyard. No title. No role. Just time stamps and scanner codes.

The job was simple. Open box. Log barcode. Place on shelf. Repeat. No essays. No safeguarding reports. No children.

At first, the silence felt sharp. Then it dulled into something like peace.

No one asked her about her past. They just handed her a hi-vis vest and pointed down the aisle. A woman in her twenties showed her the code system — yellow for fiction, blue for textbooks. Rachel didn't say she used to teach the books she now stacked.

On break, she sat alone. Tea in a paper cup. No staffroom chatter. No performance of camaraderie. Just space.

Her hands adjusted quickly. The weight of books was familiar. The rhythm — lift, scan, place — became a kind of anchor.

Occasionally, a title would catch her eye. Orwell. Baldwin. A battered copy of *Lord of the Flies*. She didn't open them. Just logged the numbers, shelved them, moved on.

No one called her Miss here.

No one called her anything.

That suited her.

The shift ended with a beep from the wrist scanner. She handed in her lanyard. Walked to her car — still scarred, still unread. The word no longer fresh, but never quite faded.

She sat behind the wheel and watched the other workers file out. Laughter, phones, smoke breaks. None of it touched her.

The engine started on the first turn. She drove home through traffic, headlights brushing her windows like insects.

In the kitchen, she made toast. Stood while she ate it.

The quiet now didn't hurt. It just was.

She looked at the card again, on the table. Still unsigned. She didn't throw it away. She didn't frame it either.

She just left it there.

Tomorrow, she'd start earlier. More boxes. More codes. No questions.

She was no longer needed in the place where she'd spoken.

Here, at least, silence was part of the contract.

The warehouse had no clocks. Just the soft tick of scan guns and the rhythm of footsteps echoing through the aisles. Time passed in boxloads. Quiet was constant, almost medicinal.

Rachel moved through her tasks without thought now. Her hands did the remembering. Labels. Shelves. Tape. Lift with your knees.

There was no classroom to prepare. No bell. No questions.

No one called her late at night to ask for cover. No parent-teacher conferences. No reports.

No voices saying her name with anything attached.

She ate lunch alone. Same seat. Corner table. The others didn't exclude her. They just didn't notice her. She was older than most. Dressed differently. Eyes that didn't scan a room for chatter — only for exits.

Once, a younger colleague asked if she'd been a librarian. She smiled, said "Sort of." He didn't press.

After her shift, the quiet followed her home. The house was clean. Too clean. She started leaving mugs out just to soften the edges.

The TV stayed off. She couldn't stand the noise of people pretending.

At night, the silence became sharper. She sometimes spoke aloud, just to hear something. Simple things.

"Kettle's on."

"Check the back door."

"Don't forget the bins."

The words sounded hollow in the small rooms.

She missed questions. Missed the mess of them. The way a student would ask something off-topic, then look embarrassed. The way it meant they trusted you, just a bit.

At the warehouse, trust wasn't required. Just stamina.

She tried to read once, before bed. Picked up an old copy of *To Kill a Mockingbird*. Made it four pages. Put it back.

The classroom was gone. The students, scattered. The lessons — hers and theirs — now suspended in time with no exam, no end-of-term feedback.

She sometimes dreamed of chalkboards. Of red pens that bled across essays. Of names she couldn't remember until she woke.

The dreams weren't nightmares.

Just echoes.

The File

It had been in the drawer for weeks. Slipped inside the brown envelope she almost threw away. A stamped cover sheet, two pages, unsigned.

That evening, Rachel pulled it out. Sat at the table with a mug of weak tea. The light above her hummed. The house was still.

The report was titled: "Incident Review – Staff Conduct and Cultural Sensitivity: Case 0403-RH"

She read slowly. Word by word. Not scanning — absorbing.

"The staff member's decision to confiscate the item in question was in alignment with safeguarding procedures. However, the tone and approach may have contributed to student distress."

She snorted quietly. *Tone and approach.*

"Given the sensitive background of the pupil, and the broader context of integration and trauma, greater cultural awareness was advised."

Advised, not offered.

Further down: *"No formal disciplinary action is being pursued. Closure has been mutually agreed."*

Closure. As if stories end that easily.

She flipped to the final page.

"This report is not to be distributed or referenced in future proceedings."

Even the paper wanted to forget.

She stared at the document. The weight of it. Not its heft — it was light, barely three sheets. But the finality. The effort of a system to reduce her into language it could manage.

She tried to remember if the boy had ever spoken to her again. He hadn't.

She placed the paper flat. Smoothed the corners.

Then, without ceremony, she reached for the shredder.

Fed the first page through. The hum rose. The paper vanished in strips. Second page. Third.

Done.

No pause. No speech. Just a hand guiding silence into ribbons.

She sat back, sipping her tea. Still warm. The shredder quiet now. A bin full of noise no longer permitted to speak.

She did not feel triumphant.

Just clean.

The shredded paper settled like dry leaves in the bin. Thin, pale strands curled and silent. Rachel watched them for a moment. No sense of victory. No regret.

Just silence.

The machine clicked softly as it cooled.

She stood, carried the bin to the back door. Stepped into the night.

The air was cool, soft with the smell of someone else's fire drifting down the road. No moon, just streetlamp glow smudging against the hedges.

She tipped the strips into the compost. No ceremony. No ashes. Just paper returning to earth by other means.

Inside, she washed her hands. Carefully. The way she used to after marking — ink on the knuckles, highlighter on the fingertips. Tonight, no colour. Just the faint smell of toner and dust.

She turned off the light. Sat on the arm of the sofa. Listened to the house creak.

It was done.

Not healed. Not forgotten. Just done.

The system had written its version. She had refused to preserve it.

There would be no archive of her refusal. No tribunal. No footnote.

Just a woman in a quiet house, who once taught children how to see through lies — and was asked to leave when she told the truth too clearly.

She opened the window. Let the air in.

Somewhere, a fox called out. Sharp, plaintive.

Rachel closed her eyes.

The page was gone. The story remained.

Part 7: Critical Essay

Discipline Under Duress

Discipline, once the spine of classroom authority, has become a terrain of deep uncertainty. In the world Rachel inhabits, rules no longer anchor — they negotiate. Her confiscation of a knife, once a clear-cut act of duty, is reclassified as "culturally insensitive," her authority dissolved not because she erred, but because she acted decisively. This is the new logic of institutional response: to police the enforcers more readily than the infractions.

The deeper collapse is not pedagogical but moral. Schools now operate under the weight of competing obligations — safety, inclusion, cultural sensitivity, legal exposure — but without clarity on hierarchy. When these values clash, as they inevitably do, the result is paralysis. In Rachel's case, the knife is not just a weapon; it becomes a symbol of the limits of institutional courage. Rather than ask who brought it or why, the system interrogates her for removing it.

This reversal doesn't simply demoralise teachers. It destabilises the entire classroom. When a student sees a teacher publicly rebuked for enforcing order, the lesson learned is not nuance — it is impunity. The classroom becomes a performance space where language is guarded, not shared; where action is weighed not by principle but by optics.

Rachel's suspension is not an isolated event but a signal. It says to staff: tread lightly. It says to students: boundaries are subject to negotiation. It says to parents, policymakers, and observers that equity, when decoupled from context, can void accountability entirely. Discipline under duress is not about balancing justice and compassion. It is about surviving the optics of enforcement.

The cost is borne most heavily by teachers like Rachel — working-class, experienced, not media-trained. She is not reckless. She is responsible. But responsibility without institutional backing becomes a trap. Once suspended, she is asked to sign a nondisclosure agreement — the final seal on her silencing. The act of discipline, and the fallout it triggers, now require erasure, not reflection.

What begins as a simple protective act ends in reputational collapse. No trial, no defence. Just the suggestion that her presence is the problem. In such a system, justice becomes spectral — glimpsed, but never grasped. And the students, watching all of this, inherit the most dangerous lesson: that authority can be dismantled not by truth, but by discomfort.

The Taboo of Truth

There is a truth at the centre of Rachel's story — plain, inconvenient, and increasingly unspeakable. A teacher, following protocol, confiscates a knife from a student. The student is a recent arrival, from a war zone, carrying trauma and memory. The object may mean different things in different contexts. But in a British classroom, it is still a knife. Still a danger.

Yet when Rachel acts, she is not protected but isolated. The response is not inquiry, but condemnation. Her actions are interpreted not through the lens of intent or

necessity, but through the loaded frame of cultural insensitivity. In this reframing, truth itself becomes a liability —
not because it is incorrect, but because it is volatile. The
system's reflex is not to examine what happened, but to
avoid what it might imply.

This is the core of the taboo: certain truths, once spoken,
are no longer manageable. And so they are recoded as
aggression, reframed as prejudice. The facts remain — a
knife in a child's bag, a teacher's intervention — but the
language around them collapses. Rachel is told not that
she was wrong, but that she was disruptive. Not that she
endangered, but that she destabilised.

Truth, in this context, is not denied outright. It is side-
stepped. It is too combustible for a risk-averse institution
that now operates more like a PR firm than a place of
learning. In such spaces, neutrality becomes performative.
Everyone must appear balanced, even when the scales are
tipping.

The danger here is cumulative. Each time a teacher is
punished for speaking plainly, others learn the lesson: stay
quiet, stay vague, stay safe. The truth becomes not only
forbidden — it becomes isolated, ridiculed, exiled. It ceases
to function as a communal reference point. Instead, it becomes the domain of the "problematic," the "divisive," the
"unhelpful."

Rachel does not speak out of malice. She acts from duty.
But duty, when truth is taboo, becomes dangerous. Her
silence at the end is not defeat — it is survival. She learns
that truth, once stripped of context and complexity, can no
longer protect her.

What is left is a vacuum. And into that vacuum pours performance, euphemism, and fear — a pedagogy of avoidance. The students see this too. They learn not to question,
but to watch what is permitted. And in that silence, the truth

— small, sharp, real — remains untouched on the floor, never to be picked up again.

Institutional Cowardice

When institutions face complexity, they often choose optics over courage. Rachel's case exemplifies this impulse. Presented with a clear breach of safety — a weapon in a classroom — her school does not ask how to protect or educate. It asks how to manage perception. The student is shielded, the context flattened, and Rachel becomes the problem to be solved.

This is not protection; it is abandonment. The school suspends her swiftly, publicly, and under the banner of sensitivity. Yet that word is a shield, not a solution. No inquiry is launched into why a child brought a knife. No questions are asked about support, fear, or background. Instead, the system short-circuits. Rachel's actions threaten institutional harmony — not because they were unjust, but because they might be *seen* as unjust.

What masquerades as caution is, in truth, cowardice. A school that cannot defend its staff when they act within duty has already collapsed in purpose. Its priority has shifted: no longer to education, but to risk containment. Its policies become masks. Its staff, expendable.

Rachel is offered a non-disclosure agreement — a quiet exit, a sealed mouth. This is not about resolution. It is about erasure. The institution's reputation is preserved by removing the witness. Such gestures are not only bureaucratic. They are moral evasions. They say: *We saw what happened. We just don't want anyone else to.*

This cowardice is not new. It thrives in all sectors where accountability might cost image. But in schools, it is particularly corrosive. Because schools are where values are shaped — where children learn what justice looks like in real time. When they see a teacher punished for doing what is right, the lesson is profound: authority is conditional. Truth is dangerous. Safety is rhetorical.

The broader impact reaches beyond one woman, one moment. Teachers retreat into scripted roles. Conversations flatten. Real engagement gives way to surveillance — not just of students, but of themselves. Every sentence weighed. Every instinct doubted.

And so, the institution survives, technically. But not honestly. It stands on foundations that crack each time someone like Rachel is pushed out for doing what needed to be done.

Cowardice here is not loud. It is procedural, quiet, and devastating. And in its silence, a generation watches — learning, absorbing, remembering.

Censorship by Policy

There was a time when censorship came in red pens and torn posters. Now it arrives in PDFs and HR procedures. In Rachel's case, it is disguised as protocol — the suspension, the nondisclosure, the soft insistence that she "reflect" on her cultural awareness. But what's being managed here is not behaviour; it is narrative. The school is not silencing harm — it is silencing discomfort.

Policy becomes the language of avoidance. It allows institutions to claim neutrality while enforcing erasure. The document Rachel is handed is not overtly punitive. It is legal, temperate, couched in concern. But its effect is absolute: do not speak. Not to the press. Not to students. Not even to colleagues. Her experience is not just punished — it is removed from record.

This is not incidental. It is structural. The very tools designed to ensure accountability have been weaponised to contain it. Safeguarding policies, equity training, complaint procedures — all of them can be turned inward, used to silence those who act in good faith but beyond the script. Rachel did not break rules. She transgressed expectations. Expectations that remain unspoken until breached.

What's censored here is not a slur, not hate, not misinformation. It is experience. It is reality. A knife in a classroom becomes unsayable because it raises the wrong questions. Because it risks aligning the institution with a "narrative" deemed politically fraught. So instead of grappling with complexity, the school opts for simplicity: suppress the witness.

This kind of censorship is more insidious than bans. It offers the illusion of consent. Rachel signs the document. She is not forced. She is "advised." And yet, the choice is false. To refuse is to be branded difficult, disloyal, unmanageable. To accept is to vanish, decorously.

For the institution, this is success. No headlines. No scandal. No need to explain. For Rachel, it is erasure. She leaves not only unemployed but unacknowledged. What she lived is now off-limits — locked behind clauses and risk assessments.

The tragedy is that this censorship does not protect anyone. Not the student. Not the staff. Not the truth. It simply delays reckoning. The silence grows heavier. The lessons harder to teach.

And somewhere down the line, another teacher will find another knife. And the question will repeat, unanswered: can I say what happened?

Orwell and Irony

When Rachel teaches Orwell in her final lesson, it is not symbolic — it is surgical. *1984* was never meant as prophecy, but in her classroom, its metaphors have already arrived. Language is policed. Thought is managed. Reality, if inconvenient, is quietly rewritten. The knife was real. The danger was real. But the record now says otherwise.

The irony is suffocating. Rachel stands before her students, discussing a novel about censorship, surveillance, and institutional betrayal — while herself being censored, observed, and erased. Her authority is crumbling as she speaks. No one listens. Not because they don't understand, but because they've already absorbed the lesson that truth is subordinate to perception.

Orwell wrote of Newspeak, a language designed to reduce the range of thought. In Rachel's world, that language is not imposed — it's internalised. Words like *concern, safety, sensitivity* are deployed not to clarify, but to blur. The vocabulary of care is used to suppress. And the students, consciously or not, perform within this new lexicon. They know what can be said. What can't. How to navigate the unspoken grid of permissible expression.

Rachel's attempt to teach Orwell is, in itself, an act of resistance. She wants her students to recognise the shape of control — not just in fiction, but around them. But the effort is too late. The mechanisms she's trying to illuminate are already in place. She is not just describing the system; she is being crushed by it in real time.

The greater irony is structural. Education, once positioned as a bulwark against authoritarianism, now replicates its traits under the guise of inclusion. Surveillance is digital. Compliance is performative. Teachers are discouraged from thinking aloud. Students are encouraged to report transgressions, not debate them. The classroom becomes a site of soft discipline, where conformity replaces conviction.

Rachel's shredding of the official report in the final scene is not petulance. It is elegy. A final, private act against the rewriting of truth. If the report stands, it becomes the version — official, sanctioned, inert. By destroying it, she reclaims a sliver of control. Not justice, but defiance.

In Orwell's world, power was loud and brutal. In Rachel's, it is quiet, bureaucratic, and polite. But the effect is the same: truth is whatever the institution says it is. And those who question it are made to vanish — not with violence, but with forms.

Violence Reframed

Violence, in Rachel's classroom, is not about blood or bruises. It is about perception. A knife is brought in. A teacher intervenes. Yet it is not the act that defines the aggression — it is the framing. The system does not ask, *What happened?* It asks, *What does this look like?* And in that question, everything shifts.

Rachel is rebranded not as protector, but as aggressor. Her intervention, motivated by safety, is recast as an act of cultural insensitivity. The presence of the weapon becomes secondary; her manner becomes the issue. She is not accused of harm, but of disruption — the subtle, institutional sin of making things difficult.

This inversion is not new. In spaces preoccupied with inclusion but allergic to conflict, clarity often becomes a threat. To act decisively, especially in moments charged by culture or race, is to risk misreading — not because the facts are unclear, but because the institution fears how others might interpret them. So the violent act recedes, and the response becomes the scandal.

Rachel's case reveals how violence is reframed to protect institutions, not individuals. The student is positioned as vulnerable, the knife contextualised, the teacher scrutinised. It is not that the child is bad, nor that the system is malicious — but that the logic of the institution prioritises image over impact. The question is never *What is true?* but *What is safest to say?*

This creates an impossible bind. If Rachel had ignored the weapon and something happened, she would be blamed for negligence. If she acts, she is blamed for overreach. In both cases, her authority is undermined. The system offers no stable ground — only a constantly shifting terrain where the rules change with the audience.

What's lost in this is the very idea of moral action. Rachel didn't react out of fear or bias — she responded to danger. But her motives are not defended, because motives don't matter in systems that fear optics. Her professionalism is consumed by institutional cowardice. The student is not punished. The knife is forgotten. Rachel is the one who must go.

Violence, then, is not what is done — it is what is named. And Rachel, in doing her job, becomes the one whose name must be quietly removed.

Working-Class Female Educators

Rachel is not just a teacher. She is a woman from a working-class background who has spent her adult life in public service. Her voice carries the accent of place, not polish. Her authority is earned, not inherited. And in the current institutional climate, that makes her expendable.

There is an unspoken hierarchy within education — not just of role, but of voice. Middle-class, managerial figures speak the language of policy. They navigate the politics of inclusion with the right idioms. Rachel does not. Her instincts are honed through experience, not training sessions. She responds to danger directly. She speaks without euphemism. And that lack of polish — that refusal or inability to speak in coded terms — marks her as dangerous.

This is how disposability is structured. Rachel is not defended because she is not seen as strategically valuable. Her class and gender make her visible only in moments of crisis — not in celebration, not in policy-making, not in staff portraits. She is expected to do the emotional labour, manage chaos, absorb failure — but when the system faces scrutiny, she is the first to be sacrificed.

Her gender compounds this. Women like Rachel are often cast in dual roles — maternal yet authoritative, compassionate yet controlled. When they break from these roles — when they raise their voices, when they draw hard lines — they are punished more harshly. Their decisiveness is called insensitivity. Their firmness, aggression. Rachel's fall is not just about a knife. It is about the system's deep discomfort with women who do not defer.

Moreover, Rachel does not have the cushion of class. No union lawyer on speed dial. No access to media platforms or sympathetic columnists. When she is asked to sign the nondisclosure, it is not just a legal act — it is the sealing off of a life's work without dignity. The message is clear: your labour mattered, your presence did not.

The deeper cruelty is that she is not even surprised. This is not her first betrayal, only the final one. And when she takes a job shelving books in a warehouse, it is not a reinvention. It is exile.

What we see in Rachel is not a scandal, but a pattern. Working-class women like her built the modern school system. But when collapse comes, they are asked not to be seen — only swept away.

Shredding the Record

The final gesture is quiet. Rachel rereads the report — the official version of her downfall — and feeds it into a shredder. Page by page, her story is consumed by thin blades, turned into unreadable strands. It is not an act of rage, but of clarity. She understands now that the document was never meant to preserve truth. It was written to overwrite it.

Institutional records carry the weight of legitimacy. They are how systems remember — or choose not to. The report likely describes her actions in careful, evasive language: "inappropriate response," "cultural insensitivity," "failure to consider context." It likely omits the knife. Or buries it. It likely praises her previous service, not as recognition, but as a soft landing into silence.

By shredding it, Rachel rejects the terms of her erasure. She does not seek vindication. She seeks to stop the lie from being enshrined. This is not about rewriting the past — it's about refusing to let it be rewritten for her.

The image is stark because it is final. No press release. No tribunal. Just paper turned to strands, the same way her career was quietly dismantled — slice by slice, under the hum of polite procedure. In a system that speaks in records, to destroy one is to speak for yourself.

There's something painfully intimate in this act. Teachers file reports. They build records. They teach students that documentation matters. And now, Rachel sees that hers was built not to protect, but to contain her. The system took what she did, translated it into a language that erased her motive, her fear, her humanity — and filed it away.

She does not burn it. That would be too dramatic. Too loud. The shredder is bureaucratic, domestic — fitting. The record that tried to end her ends in the same language it was written: quiet, mechanical, efficient.

What remains is not a replacement story, but absence. She chooses not to fill the gap. Just to preserve the truth by denying the lie its permanence.

In the end, there is no redemption. No return to the classroom. Just silence and a stack of shredded paper, fluttering in the bin like a thousand unsent messages.

Part 8: The Blue Light

Missed Call

Kev sat in the cab, thermos in hand, eyes on the map. The screen blinked once, quietly — a soft tone, barely urgent.

CODE: R4 – Respiratory Distress. LOCATION: RIVERTON BLOCK CSTATUS: OUT OF COVERAGE ZONE

He sipped the tea. Still hot. Still too sweet. The call hung on the display, red lettering flashing slower with each second.

His partner, Lee, leant forward. "That's outside the grid."

Kev nodded. "Reroute'll catch it. Eventually."

"Looks bad."

Kev didn't answer. He tapped the screen once — *Acknowledge but not attending*. The alert dimmed, vanished. The cab returned to quiet.

Outside, the housing blocks loomed. Riverton was less than two miles away. Fifteen minutes with traffic. Ten with lights. But it wasn't on the new coverage map. Not anymore.

Lee adjusted his seatbelt. "Used to be our patch."

"Not since the restructure."

They watched a fox dart between bins. Its eyes caught the morning glare. Then it was gone.

Kev leant back. His fingers tapped the steering wheel. Not nervously. Just out of habit.

"You okay?" Lee asked.

Kev didn't answer right away. "It's just a call."

Lee nodded. Said nothing more.

The radio buzzed again — a job in a hotel by the bypass. Private contract. Guaranteed response.

Kev clicked *Accept*. Shifted gear. Pulled out slowly.

The blue light wasn't needed. Not yet.

As they turned onto the ring road, Kev glanced in the side mirror. The towers behind them faded into fog. He imagined the sound of a phone ringing in one of those flats. A child coughing. A mother waiting by the window.

They'd be told an ambulance wasn't available. Maybe later. Maybe not.

Kev kept driving.

"You sure you're alright?" Lee asked again.

Kev nodded once. "We go where we're sent."

Neither of them said the rest.

They arrived at the hotel seven minutes later. The patient — a minor panic attack — was already being helped by on-site staff.

Kev stepped inside, clipboard in hand. Smile ready.

The siren never went on.

The call from Riverton never came back.

The lobby was spotless. Smelt of antiseptic and cinnamon. Kev stepped inside, boots muffled by polished tile. A security guard nodded, holding the door. Lanyard, clipboard, two radios clipped to his vest.

"This one's on Floor 2," the man said. "Room 214. They've calmed down. Just protocol now."

Kev nodded. Lee followed, already filling the form.

Upstairs, a staff member — blue scrubs, NHS badge — waited outside the door. "He's fine now. Bit of breathlessness. Anxiety spike. First week here."

Kev gave a thin smile. "Vitals?"

"All logged. I've emailed the readings to dispatch."

Kev entered. A young man sat on the edge of the bed, eyes wide, chest rising and falling too fast. He clutched a phone. Language barrier. But the fear was clear.

Kev crouched gently. "You're alright. No emergency."

The boy didn't understand the words, but the tone worked. His breathing slowed.

Kev checked the chart. Everything stable.

"We'll log it," he said to the nurse. "No transport."

The woman nodded. "Appreciate it. We've had five today. They panic. New setting, no control. Anything feels like collapse."

Kev looked around. The room was clean. Warm. Basic care kit in the corner. Bottled water on the shelf. A folder marked *Medical Provision – Urgent Access* sat on the table.

"Does this place have a full contract?" he asked.

She nodded. "24/7. Signed last year. You guys are their first line."

Lee scribbled. "They're faster than A&E most days."

Kev said nothing.

Downstairs, the reception staff offered coffee. Kev declined.

Outside, the van idled quietly. The fog was lifting.

As they pulled out, he looked back. The hotel shimmered in the afternoon light — bright, orderly, ringed by private security. A refugee centre, dressed like a clinic.

Across the road, a group of local kids kicked a flat ball down the pavement. One glanced up as the ambulance passed. No wave. Just eyes tracking the blue stripe along the van's side.

Kev turned back to the road.

"Five calls in one building," Lee said.

Kev didn't reply.

He was still thinking about Riverton. Still hearing a cough behind closed walls. Still wondering if anyone would call back.

He didn't say it.

The system had already answered.

The Fire

The first call came at 19:42.

Flames seen from a bedroom window. Screams. A woman on the line saying, "Please — they're still inside." The address: Vine Street, Number 48. A place Kev had been to dozens of times. Block housing. No lift. Peeling paint. Not on the new coverage grid.

The job was flagged as *delayed response – resource prioritised elsewhere.*

Kev's unit didn't get it.

Another team, coming off shift, caught the alert 12 minutes in. They were rerouted — already heading to a call in a better-ranked district.

At 19:59, the first crew arrived.

By then, the fire had breached the upstairs hall. Smoke poured from the broken windows. A neighbour was screaming from the front garden. Sirens echoed from far off, too late.

A man tried to go back in — bare feet, no coat. A child's voice was heard, then swallowed.

At 20:01, dispatch updated the file: *fatalities suspected – awaiting confirmation.*

Kev wasn't there. He read the log the next morning. Quietly. Alone in the breakroom, eating a sandwich he didn't want.

Three children. Siblings. Ages five, seven, nine.

He stared at the screen until the text blurred.

Lee came in, holding two coffees. "You see it?"

Kev nodded. "Seventeen minutes."

Lee sighed. "Not our call."

"I know."

"Not our fault."

Kev said nothing.

Outside, the rain started lightly, then steadied. Someone had left their boots by the van, water collecting in the toes.

That night, Kev didn't sleep. He sat in the living room with the lights off, the television glowing without sound. His phone buzzed once — an article, already live: *Tragedy in Eastborough: Emergency Delay Under Review.*

Review. Not apology.

He turned the screen over, face down.

At 02:11, he thought about the mother. About the breath she held between sirens. About the moment she realised no one was coming fast enough.

He got up. Made tea. Didn't drink it.

Just stood at the window.

The street was empty.

No lights flashing.

No one on the way.

They weren't even dispatched until twenty minutes in.

By then, the fire was "contained," according to Control. Still, they were sent to assist — not as first responders, but for visibility. For presence.

Kev drove. Lee was quiet, flicking through the call log. When they turned onto Vine Street, the sky was orange at the edges. Wet ash clung to the windscreen.

The house was gutted. Blackened windows like empty sockets. Police tape. A blanket folded on the kerb, stained.

Someone had chalked flowers onto the pavement — child-like, too bright.

Kev parked without speaking.

A fire officer waved them over. Red helmet, soot on his cheeks. "We're past it. Three confirmed. Two DOAs. One taken out but didn't make it. Parents survived."

Kev just nodded.

"Med teams already cleared," the officer added. "You're here for scene support."

They stepped through the debris field. The air still smelt hot, even as the rain began.

In the hallway, a single shoe sat by the stairs. Small. Blue. Melted slightly at the toe.

Kev turned away.

Outside, the mother was sitting in the back of a squad car, wrapped in foil. Her face was grey. Hands limp. No one was talking to her. A paramedic had logged her vitals, stepped back. Nothing more to do.

Kev walked over.

He crouched beside the open door, said nothing. Just sat on his heels.

The woman didn't look at him. Didn't cry. Just blinked slowly, as if time had thickened.

"I'm sorry," Kev said.

She didn't move.

"I should've come sooner," he added, quieter.

A police officer gave him a look — too long. He stood, nodded once, stepped back.

Lee was already logging the report: *No medical action taken. No transport. Emotional distress noted.*

Kev signed it.

They drove back in silence. The fog returned. The street-lights glowed without warmth.

At the depot, Kev didn't clock out right away. Just sat in the van, engine off, watching the rain pool in the car park.

The blue light hadn't gone on that night.

Didn't seem right to use it anymore.

That should've been the end of it — the sirens, the silence, the shoe on the stairs. But it wasn't.

By morning, the fire was still burning — in headlines, in inboxes, in every room where no one dared say what they actually felt.

Inquiry

Kev had barely slept. The house still burned in his head. Three children. A mother blinking in silence. And a shoe by the stairs.

Their faces were on every screen.

Local surname. Known at the primary school, pictured once in a fundraising newsletter. Photos surfaced — school uniforms, wide smiles, the youngest missing front teeth.

The headline read: *Local Tragedy Raises Response Questions.*

The article didn't mention coverage zones. Or reroutes. Or the contract that had sent Kev to the hotel while the fire took hold.

But everyone knew.

The family lived two streets from the depot. Their grandmother used to bring the kids to the ambulance bay on open days. Kev remembered them — faintly. A girl who liked the siren. A boy who asked to see the bandages.

At the station, no one said much. A few printouts were pinned to the board — policy reminders, fire protocol updates. Above them, someone had written in pen:

WHERE DID WE GO?

It was crossed out by lunch.

That afternoon, Kev was called into a meeting. A small room. One senior. One clipboard. One phrase repeated three times:

"Don't personalise the incident."

He said nothing.

"We're being reviewed," the officer added. "Externally. Just stick to the notes."

Kev nodded. Not out of agreement — but because the sentence wasn't meant to be answered.

Later, at the petrol station, he saw a woman staring at him. Not angry. Just fixed. She didn't speak. Just got in her car and drove off.

That night, he read the names again.

They weren't foreign. Weren't part of a resettlement list. No contract. No flagged status. Just local. Unremarkable. British.

And dead.

He wondered what the report would say. How the delay would be explained. Whether it would be worded softly, or just omitted entirely.

He didn't ask. He didn't sleep.

He sat in the kitchen with the lights off, one boot still on, the radio murmuring updates from somewhere else.

The blue light wasn't spinning.

Not that night.

Not for them.

It was supposed to be a "wellness check in."

Kev was led into the HR room — pastel walls, pot plant wilting, a bowl of mints on the table no one touched. Across from him sat Sharon, clipboard in lap, voice soft.

"How are you coping?" she asked.

He shrugged. "Fine."

A pause.

"About the Vine Street fire," she continued, "we're preparing a response. Media attention's high. Emotions are running."

Kev looked at the window. Closed. Blind drawn. No light in.

She went on. "I want to remind you — all staff — to avoid sharing commentary. On or off duty."

He raised an eyebrow. "Commentary?"

"Statements. Opinions. Anything that might be misread as criticism of operational policy."

He didn't respond.

Sharon folded her hands. "You were not assigned to that call. You followed protocol. I just want you to be aware of optics. It's a sensitive time."

There it was. The phrase.

"Don't politicise the incident."

He repeated it aloud. Flat.

Sharon hesitated. "We're being looked at. If staff start assigning blame publicly—"

"I'm not going public."

"Good," she said quickly. "Because it's not about blame. It's about process."

Kev stood up. "Three kids died."

Sharon nodded, slowly. "It's terrible. But we can't afford emotional narratives right now."

He stared at her.

"Is that what you think I am? A narrative?"

She didn't answer. Just looked at the notes in her lap.

Outside, the corridor hummed. Voices passed. A laugh. A door closing.

Kev left the room. Didn't take a mint.

In the breakroom, someone had turned off the news.

The screen was black. The silence full of things no one was allowed to say.

Shift Swap

They were halfway to a call — a fall in a care home, standard response — when Lee pulled the van over.

Didn't say anything. Just slowed, blinkers on, stopped beneath a railway bridge. The road ahead shimmered in heat. No traffic behind.

Kev looked over. "What is it?"

Lee's hands stayed on the wheel. Knuckles white. His head tilted forward slightly, like something had knocked him inward.

"I can't," he said.

Kev blinked. "Can't what?"

Lee's breath came in short pulses. "I can't go in. Not again. Not today."

Kev reached over, turned down the dispatch radio.

"You alright?" he asked, gently.

Lee shook his head. "I dreamt about them. The kids. I wasn't even there. But I saw it. In the hallway. Smoke. I couldn't find the stairs."

He covered his face. No sobs. Just stillness. Like something was leaking out without noise.

Kev sat quietly.

They waited like that for a full minute.

Then Kev tapped the wheel. "Swap with me."

Lee nodded. Moved slowly, got out. Kev took the wheel. They didn't speak during the switch. Lee climbed into the passenger side like he was made of paper.

The care home was only ten minutes out. When they arrived, Kev went in alone. Handled the lift. Logged the vitals. Nothing urgent.

When he came back, Lee hadn't moved.

Kev drove them back to depot.

In the parking bay, Lee turned to him. "I'm gonna take a few shifts off. Say it's flu."

Kev nodded. "I'll cover if they ask."

Lee looked at him. "You sure?"

Kev didn't answer right away.

Then: "I'll manage."

Lee left quietly, bag over shoulder. The sky was low and yellowing. A bus hissed past without stopping.

Kev stayed in the van a little longer.

Not to rest.

Just to feel what it was like to sit in silence without breaking.

The next morning, Kev took Lee's slot.

No one asked questions. Just a nod from dispatch. A scribbled update on the rota board. He was now pulling doubles — early to late, four shifts running.

By noon, his stomach burned from bad coffee and emptiness. He stopped at the corner shop near the depot. Bought a sandwich he wouldn't eat. And a small bottle of vodka he slipped into his coat pocket.

He didn't plan it. Didn't think of it as a turning. Just a pause.

The depot canteen was half-lit. Two drivers played cards in the corner. A trainee watched something loud on his phone with earbuds in.

Kev sat by the window. Poured two fingers of clear into a paper cup. Stirred it into the juice he'd brought from home.

No one noticed.

The first sip was nothing. Just warmth. Second, quieter. Third, he stopped counting.

The juice was gone. The ache in his shoulders softened. His chest loosened — slightly.

He went back out to the van. The world still moved. Sirens still sang somewhere in the distance. His screen blinked with a new dispatch: minor injury, industrial park.

He drove.

He wasn't drunk. Not yet. Just duller. Just far enough from feeling sharp.

That night, he tossed the bottle in a bin on the walk home. Didn't look back.

The next day, he bought another.

By the fourth shift, he didn't need the juice. Just the cup. No one asked.

At briefing, someone said the service was understaffed by 30%. Everyone nodded. No one questioned why the maps had been redrawn. Why the calls came slower but felt heavier.

Kev worked like nothing was wrong.

He smiled when needed. Lifted cleanly. Logged the right codes.

But inside, he was quieter.

And the cup in his locker said enough.

The Dispatch Room

The new software rolled out on a Monday.

A presentation in the depot briefing room. Flat voices. Corporate slides. *"Optimised Response Allocation: Powered by Predictive Needs Assessment."* Kev sat in the back, arms crossed, cup in hand.

The screen showed a map — clean, bright, full of coloured zones. Blue for high-priority. Yellow for monitored. Grey for "non-urgent clusters."

Kev watched as familiar postcodes faded into grey-scale.

Someone raised a hand. "So... Eastborough's not covered?"

A presenter smiled. "Eastborough has low recorded call volume and high non-response risk. The model reroutes to higher-efficiency corridors."

Another asked, "What about Vine Street?"

A pause. "It's now part of a legacy zone. We'll monitor. But live units won't be dispatched unless secondary confirmation comes through."

Kev leant forward. "People live there."

The room went quiet.

The presenter nodded, thinly. "Of course. But the model accounts for outcomes. Resource concentration is key."

Afterward, Kev stood in the dispatch room. Watched the new software in motion. Calls came in. Dots blinked. Lines redrew. The system pulsed — fluid, impersonal.

He noticed something else. Some streets — whole blocks — didn't trigger the alert tone anymore. If a call came from one of them, it blinked silently. Waited for manual override.

Most times, none came.

The map was learning. But what it was learning to do was not see.

Kev tapped the screen. "Why's this one dim?"

A dispatcher shrugged. "Low yield. System deprioritises unless a second call confirms severity."

"And if there is no second call?"

The dispatcher looked at him. "Then it's not an emergency."

Kev walked out.

Outside, he stood by the van, engine off, hand in pocket.

The sky above was overcast, flat. A single gull circled once and vanished.

He thought of all the streets he used to know by smell — chip oil, dust, damp brick. Places that weren't great, but still mattered.

Now they were greyed out.

Invisible.

Unrescued.

The tablet on Kev's dashboard used to display the whole city — gridlines stretching out in every direction, little pins for calls, circles pulsing when urgent.

Now, half of it was grey.

Every week, a new patch faded.

The screen didn't announce it. There was no alert. Just one day, a neighbourhood would be gone. No calls from there. No routes through it. Just emptiness.

Kev swiped across the map during a lull in calls. North-bank, gone. Parts of Woodmere, gone. Vine Street already erased.

Only the high-priority corridors remained — the hospital loop, the migrant housing complexes, the transport hubs. Clean routes. Contracted zones.

He zoomed out. The city looked smaller.

No — not smaller.

Hollow.

Lee walked past the van, tapped on the glass. Kev rolled down the window.

"You seen the new rollout?"

Kev nodded.

Lee exhaled. "Feels like they're drawing a line. Between who gets saved, and who gets logged."

Kev didn't reply.

That evening, while parked outside a supermarket on standby, he watched two kids argue near the bins. One fell. Cried out. A woman nearby pulled out her phone.

Kev's screen stayed blank.

No call was dispatched.

The child stopped crying. Got up. Limped off.

Kev stared at the screen.

Still blank.

He opened the old A-Z map from the glovebox. Paper. Cracked spine. Streets still printed, still real.

He traced his finger along a line — his old route from three years ago. He could still remember which lights took longest. Where Mrs. Hadley used to wave from her porch. Where they'd found a man passed out in a stairwell and brought him back.

None of those addresses showed up anymore.

The map glowed faintly beside him. Shrinking, silent.

A tool designed to save had become a mirror.

It reflected back what the system had chosen to forget.

Blue Silence

Kev didn't plan to stop.

He was driving back from a cancelled call — flagged, then pulled, reassigned without reason. The van was quiet. The radio chatter had gone thin. Just static and silence.

The bridge came into view, low and unmarked, cutting over the motorway like a forgotten stitch.

He pulled over.

Engine running. Blue light off. Just the dull hum of idle.

Below, the traffic moved like breath — in, out, in, out. Headlights streamed in both directions. Nobody looked up.

Kev sat in the driver's seat, hands on the wheel, eyes unfocused. He didn't cry. Didn't speak.

He just sat.

The city behind him pulsed with unseen calls. The screen blinked softly — standby, reposition, hold. He didn't touch it.

He thought of the first time he'd ridden in an ambulance. Student placement. White uniform, fresh clipboard, nerves masked by eagerness. The call had been a domestic — nothing dramatic. But he remembered the way the driver moved. Quick. Decisive. As if every second still mattered.

Now, the seconds drifted.

He turned on the blue light.

Just the light.

It spun against the dark, reflected in the van's mirror. A glow with no direction. No siren. Just rotation. Silent. Aimless.

Cars below didn't slow. Didn't notice.

Kev rested his forehead on the steering wheel. The engine ticked. The blue light turned the inside of the cab a soft, rotating wash of colour.

He stayed there.

Not gone.

Not okay.

Just still.

The van breathed with him.

And no one called him back.

The van remained on the bridge.

Lights still on. Engine still ticking. The blue beacon spun quietly above, casting slow, rhythmic flashes onto the tarmac, the metal railing, Kev's face.

He didn't move.

The seat creaked slightly each time he shifted, but otherwise, the silence held. Not heavy. Not waiting. Just full.

The motorway below throbbed with motion. Lorries surged beneath him, headlights cutting tunnels through the dark. Nobody stopped. Nobody looked up.

Kev stared through the windscreen. Not at anything. Just through.

The radio crackled once — a name half-spoken, a code half-issued — then fell quiet again. He reached toward it, then let his hand drop.

His coat hung open. His badge still clipped to the breast pocket. His boots scuffed. His breath even.

No call came.

No knock on the glass.

He wasn't asleep. But he wasn't fully here either. Somewhere in between. Held.

Above, the sky shifted to that pre-dawn grey — colourless, expectant. The kind of light that makes everything look paused.

The van idled.

Fuel low. Battery steady.

Kev blinked once. Rested his hand on the steering wheel. The blue light continued its slow rotation — casting its glow in circles too wide to reach anyone.

And still, the engine ran.

Part 8: Critical Essay

Emergency Access Inequality

The blue light — once a symbol of universal urgency — has become a signal of selective response. In Kev's world, working as an ambulance driver, it no longer means *help is coming*. It means *help is coming — if you're on the right list*.

Scene by scene, the story reveals a truth long understood but rarely spoken: not all emergencies are equal. Not all addresses are treated the same. The family in the fire waits seventeen minutes. Three children die. A migrant hotel, meanwhile, is contractually guaranteed 24/7 cover. The discrepancy is not accidental. It is built into the routing software, into funding flows, into the logic of privatised triage.

What's framed as efficiency is, in practice, abandonment. The state has outsourced care to contracts, and in doing so, has relinquished judgment to algorithms. Decisions are made not by medics, but by metrics — response-time quotas, cost-per-callout models, high-priority zones defined not by need but by liability exposure.

This is what emergency access inequality looks like: a system where urgency is mediated by geography, race, status. Kev doesn't refuse the call because he's cruel. He does it because he's instructed to. The rules are clear, even if the consequences are devastating. And when he does arrive — late, broken, too human — he is told not to politicise it. The language of neutrality protects the system, not the citizen.

The deeper collapse is moral. The uniform still implies service, but the routes are shrinking. The siren means less. Its sound becomes ambient, not alarming. It passes by, often without stopping.

For working-class responders like Kev, the contradiction corrodes from within. He knows what the job used to mean — he remembers entering still burning homes, not questioning coordinates. Now he's watching the map get smaller. He's told to drive around grief. The blue light, once a promise, becomes an emblem of selection.

And for those on the outside — the citizens waiting for care that doesn't come — trust erodes silently. Not through protest, but through the long, slow realisation that urgency has been privatised.

The tragedy is not only who is saved or lost. It's who is seen as worth the call — and who no longer qualifies for the sound of help.

Privatisation of Urgency

In Kev's world, urgency is no longer a moral imperative — it is a contractual term. The story reveals a profound shift in the architecture of care: emergencies are no longer judged by need, but by billing code. The ambulance service, once a symbol of public promise, now operates under a logic of deliverables and efficiencies. Time is measured not in lives saved, but in compliance with key performance indicators.

The migrant hotel in the story is not a villain, nor its occupants undeserving. But it is part of a newly tiered system: covered by private contracts, guaranteed response, embedded within a framework of liability and optics. The irony is sharp. A space designed for the displaced becomes the most secure node in the network — not because of moral obligation, but because the funding is ring-fenced.

Meanwhile, the local family burns.

This is the heart of the privatisation of urgency: the quiet redefinition of who matters most, written into agreements no one voted for, administered by software, shielded by bureaucracy. The response time isn't slower because the service has failed — it's slower because the family wasn't on the list. They weren't a risk to the government. Just a tragedy waiting to be absorbed by another headline.

Privatisation doesn't just alter access; it reconfigures intent. Kev is no longer responding to need. He is fulfilling obligations. He drives not where his instinct leads, but where the system allows. In this, his own role is hollowed. He is a driver with a siren, not a responder with purpose. And when tragedy strikes — when children die — the institution's priority is not justice or explanation. It is containment.

The emotional cost to workers like Kev is acute. Not because they don't care, but because they are forced to simulate neutrality while carrying guilt. They are made complicit in a system that asks them to forget the difference between rules and right.

This is not just a policy shift — it's a philosophical one. Urgency used to mean the collapse of hierarchy: all else stops, because someone is in danger. Now, it reinforces hierarchy: only some emergencies pause the machine.

And the rest?

The rest wait in silence, smoke curling above them, sirens passing on the other side.

Spatial Discrimination

In Kev's shifting map of service, not all spaces are equal — and increasingly, some are not serviced at all. The story reveals how discrimination in public services has moved from overt policy to coded logistics. It is no longer who you are, but where you are that determines your worth. And yet, even that geography is not neutral. It is drawn, edited, and erased by unseen hands.

When the new AI dispatch system comes online, Kev watches his coverage area shrink. Neighbourhoods disappear from the response grid — not because they're empty, but because they're inconvenient. Low-income housing blocks, outer estates, rural pockets once covered by habit and instinct are now marked low-priority. The algorithm routes resources elsewhere. Efficiency, it says.

But what it really means is: less care for certain people in certain places.

This is spatial discrimination — the quiet re-mapping of who is protected. It doesn't announce itself. It arrives through software updates, internal memos, subtle delays. It cannot be challenged in court, because it is not declared. Yet its effects are immediate: slower response times, longer waits, more deaths.

The emergency map becomes a palimpsest — a city rewritten according to cost-benefit, not compassion. Migrant hotels, affluent developments, and contract-tied institutions remain illuminated in blue. The rest fade into grey.

Kev sees it in real time. He knows these streets. He's served them for years. He sees who has vanished from the grid — not by moving, but by being moved off the map. His growing despair is not just about institutional failure. It is about the erasure of presence. The idea that some places — and by extension, some people — no longer register as urgent.

What's more, this discrimination doesn't feel malicious. It feels technical. That's its strength. There is no one to blame. No face to confront. Just the machine rerouting attention elsewhere. And when someone calls to say their mother has collapsed, and the ambulance doesn't come, the failure is framed as system overload — not system design.

In this context, Kev's blue light becomes a kind of moral spotlight: not illuminating need, but exposing absence. The places he used to rush toward are now behind glass — visible, unreachable, disallowed.

And when space itself determines who lives and who waits, what's being discriminated against is not just address — it's belonging.

Morale in the Emergency Sector

Kev doesn't break all at once. His collapse comes in increments — missed calls, short tempers, longer lunches, and finally, stillness. His arc is not about trauma from singular events, but from the erosion of purpose. In the emergency sector, morale isn't lost in crisis. It's lost in repetition — of failure, of futility, of being told not to care too loudly.

Once, his work carried meaning. Lives saved. Situations stabilised. Purpose was found in movement, in arriving just in time. Now, his shift begins with limits: calls he can't answer, streets he can't enter, deaths he'll be blamed for only in silence. There's no scandal, just a quiet, managerial drift. Each restriction is framed as policy. Each absence, an efficiency.

And so the workers stop speaking. They stop asking. They learn to document instead of intervene, to write reports instead of grieve.

This is what morale collapse looks like. Not chaos. Not rage. Just detachment.

Kev's colleague cries mid-shift and walks off the job. No one chases him. No debrief follows. That kind of exit has become common. Temporary. Rotational. The assumption is that someone else will fill the seat. Or not.

The system doesn't respond to emotional fatigue. It translates it into staffing gaps. Coverage metrics. Temporary agency hires. It tracks everything but meaning.

And the deeper Kev slips into disillusionment, the more the system misreads him. His silence is marked as compliance. His numbness mistaken for resilience. No one notices that he's stopped caring — because the structure no longer requires care, just functionality.

The irony is brutal: the people most relied upon to bring others back from the brink are being pushed silently toward their own.

What makes it worse is that they know. Kev knows. His despair isn't born of ignorance, but of clarity. He sees the gap between the ideal and the real. And every day that gap widens, his work becomes not just a job, but a ritual of pretending.

In the end, the siren still works. The blue light still spins.

But the driver beneath it is no longer sure why.

Tragedy as Routine

The fire is not exceptional. Three children die, and the system absorbs it without rupture. There are no protests. No resignations. Just a quiet note logged under "delayed response," and a dispatch report closed by shift's end.

In Kev's world, tragedy has become procedural. What once would have shocked now merely updates a file. Death is not denied — it is administrated. A tragedy is something to move through, not to be moved by.

This routinisation is not born of cruelty, but of defence. The emergency sector is so overwhelmed, so structurally depleted, that it can no longer afford full emotional engagement. Grief is not sustainable when the next call is already waiting. And so Kev, like many in his role, learns to compartmentalise. To name things clinically. To describe fire as "incident," death as "outcome," delay as "triage pressure."

But language doesn't protect him. It isolates. The more he speaks in euphemism, the more removed he becomes from the reality of what he's witnessing. The child in the fire is real. But the form says "minor fatality." A life becomes a number. A delay becomes a metric. And grief becomes a private, unfiled emotion.

The system encourages this. Bureaucracy trains responders to keep moving. Even Kev's quiet moment on the bridge is framed as a lapse, not a signal. There is no space in the shift pattern for mourning. No protocol for conscience.

The broader cost is a workforce hollowed out from within. Men and women like Kev once saw themselves as lifesavers. Now, they're told to be efficient. To trust dispatch. To follow the map. What's removed from them isn't just time or pay — it's moral agency.

When tragedy becomes routine, two things happen. First, society stops noticing. Accidents become background noise. Delay becomes expected. Death becomes another line in the news scroll. Second, the responders stop feeling. Not because they don't care, but because the system punishes those who still do.

Kev is not broken because he sees too much — but because he's been taught that seeing must not change anything.

And so he drives. He logs calls. He hears the sirens blur into traffic. What was once an alarm has become ambience.

The tragedy, now, is not the accident.

It's that the accident is just another Tuesday.

Language of Neutrality

The bureaucracy Kev works within does not deny inequality. It simply names it differently. The call that was skipped becomes a "resource reallocation." The area not reached is flagged as "low-priority zone." The child who dies is noted under "non-viable casualty." This is the language of neutrality — words designed not to lie, but to flatten.

What makes this language dangerous is its tone. It speaks softly, professionally, rationally. It removes urgency from the urgent, pain from the painful. It does not deny that harm has occurred — it just ensures no one feels too responsible.

In Kev's case, language is used to sanitise abandonment. After the fire, he's told not to "politicise the incident." That sentence does more than censor — it redefines. His grief, his frustration, his very act of noticing a pattern becomes inappropriate. The system demands neutrality from its workers even as it practices selection in its service.

But neutrality, in this context, is not balance — it is betrayal. It allows the institution to continue functioning without ever confronting the consequences of its decisions. It permits tragedy to pass without naming the conditions that created it.

This is why the new routing software matters. Not just for where it sends ambulances, but for how it justifies its choices. It's described in meetings as "optimised" and "data-informed." Yet what it optimises is abandonment. What it informs is a hierarchy of care — not based on need, but on policy.

Kev feels this dissonance in his body. Every time he drives past an estate he used to serve. Every time he hears that a colleague is "under review" for deviating from protocol to help someone. Every time he's asked to tick a box that erases what really happened.

This isn't censorship by force. It's erasure by format.

The deeper effect is internal. Kev stops trusting his own instincts. He begins to second-guess what used to be moral certainty. The blue light still spins, but it no longer points anywhere solid.

Language, once a bridge between experience and meaning, has become a barrier. The words protect the system, not the people. They allow injustice to continue — quietly, logically, with just enough distance to avoid blame.

And in that distance, the truth dies quietly, unsigned.

PTSD and the Blue Light

Kev doesn't flinch at violence anymore. It's not that he's numb — it's that he's learned to expect it. Trauma, for him, is not an event. It's the residue of chronic exposure to failure. Not just witnessing death, but being told to ignore it. To explain it. To move past it.

The blue light, once a call to action, now triggers dread. For Kev, the sound of the siren is no longer the sign of arrival — it's the beginning of blame. When the radio crackles, he doesn't brace for what he'll find, but for what he'll miss. The dying mother. The unreachable address. The call he couldn't answer because another contract took precedence.

This is what PTSD in the emergency services often looks like: not flashbacks, but corrosion. A slow undoing of confidence, purpose, clarity. The sense that nothing matters because the outcomes are predetermined — by politics, software, budget.

Kev's trauma is bureaucratic. It accumulates in reports, in apology scripts, in the memory of roads he was told to bypass. It's worsened by the demand for composure. When responders crack, they are not seen as human — they are seen as risks. Complaints waiting to happen. Incidents to be managed.

So they keep it inside. Until the inside hollows.

Kev starts drinking at lunch. Not to forget, but to take the edge off the knowing. The knowledge that someone will die tonight, and he might not be sent. Or worse — that he might be, and it won't matter.

The blue light becomes a symbol not of help, but of selection. It shines not where the need is greatest, but where the policy directs. And so every call becomes a moral question he's not allowed to ask.

What Kev suffers from is not just PTSD — it's institutional betrayal trauma. The injury of being asked to serve, then punished for trying to do so fully.

There is no therapy for this. No debrief. Only shifts. And silence.

By the end, when Kev sits alone on the bridge, the siren still pulsing in the distance, he is not imagining jumping.

He's imagining never having to hear it again.

Suicidal Systems

Kev parks the ambulance on the bridge. Lights still spinning, engine running, radio silent. It's not a cry for help — it's a portrait of collapse. Not personal collapse, but systemic. The story ends not with a jump, but with a stillness that speaks of something broader: a system that no longer wants to live by its own values.

This is what a suicidal system looks like: not one that explodes, but one that abandons its purpose while continuing to operate. The sirens still wail, the software still routes, the uniforms are still worn — but the mission is gone. The illusion of service remains, but underneath it is a machinery that has stopped believing in rescue.

Kev's breakdown is not the cause of failure — it is its proof. He is the last honest part of a dying structure, reacting exactly as one should to betrayal, absurdity, and helplessness. His presence on that bridge is not an anomaly. It is a diagnosis.

The system asks for silence. It trains responders to suppress grief, to obey policy, to drive faster past need. In doing so, it engineers their disappearance — emotionally first, then practically. Some burn out. Some vanish. Others, like Kev, stall in place, engine on, unsure whether stopping is treason or mercy.

There is a myth that suicidality belongs only to individuals. But systems can self-harm too — by cutting off feedback, punishing dissent, denying reality. By prioritising image over truth until no one inside it believes in its function anymore. What remains is ritual. And beneath that, void.

The ambulance, parked and pulsing, becomes a metaphor. The blue light is still there, but no longer signals arrival. It is the last flicker of a promise being extinguished.

And as Kev sits in that vehicle, watching traffic pass below, we are left with the realisation: not everyone who dies jumps. Some are walked there. Slowly. By shifts. By forms. By silence.

The tragedy is not just Kev's.

It belongs to every injury left waiting.

Every responder asked to abandon instinct.

Every society that lets urgency become selective.

And every system that, faced with its own decay, chooses not to change — but to carry on dying in plain sight.

Part 9: Gates of Dover

Morning Watch

The light came slowly over the docks, blue-grey and diffused, the kind that flattens everything. David zipped his jacket higher, collar rough against his chin, and took his place by the gate. A clipboard hung from his hand, already damp. The wind tasted of salt and diesel.

The ferry had docked just after five. Another overnight crossing. He watched as the first cluster of passengers stepped onto the asphalt — quiet, hunched, blinking at the morning.

He didn't speak at first. Just nodded. Hands out. ID.

Some had passports ready, held forward like apologies. Some looked away. One man handed over a folded paper that was damp and half-torn, the ink smudged at the edges. David turned it in his hand, uncertain if the name had been there in the first place.

"Step to the side," he said.

The man obeyed. No protest.

Another group followed. Eleven this time. Only four had documentation. The rest murmured when prompted, gave names David didn't catch. One woman pointed to her baby, then to the sky. Her other hand clutched a laminated card, years out of date.

He logged what he could. "Unknown Male." "Claimed Syrian." "No proof." The tablet lagged in the cold, blinking red before saving. He re-entered three forms.

Behind him, a seagull screamed, then landed on the roof of a shipping container and stared.

The line kept moving.

By six, he'd counted twenty-seven. Eleven without papers. One child holding a photo instead of ID — a picture of himself, possibly, in a jacket three sizes too large, eyes too wide.

David let him pass.

Another officer glanced at him. Said nothing.

The sun, pale and slow, began to rise over the lorry yard.

David looked at the clipboard. His handwriting had changed. Tighter. Less precise. The word *Unknown* repeated six times in the first column alone.

He flipped to a new sheet.

The ferry doors clanged shut behind the last passenger.

He rubbed his eyes. Pocketed the pen.

The gate held. The sea behind it glimmered like steel.

David sat in the booth, hunched over the intake logs. The heater buzzed softly behind him, struggling against the cold that seeped through the steel frame. His gloves lay beside the terminal, fingertips worn from overuse. He typed slowly, double-checking each entry.

Arrival Manifest: 27 Individuals.Confirmed IDs: 16.Unverified: 11.

The terminal flagged the discrepancy. A small yellow triangle appeared in the corner of the screen, offering help: *"Would you like to log a secondary review?"*

He clicked *No*.

Down the quay, another officer was questioning a man in his twenties, wrapped in a jacket two sizes too small. The man pointed to a plastic wristband, blue with white lettering — a hospital tag, not a visa. David could see the conversation from the booth window. It wasn't going anywhere.

He returned to the log. Beside each unverified arrival, he typed "Unknown Male." He didn't bother with physical descriptions anymore. It all became noise — "short hair," "medium build," "brown eyes."

They blurred together.

One of the arrivals — a boy maybe sixteen — had smiled at him earlier. Just briefly. No words. The smile wasn't warm. It was something else. A question, maybe.

David hadn't smiled back.

He clicked "submit." The yellow triangle disappeared.

The printer whirred, spitting out a page he didn't need. He glanced at it anyway. Row after row of assigned ID numbers for people who had none.

The boy's smile returned to him. How out of place it had looked.

He stood, stretched, stepped out of the booth.

The sun had fully breached the horizon now, turning the warehouse roofs gold. Gulls swirled above the lot, feeding on the leftover debris from cargo loads.

He watched one of the unverified men sit on the kerb, pull off his shoes, and flex his toes. No socks. Just skin hardened by travel.

David reached for his radio.

"Central, this is Gate Post Three. Morning intake confirmed. Eleven without documentation. Awaiting further instruction."

A pause. Then a crackling response: "Roger that. Proceed to processing. Files pending."

He returned the radio to his belt. Turned back toward the booth.

The boy was still standing there, alone now, eyes fixed on the water.

David pretended not to see.

The Board

By Friday, David had written "Unknown Male" one hundred and thirteen times.

He noticed it when he reviewed the weekly summary — a thick sheaf of printouts with staggered arrival logs, times, and initials. He hadn't meant to count. But the repetition drew him in, compelled him to follow it row by row.

Sometimes the names were offered but unverifiable. Other times, they were never spoken. Language barriers, intentional silence, or simply too much noise between questions and answers. It didn't matter. Protocol dictated clarity, and clarity in absence was marked as *unknown*.

He stared at the list. Each line blurred into the next. 08:13, 08:17, 08:20. Row after row of men without papers, without proof.

The border had become a mirror of itself — reflecting the same outline again and again.

He got up from his desk, walked to the wall-mounted board in the intake office — a laminated chart meant for trend tracking. It still had markers in the tray, different colours for different risk levels. No one had updated it in days.

He picked up the red marker. Drew a single line.

Then another. Then again.

Eleven tallies for Monday.

Nineteen for Tuesday.

He stopped after Thursday. Left Friday blank.

Behind him, an officer muttered into a phone, reading out codes without emotion.

David sat down and opened his drawer. Inside: his notebook. Not official. Just spiral-bound, private. He flipped through the pages. Names he had tried to write — phonetic guesses, drawn from accents and gestures. Notes beside them: *reappeared?*, *same eyes*, *too clean to have crossed alone*.

He'd stopped logging names two weeks ago. They didn't hold.

Now, he just drew faces. Not portraits. Just outlines. Variations on the same figure.

He added one more.

Later, he stood by the holding bay as another group arrived. The same shuffle, the same hesitations. One man looked up — dark hair, cheek nicked, scar across the brow. David felt something tighten. He had logged that scar before.

Or thought he had.

He stepped forward, ready to ask, but the man looked through him.

David paused. Opened his mouth. Closed it again.

He wrote: *Unknown Male. Scarred. Possible repeat.*

Then walked away.

The official forms weren't enough anymore. Too rigid. Too slow. They filed the bodies but missed the patterns.

David started using his own notebook — small, spiral-bound, soft-backed. He bought it on a break from the WHSmith by the terminal, telling the cashier it was for "shift notes." That was true, in a way.

On the first page, he drew a grid: Date. Estimated Age. Distinguishing Features. Seen Before?

It wasn't protocol. But the system hadn't noticed the repetition—so someone had to.

On Monday, he logged three men with identical tattoos on the left wrist: black triangle, faded. All claimed different nationalities. All had no documents.

On Tuesday, he noted two arrivals with the same birthdate. Same height. Same grey hoodie.

By Thursday, he stopped filling in the nationality column.

It felt performative.

The notebook never left his pocket. During breaks, he jotted between calls. In the booth, he scribbled after finishing digital entries. Sometimes it was just a word: *scar. silent. same voice.* Once, he wrote: *Is it me?*

That night, he flipped through the pages before sleep. One face kept recurring—not fully drawn, just suggested: strong brow, narrow chin, downturned mouth. It showed up again and again in sketches made on different days.

He stared at the lines, wondered if he'd copied the same person each time. Or imagined him.

At the depot, he asked a colleague—Stevens, two years younger, easy smile—if he'd noticed anything odd.

"Odd how?" Stevens asked, chewing gum.

"Repeat entries," David said. "Men coming back. Same features. Different names."

Stevens shrugged. "They all look the same after a while."

David flinched at that. Not out of offence, but recognition.

They did. But not in the way Stevens meant.

They blurred because the system refused to see them. David was trying to look.

Back in the intake booth, he logged another arrival: no ID, no language, but the same slouch, same slow blink, same pause before stepping forward. He flipped to his notebook, checked back four pages.

It matched.

He stared at the man.

"Have you been here before?"

No answer.

He wrote: *Repeat? Circle left eye. Still silent.*

The man was ushered on.

David held the pen in his hand for a moment longer, then added, softly:

They're coming back different.

The Dream

He woke before dawn, soaked in sweat, the air in his flat stale and unmoving. The dream was still with him — clear, compressed. A face at the end of a hallway. Not menacing. Just still. Watching.

He sat at the table with the notebook, flipping pages fast. Not looking for words. For lines. The sketches, scattered across days, stared back at him. Each one slightly different. But together — they formed something singular.

The same face.

He hadn't drawn it consciously. Sometimes just a brow. Sometimes a nose, sloped in a way that caught him off guard. A scar he kept replicating near the jawline, as if he'd seen it before.

He had.

At the terminal, during Tuesday's intake. And again, on Wednesday, from the ferry. Different names. Different accents. But the same way the man stood. Same pause before responding. Same eyes — unreadable, but certain.

David closed the notebook.

At the depot, he asked for access to archived photos. "Cross-check," he told the shift manager. "Training review." A lie. No one questioned it.

He scrolled for an hour.

Different files. Same face. The same geometry. Hairline adjusted. Weight shifted. But the eyes — always the eyes. Still. Heavy.

He printed three images. Taped them to his locker.

Later, by the intake barrier, a new group arrived.

And there he was again.

Younger. Maybe. Or just thinner.

David stepped forward.

The man handed nothing. Said nothing. Just looked at him.

David held the stare.

"Have you been here before?"

The man blinked once. Then shook his head. A soft, practiced movement.

David didn't argue. He just nodded, logged "Unknown Male," and watched the figure disappear into the waiting zone.

That night, he didn't sleep.

The flat was too quiet.

He opened the notebook again. Added a date. A page number. Then wrote:

He keeps returning. Or I keep seeing him.

He didn't draw the face this time.

He didn't need to.

It was already there, behind his eyelids, perfectly formed.

It happened while David was scanning the queue.

The line was long, drawn tight across the tarmac. Rain threatened but hadn't fallen. The usual shuffle of boots.

Coughs. Hushed conversations in languages he didn't know. Faces he half-recognised.

Then—there he was again.

Fourth from the front. Same cheekbones. Same grey jacket. No ID in hand. Just eyes fixed on David.

David's breath stalled. He gripped the clipboard tighter, fingers whitening.

The man stepped forward.

David raised his hand. "Wait."

The man obeyed.

They stood like that for a beat. No words. Just the wind shifting through the shipping containers behind them.

David leant in slightly. "We've seen you before."

The man tilted his head.

David said it again. "You were here. Three days ago. Different group."

The man opened his mouth. No sound.

Then slowly, deliberately, he shaped the words:

You don't know my name.

No voice. Just lips forming the sentence with perfect clarity.

David blinked. "What?"

The man repeated it — silent again.

You don't know my name.

And smiled.

Not kind. Not cruel. Just *there*.

David stepped back.

Another officer approached from behind. "Problem?"

David shook his head. "No. Language thing."

The man moved on, slotted back into the queue. The spell broke.

But David couldn't let it go.

Later, in the intake room, he pulled up the CCTV.

He froze the footage at the exact moment the man had mouthed the phrase. Rewound. Played it again.

The same sentence.

You don't know my name.

He pressed print. The image came out grainy and grey.

He taped it into the notebook. Drew a circle around the mouth.

Then, underneath: *He knows I don't know. He's right.*

He sat there long after his shift ended. Booth empty. Screen blinking. The rain had started, a soft tapping against the roof.

His radio buzzed once, then fell silent.

He flipped to a fresh page and wrote just four words: *What does he want?*

The answer didn't come.

Only the face. Over and over.

Midnight Inspection

The restricted zone lay behind the intake lot, bordered by rusting fencing and CCTV cameras that didn't always work. Old processing containers stood idle there — decommissioned offices, portable toilets, stacked pallets draped in tarps. No foot traffic. No noise. Just wind, whistling through the cracks.

David volunteered for the midnight patrol. Said he needed the quiet. The supervisor barely looked up from his tablet. "Keep your radio on."

He passed the checkpoint with a flick of his badge. The gate creaked open, metal teeth grinding.

The torch cut a narrow cone through the dark. Every surface seemed damp — with sea air, or something older.

He moved slowly, boots crunching over gravel and spent wrappers. A single gull squawked somewhere overhead.

He didn't expect to find anything. He just needed space.

The wind picked up. Something shifted on the far side of the lot — a door ajar, tapping lightly against its frame.

He approached, careful, breathing shallow.

It was the back of an old intake unit. Long disused.

He pushed the door open.

Empty.

Dust. A broken chair. A file cabinet with no drawers.

He turned to leave—

And heard it:

A voice. Close. Just behind him.

"You missed me."

He froze.

Turned slowly.

No one.

Just the door swaying.

Torch beam scanned the dark — nothing.

His breath came fast now.

"You missed me," the voice repeated.

Soft. Familiar.

But there was no one in the room.

He stepped back outside, into the open air, heart pounding.

The lot was still empty.

The gate in the distance stood where he'd left it. Unmoved.

He looked at the booth — far off now — lights low.

No one waiting.

No one watching.

He steadied himself, tried the radio.

"Post Three to base."

Static.

"Post Three, copy?"

More static.

He exhaled. Put the radio down.

Looked up at the sky — blank, starless.

Then turned and walked slowly back toward the light.

Behind him, the door swung once more.

And the wind whispered:

You don't know my name.

The voice came again as he reached the gate.

"You missed me."

Clearer this time. Not a whisper. A statement.

David spun around.

Nothing behind him but fog and fencing, the beam of his torch trembling slightly with the motion.

"Who's there?" he called, voice louder than intended.

No answer.

He swept the light across the gravel, over the containers, into the crevices of metal and plastic. Empty. Still.

But he felt it—something behind him, not physical, but present.

He turned back toward the gate. Took a step.

"You missed me," the voice said again, closer now.

He stopped.

His body knew something his mind couldn't explain. The hairs on his neck lifted. His hands tightened around the torch. He didn't turn.

He didn't need to.

He knew whose voice it was.

It wasn't any one man. It was all of them.

Every unrecorded. Every unknown. Every face that blurred into the next.

The face he kept drawing in the notebook.

The voice he'd never heard but had always imagined.

"I was here before," it said.

David swallowed.

"You said I was no one."

He turned slowly.

Still nothing.

But the fog felt thicker, pressing in against his chest, like the air itself was waiting.

He pulled the notebook from his pocket with shaking fingers. Flipped through. There it was — the sketch, slightly smudged from the cold. The eyes that wouldn't leave him.

He tore the page out.

Let it fall.

The paper fluttered down, slow, then settled against the gravel.

The voice spoke again. Soft. Unhurried.

"I'll keep coming."

David turned off the torch.

The dark felt honest.

He walked the rest of the way back without looking behind him.

At the booth, the lights seemed too bright. Too artificial. The radio buzzed again — nothing urgent. Just shift updates.

He sat down, placed the notebook on the desk, and didn't open it.

For the first time in weeks, he didn't write anything.

Outside, the fog pressed gently against the windows, patient and sure.

Crossing

The request came in before sunrise. A report from the night crew: lights spotted offshore, movement past the markers. Possible drop. No confirmation. No drone footage.

David offered to follow up.

"No backup?" the port officer asked.

David shrugged. "Just a sweep. I'll radio if there's anything."

He signed the slip. Picked up the keys.

The speedboat sat low in the water, engine silent, hull slick with dew. He climbed in slowly, flicked the switches. The cabin screen blinked awake — tide charts, wind speed, fuel.

He pulled out from the dock without a sound. No siren. No lights.

Only the dull thrum of the motor as the shoreline fell behind him.

The water was calm, wide as a lie.

Out here, the paperwork didn't matter. No logs. No files. Just space.

He moved toward the open channel, following instinct more than coordinates. The fog drifted in, low and close, the kind that swallows time.

Ten minutes in, he slowed.

There was no sign of life.

No vessel.

No drop.

Only the quiet churn of his wake, folding back on itself.

He cut the engine.

Let the boat drift.

He stood at the helm, staring into grey.

The sea looked like the air — indistinguishable, depthless.

He reached into his coat. Pulled out the notebook. Thumbed through it, pages rippling in the salt wind.

Sketches. Notes. Questions.

At the back, a loose photo — grainy CCTV still. The man from the queue. The one who mouthed the words.

David stared at it for a long time.

Then let it go.

The paper lifted, caught the breeze, skimmed the surface like a skipped stone, then disappeared into the fog.

He looked down at the dash. The comms were still on.

He pressed the button.

"Coastal Three reporting," he said, voice steady. "Negative visual. No contact made."

A pause. Then static.

"Copy that, Coastal Three. Return when ready."

He didn't respond.

He stared ahead.

The fog thickened.

The shore was gone.

And still, he waited.

The shoreline vanished behind him, swallowed inch by inch by fog and memory. The motor idled, its pulse steady beneath the silence, more felt than heard.

He stood at the bow now, both hands gripping the rail.

Ahead—only grey.

Not weather, but texture. A fog so thick it erased even the idea of direction.

He'd radioed in, marked himself as "still sweeping." No one would expect him for at least an hour.

The notebook sat open on the seat behind him. Pages lifted by breeze, then dropped.

He hadn't written anything new.

There was nothing left to log.

Everything blurred now — names, days, faces. Even his own.

He leant forward, eyes searching for a horizon he no longer trusted. A boat could be twenty metres off and he'd never see it. A man could be waving from the water's edge and remain invisible.

He found that comforting.

The fog closed in tighter. The sound of gulls faded. Even the sea itself seemed to hush.

David closed his eyes.

The face appeared immediately — not threatening, just constant. The one he'd seen too many times. The one no system ever caught.

He whispered something. Not a prayer. Not a name.

Just a line he couldn't forget:

"You don't know my name."

He opened his eyes again.

Still fog.

He stepped back into the cabin. Flipped the switch for the motor. Nothing. Switched again. No click. Battery light flickered, then died.

He didn't panic.

He sat down.

Looked at the open sea.

He thought of the others who had vanished here. The boats never found. The logs closed with a dash. The ones who entered the water without origin and left it without trace.

Now, perhaps, he'd be one of them.

Not protest.

Not surrender.

Just a man stepping out of the system that failed him.

He reached for the comms. Then stopped.

There was nothing left to report.
He stood once more at the bow.
Hands steady.
The notebook fluttered behind him.
The fog thickened again, closing like a door.
And then—
he was gone.

Absence

They found the notebook two days later.

His locker was half-empty. Uniform folded. Boots tucked beneath the bench. No sign of rush, no note of goodbye. Just the notebook, spine split, tucked behind a rolled pair of gloves.

Stevens opened it first, standing in the breakroom while others watched the news. The report said: *Coastal agent presumed lost at sea. Vessel found adrift. No foul play suspected.*

The locker room was quiet. No one said his name.

Stevens turned the pages slowly.

Faces sketched in graphite. Dozens. Some detailed, some not. Notes in the margins: "Possible repeat." "No match in file." "Same posture. Same eyes."

Further in—maps of the intake area. Marked with Xs. Dots. Times. Arrows.

Then fragments of thought:

"I'm being watched, but not by who you think."

"The pattern is real. I don't know if they know it."

"The name keeps changing. The face does not."

Stevens stopped at the last page.

Only one line:

"They're already here."

No signature. No explanation. Just that.

He shut the book. Held it in his hand like it might warm.

Behind him, a rookie asked, "Is it true? He didn't call for help?"

"No," Stevens said.

"Did he jump?"

Stevens shook his head. "No one knows."

Outside, the sea pressed against the harbour wall. Tide high. Weather clear.

The boat had been found near a navigation buoy, empty. Engine off. Lights still flickering when the coast guard reached it. Nothing inside but a clipboard, sealed comms, and a mug half full.

The official report called it "operator disorientation."

The staff didn't say much.

David's name was removed from the schedule the next day. His file archived. His badge deactivated.

But the notebook stayed.

Stevens kept it in his locker. Said nothing.

Sometimes, he would open to the last page again.

Stare at the line.

They're already here.

And wonder—not what it meant, but what it saw.

After the incident, no one had been told what to do with it. The notebook remained in Stevens's locker, wrapped in a freezer bag to keep out moisture. It wasn't official evidence—just something found. No one filed it. No one claimed it.

Still, people talked.

Some said David had lost it months ago. That the sketches weren't real. That he'd been "too close to it for too long." Others said the opposite—that he had noticed something no one else dared to name.

The rookies asked questions quietly, always with a glance over the shoulder.

But no one denied the page.

The final one.

Black ink. Heavy hand. The words etched rather than written:

They're already here.

Stevens read it again during a late shift. Rain tapped the depot roof. The radio was silent. A ferry due at four.

He held the notebook like it might explain something if he stared long enough.

He flipped back through the sketches. The faces looked more deliberate now. Less like guesses, more like memory. Variations of the same expression, repeated in new skin.

He thought about David's quiet mornings. The way he stared at people—not with suspicion, but with attention. Like he was trying to remember them before they disappeared.

That kind of attention costs something.

At the next staff meeting, no one mentioned the boat.

The manager said, "We move forward."

Someone coughed.

The ferry arrived late. A new cluster came off. Twelve men. Three women. Eight children. Six with ID. The rest without.

Stevens processed them, pen tight in his grip.

When he logged the fifth *Unknown Male* of the day, he paused.

Looked up.

One man in line met his eyes.

Familiar. Not identical. But close.

Something in the way he tilted his head. The slow blink. The silence.

Stevens stared too long.

The man mouthed something.

Stevens didn't hear it.

But he thought he knew.

He finished the intake. Filed the sheet.

Later, back in the locker room, he pulled out the note-book.

Opened to the last page.

Ran a thumb across the words.

They're already here.

Then closed it.

And said nothing.

Part 9: Critical Essay

Untracked Bodies and Broken Borders
Dover is more than a location in this story — it is a membrane, straining. It stands for the national threshold, both geographic and symbolic, through which bodies arrive, vanish, accumulate, and blur. In the world of *"Gates of Dover"*, the border no longer separates inside from outside in any coherent sense. It is porous yet impenetrable, visible yet functionally meaningless. What matters now is not the wall, but the record. And increasingly, the record is failing.

David, a customs officer, becomes not a gatekeeper, but a witness to the slow breakdown of tracking itself. Migrants arrive in waves. Some are processed. Some are turned back. But many fall into the grey — undocumented, unnamed, uncounted. The ledger grows blank spaces. The spreadsheet fills with "Unknown Male," repeated so often it becomes liturgical. Bureaucracy becomes overwhelmed not by volume alone, but by a crisis of identification. Identity, once required to pass the border, is now optional — or worse, assumed.

In this context, the untracked body becomes the most dangerous symbol. Not because of threat, but because it exposes the state's helplessness. To govern a border, the state must be able to say: who, from where, and why. When it cannot, the idea of the border collapses conceptually, even if it still holds militarily. This is not just a failure of control, but of narrative. The nation no longer knows its edges.

David's growing unease is not rooted in hostility, but in incoherence. He cannot do the job he was trained for because the job no longer exists in a meaningful way. His role shifts from enforcement to repetition. He scans documents that do not exist. He logs entries that contain no substance. The rituals remain — the inspections, the files, the stamps — but the content has dissolved.

Meanwhile, the bodies continue to arrive. They are not threats. They are simply there. Not as enemies, but as data points that resist becoming meaningful. The political discourse may rage about borders, but David's daily experience is one of quiet erasure. The body in front of him cannot be named, and therefore cannot be placed. And if it cannot be placed, then nothing can be secured.

The untracked body, in this sense, is not just a migrant. It is the future — visible, undeniable, and unassimilated.

The Absurdity of Vetting

The act of vetting presumes the presence of facts. It assumes there is a history to inspect, a file to review, a trail that precedes the body standing at the gate. But *"Gates of Dover"* strips that illusion bare. In David's world, the migrants who arrive often bring nothing. No documents. No names. Sometimes, not even language. They arrive in the form of presence alone — real, breathing, and unknowable.

This shatters the very foundation of the vetting process. The systems in place require inputs: name, date of birth, country of origin, political status. Without these, the state flails. It reverts to instinct, stereotype, fear. The questions remain — "Where are you from?" "Why are you here?" — but they are asked with less and less conviction, their answers less and less useful. Vetting becomes pantomime, a ritual of control performed in the absence of control.

David begins to see this. He logs names that aren't names, accepts stories that shift daily, records facial details that match half a dozen others. His notes become rote, recursive, meaningless. And yet he is told to continue. The system doesn't adjust for the loss of certainty — it doubles down. It refines its procedures, sharpens its software, as if more precision could retrieve what no longer exists.

What's absurd is not that the process fails, but that it continues despite failing. A kind of institutional farce emerges: officers pretending to assess risk, authorities pretending to make informed decisions, paperwork passed from desk to desk as though belief alone could fill the gaps in knowledge. The state becomes a theatre of certainty, playing to itself, while the real flows of movement occur outside its lines of sight.

This absurdity has a cost. Not only does it fail to serve the function it claims — it begins to erode the credibility of governance itself. When the public sees that identity can be unverifiable, when enforcement becomes erratic and symbolic, trust weakens. The question becomes not *who got in*, but *how no one knew who they were.*

David's breakdown begins here — not in violence, but in futility. He is not cruel. He is careful. But care has no effect when the material of truth is absent. In its place: a parade of unknowns, each met with forms that no longer match the shape of reality.

The Spectre of Loss of Control

Borders have never merely been fences or checkpoints; they are symbols — projections of sovereignty, control, and narrative cohesion. In *"Gates of Dover,"* what unravels is not the physical threshold, but its symbolic power. The border still stands, the officers still operate, but the idea of control has fractured. What replaces it is performance, unease, and a creeping sense that something irreversible has taken place — quietly, offstage, and too late to halt.

David embodies this collapse. His role, once clear, now feels ceremonial. He checks names that repeat endlessly — *"Unknown Male"* scrawled into the log over a hundred times in a week. The more he records, the less he knows. He begins to see faces repeated — not in actuality, but in essence. A pattern haunts him: sameness without identity. Each man different, but all arriving from the same fog of unverifiability. The spectre of loss is not physical — it is epistemic.

This is what the story makes painfully clear: the fear is not of invasion, but of disorientation. David is not overrun by migrants. He is undone by the disappearance of structure. He used to trust the systems that trained him. Now, they echo with uncertainty. The vetting process fails not just because people lie — but because the state no longer believes in its own tools. And the moment that belief falters, the border becomes porous not in space, but in meaning.

Dover, in this narrative, is not a port. It is a metaphor for Britain itself — a nation wrestling with who it is, who gets to belong, and whether its institutions still function. The language of control persists — politicians speak of "crackdowns," "zero tolerance," "sovereignty" — but the practice underneath is frail. Boats arrive. Bodies are processed. Names are lost. And nothing is resolved.

David's psychological erosion mirrors this broader unravelling. He begins to question not just what he sees, but what is real. If names mean nothing, if identities dissolve, if faces repeat, then the self itself becomes unstable. He is haunted not by threat, but by the collapse of orientation.

In the end, control isn't lost through breach. It is lost through ambiguity — a slow, silent erosion of clarity, where every name might be a mask, every file a fiction, and every uniformed gesture a performance for an audience that no longer believes.

The Madness of Patterns

David begins to see the same face everywhere. In the queues. In the holding rooms. Across days and names and declarations, the features repeat — eyes too still, jawline too familiar, voice too precise. This is not paranoia in the usual sense. It is the logical endpoint of a world saturated with incomplete data, in which human difference becomes indistinct under the strain of repetition.

The madness of patterns is not in their falsehood, but in their seduction. David isn't imagining what isn't there — he's seeing too much of what is. Men arriving without papers. Declaring identical stories. Claiming similar routes. The details blur. The patterns compound. And with no way to confirm or disprove them, his mind begins to spiral. What's haunting is not one lie, but the accumulation of half-truths that begin to echo across bodies.

He starts to keep a separate notebook — a private archive of anomaly. Eyes that match. Birthdates reused. One man who comes back two weeks after he was supposedly deported, with a different name but the same scar. The system doesn't flag it. The log accepts the data. The pattern, official and unofficial, remains unseen.

This is how madness forms in institutional space: not through trauma, but through incongruence. David knows something is wrong, but no one else seems willing to name it. To colleagues, these are just coincidences. To supervisors, they're clerical echoes. To David, they are evidence of a deeper breakdown — the border not just breached, but bent.

The story invites the reader into this mental shift. What begins as documentation becomes obsession. The notebook fills. Dreams change. Faces follow him home. The unreliability of the system turns inward, and David no longer trusts even his own perception.

And yet, the patterns remain.

There is a quiet horror in this. Not dramatic, not explosive. Just a slow unreeling. If the state cannot verify, and if the officer cannot believe, then reality itself becomes porous. The line between vigilance and delusion thins.

David's madness is not individual failure. It is a symptom of institutional refusal. When patterns emerge and no one looks, when records loop and no one listens, those who do notice are left to break in isolation.

The face repeats.

The name repeats.

And somewhere in that recursion, David begins to vanish, too.

Paper vs. Flesh

The modern border is not patrolled by guards alone, but by paperwork. Passports, biometric scans, intake forms — the promise is that identity can be captured in text. But in *"Gates of Dover,"* this promise fails. The state clings to the fiction that a person without paper is a person without substance, and yet the flesh remains — present, breathing, beyond deletion.

David lives within this contradiction. He is trained to verify. To match face to file. But day after day, men appear with no documents. Or with documents that contradict each other. Or with details so vague they may as well be blank. The temptation — bureaucratic and psychological — is to treat these men as less than real. If the paper is incomplete, then so is the person.

But the story resists this logic. It insists on the undeniable presence of the body. The migrants do not vanish when their names are uncertain. They queue. They eat. They sleep on folding beds. They take up space. And yet, in the eyes of the institution, they remain suspect precisely because they refuse to resolve into data.

This is the quiet violence of bureaucratic thinking: it privileges the record over the person. Flesh is seen as unreliable. Paper is trusted — even when it is clearly false, forged, or fabricated. David feels this dissonance acutely. A man can be coughing, bleeding, alive in front of him — and still be logged as "Unknown Male #43." There is no grief for unknowns. No memory. Just numbers.

Over time, this inversion corrodes David's ability to relate to either side. The migrants are reduced to forms he no longer believes in. His colleagues, fluent in the language of protocol, treat irregularities as routine. He finds himself caught between presence and proof, unable to locate where truth resides.

The distinction between paper and flesh becomes more than metaphor — it becomes a rupture in how meaning is made. The state requires documentation to act. But when documentation fails, it does not adapt. It defaults to indifference.

The human body, once a site of moral attention, is now merely a placeholder for missing information.

David watches as the system writes over these absences with silence. But he cannot forget the faces. The weight. The sweat. The sound of the same voice, day after day, saying nothing that can be written down.

Collapse of National Imagination

A nation is not held together by geography alone. It is maintained by shared belief — in borders, in belonging, in a coherent sense of inside and out. *"Gates of Dover"* explores the disintegration of that belief. The border still functions as a process, but not as a narrative. There is no longer a clear story of who "we" are — and in that absence, control falters not only institutionally, but imaginatively.

David's role is meant to reaffirm the nation's perimeter. His job is to distinguish between citizen and outsider, legal and illegal, known and unknown. But the definitions blur. Every day he logs new arrivals who do not fit the nation's self-conception — not because they are threatening, but because they are unplaceable. There is no mental architecture left to house them. They don't challenge sovereignty — they challenge *comprehension*.

This is the collapse of national imagination: when a country can no longer picture its future in coherent terms, when it no longer recognises the shape of its own edges. The migrants in the story don't break the system. They arrive in silence, in exhaustion, with no demands. What cracks the system is the state's inability to absorb this presence into a functional narrative.

David begins to see this early on. The language around him grows thinner. Colleagues speak in euphemism. Politicians on the depot's small wall-mounted TV cycle through slogans: "Take Back Control," "Secure Our Future." But the slogans float above a reality they cannot reach. The control is gone. The future is unclear. The story no longer fits the scene.

The border becomes theatre. Uniforms still worn. Files still printed. But belief has withered. What used to be imagined as a line is now a fog — too many exceptions, too many anomalies, too many quiet arrivals that cannot be refused, cannot be remembered, cannot be resolved.

In this narrative void, paranoia grows. David's mind begins to fragment because the country around him no longer makes narrative sense. It is a border without myth, a perimeter without shape. All that remains is motion — people arriving, disappearing, looping back. A ghostly repetition.

Without a national imagination, policy becomes reaction. Law becomes gesture. And people like David, left to enforce a story that no longer exists, begin to fracture under the weight of their own disbelief.

Migration and Male Anxiety

The crisis at the border in *"Gates of Dover"* is not only logistical or legal — it is psychological, and gendered. David's unravelling reflects a deeper undercurrent of male anxiety in the face of migration, particularly in a post-industrial Britain where identity has grown precarious. His authority, once linked to uniform and function, begins to erode. The figures arriving — nameless, faceless, endlessly recurring — become not just undocumented migrants, but reflections of dislocation, of a masculinity that no longer commands space with certainty.

The narrative draws a subtle but potent line between control and fear. David's sense of self is intimately tied to the idea that the world can be sorted — bodies processed, threats identified, outcomes managed. But migration defies that. It is fluid, repetitive, unscheduled. It introduces not just strangers, but uncertainty. And for a man raised in a culture that promised stability through order, through work, through borders — the collapse of those frameworks becomes a personal undoing.

There is no open hostility in David. No ranting, no cruelty. Instead, his anxiety manifests as a quiet, spiralling surveillance — of others, of the patterns in his notebook, of his own mind. The fear is not of the migrant himself, but of what he represents: a shift in the balance of visibility and relevance. Who is seen? Who is recorded? Who is still legible in the national script?

This is a story of parallel erasures. The migrant arrives with no papers. David files him as "unknown." But over time, David too becomes less visible — not to the system, but to himself. He watches new men arrive and replace him in presence. He sees his authority narrowed to mechanical roles. His knowledge no longer equips him to interpret what he sees. His instincts betray him.

The migrant and the officer, then, are not opposites, but mirror figures — both operating within a framework that no longer honours their complexity. One is reduced by statelessness. The other, by irrelevance.

Migration here is not just movement of bodies — it is a confrontation with change. And David's anxiety is not about threat, but about displacement of self: a man trained to guard the border now finds the border inside him — blurring, receding, rewriting what he thought he knew.

Symbolic Suicide

The final act of *"Gates of Dover"* is not a declaration, but an erasure. David drifts off into the fog, alone, piloting a speedboat into the Channel under the guise of tracking smugglers. No body is recovered. No report is filed. Only a notebook is found in his locker, its final page reading: *"They're already here."* The moment resists analysis because it was never designed to be read as logic — it is a gesture. A quiet, unclaimed exit. A symbolic suicide.

David does not end his life in protest, or even in despair. He disappears in response to incoherence. The system around him has broken the link between perception and action, between truth and record. He sees patterns no one else acknowledges. He speaks into silence. He writes names that are deleted. Eventually, the only remaining form of agency is to remove himself from the page entirely.

This is not an act of spectacle. There are no speeches, no manifestos. Just the simple fact of absence — the thing the state most fears and most creates. In a system obsessed with tracking, David becomes untraceable. His exit mirrors the very crisis he was charged with managing: bodies that vanish, presence without paperwork, names unconfirmed.

The symbolism deepens in the act of choosing the water. The Channel, which divides and connects, which has become both a grave and a gateway, now receives him. He joins the unrecorded. No uniform. No ID. No traceable narrative. He becomes, in the end, one of the unknowns.

What David enacts is not surrender, but alignment. His disappearance is a way of making visible the disappearance of meaning around him. If the state cannot recognise truth, if the institution no longer listens, then leaving becomes the most coherent response. Not as punishment, but as mirror.

There is tragedy here, but also clarity. David's final act is not madness — it is an indictment. He does what the system cannot: he stops pretending. The state continues to process shadows. David chooses to become one.

In the logic of the story, this is the only end possible. A man who sees too clearly cannot remain. He does not die in rage. He dies in quiet symmetry with the world he tried to understand — by becoming its most truthful fiction.

Part 10: The Firestarter

The Cell

Lewis joined *The Reklaimers* at 1:42 a.m. The invite came through a forwarded link on Telegram, sent by someone he didn't know, with a username that looked like a spelling mistake. He clicked without thinking. The group banner showed a lion's head in black and white, pixelated, with a slogan underneath: *We Remember What They Erased.* There were 236 members. The latest message read: *Another centre approved. North Road. Burn or be replaced.*

He stared at the screen, thumb hovering. His bedroom was quiet except for the low whir of the radiator, the rustle of wind through the cracked vent. Posters on the wall — a footballer mid-strike, a UFC fighter bleeding from the eye — curled at the edges. In the corner, a small desk lamp lit his phone's face in blue.

Downstairs, the kettle clicked off. His dad always boiled water before bed, then forgot about it. Their rhythms no longer touched. Lewis hadn't eaten dinner; his father hadn't asked. In the silence, the join request went through. He was in.

The chat fed on itself. Images of burnt-out vans, a grainy video of a man shouting outside a council office, maps annotated with red dots and phrases like *clearing required.* Some of it looked fake. Some of it didn't. One message stood out: *Don't just scroll. Act. Your father won't fix this. Your mother already left.*

Lewis swallowed. His mother hadn't left, not exactly — she just wasn't home much. Worked double shifts at that place by the viaduct. Intake something. Always came back late, eyes heavy, smelling of antiseptic and mint.

A knock at the door.

'Turn off the Wi-Fi, yeah?' his dad said. 'I'm knackered.'

Lewis didn't answer. Just stood and pulled the router's plug from the socket. The light dimmed. Connection gone.

Back upstairs, his phone still glowed. Messages continued in grey silence. He couldn't reply — not without data — but he watched the feed unspool. Angry words, half-baked plans, names he didn't recognise. Then one message blinked: *You in North? Need action by Friday.*

He didn't respond. But he didn't look away, either.

His dad stood in the doorway a moment longer than usual.

'Wi-Fi off, right?'

'Yeah,' Lewis said. He turned to show the blank light on the router, though his father didn't look. Just nodded vaguely and scratched at his jaw.

The hallway light cast a long shadow across the carpet. His dad wore the same joggers he'd slept in the night before, a faded jumper with a missing cuff. His face sagged slightly, like a man not quite sick but not quite well. Behind him, the house yawned into silence — kitchen light still on, tea gone cold.

'You alright for tomorrow?' his dad asked. The way he asked questions now — like he was borrowing them.

Lewis shrugged. 'S'pose.'

'You've been in a bit lately. You going out at all?'

Lewis kept his eyes on the wall. 'No one's about.'

His dad hesitated again, then exhaled through his nose and turned. 'Alright then. Sleep if you can.'

The door clicked shut. No lock, no shout, no correction. Just absence in slow motion.

Lewis sat back on the edge of the bed. In the absence of Wi-Fi, the room felt quieter, heavier. The phone in his hand dimmed and locked. He didn't unlock it. Just stared at the dark screen like it might stir.

Downstairs, the kettle clicked again — reheated by mistake. His dad wouldn't notice.

In the corner of his room, the desk lamp buzzed slightly. Lewis stood, reached to switch it off, then stopped. He looked around the room as if seeing it from outside: the worn posters, the laundry pile, the cracked socket with the plug still half in. The place didn't look lived-in. It looked paused.

He pulled the curtain aside. Outside, the street was empty. The old lamppost flickered. A fox darted across the tarmac and vanished under a hedge. Far off, the faint rattle of a train. The night made everything thinner.

He let the curtain fall and sat again. On the floor now. Legs crossed, back against the wardrobe. He didn't reach for his phone. Instead, he mouthed the words he'd read earlier, under his breath.

'Burn or be replaced.'

They sounded stupid when said aloud. But they lodged in his chest all the same.

Target

The plan wasn't a plan. It was a suggestion, floated in the grey half-speech of online threads. No names, no dates — just a postcode and a phrase: *unclaimed opportunity.* Beneath it, a grainy photo of a brick building behind temporary fencing, with bins clustered like sheep near the entrance. The windows were mostly dark. A single upstairs room showed light.

Lewis stared at it for hours. He screenshotted it, deleted it, typed the address into Maps, then cleared his history. He didn't tell anyone. Not his mate from school, not the boy at the gym who sometimes nodded at him. The thing growing inside him didn't want company. It wanted direction.

On Thursday, he walked past the building just after sunset. It looked smaller than the photo — more ordinary. The kind of place you wouldn't notice unless told to. A woman in uniform stood outside smoking. She leant on the wall, one foot folded behind her ankle, phone pressed to her ear. Lewis didn't look at her face. Just kept walking, hands in pockets, heart skidding a little.

He passed again an hour later. She was gone. A blue security light blinked above the door.

That night, in his room, he opened the app again. The chat had shifted. No one used words like *burn*. Now it was *action* and *final shift*. One voice said, *just one more and we go dark*. Another posted a photo of lighter fluid beside a kitchen sink.

Lewis checked the cupboard under his own sink. Nothing there. In the garage, he found an old canister for the barbecue — mostly empty, but it would do. He didn't tell his dad. Said he was going out for a late walk. His dad nodded from the sofa, didn't ask.

Back in his room, he prepared the bottle. Glass. A sock from the drawer. Not soaked yet, just set aside. He tucked it under the bed in a shopping bag. The smell was faint, but present. Acrid. Like something getting ready to speak.

The phone buzzed once: *North Road. Window side. Friday. 10pm.*

He didn't reply. Just placed the phone screen-down on the desk and stared at it.

It didn't buzz again.

He waited until his dad fell asleep. The snore was faint but rhythmic, rising from the living room like a metronome in another room. Lewis moved slowly — no panic, no ceremony. The rucksack was already packed. The glass bottle inside was double-wrapped in an old hoodie. The sock lay curled like a tongue.

In the kitchen, he found a half-used bottle of white spirit under the sink. He didn't check the label. Just uncapped it and poured, careful not to spill. The smell rose like a signal — synthetic, sharp, unforgiving. He sealed the bottle, wiped the sides with a tea towel, and stuffed it deep into the bag.

Upstairs again, he changed into black jeans, dark hoodie. Not camouflage — just quiet. He looked at himself in the mirror. Pale face, blank eyes, a faint line of stubble where a beard was trying to start. He didn't look angry. He looked tired.

He pulled the hood up, slung the bag over one shoulder, and paused at the door. The house was silent except for the fridge hum and the intermittent cough from the living room. No drama. No goodbyes.

Outside, the air was damp, not quite cold. The pavements glistened faintly from an earlier drizzle. He walked quickly, not fast. He knew the route without checking. Past the shuttered vape shop, the betting place with the smashed window, the kebab van closed for the night. No people. Just lights and shadows.

At the alley behind North Road, he stopped. The building rose like a lump in the dark. Unremarkable. Ordinary. A light flicked on upstairs, then off again. Somewhere, a cat mewed and scratched at a bin.

He crouched behind a wall, unzipped the rucksack. Pulled the bottle out. The sock was soaked now, stuffed into the neck, frayed slightly at the end. His hand trembled, but only a little. He gripped the lighter. Plastic, orange, from a petrol station.

He struck it once. A faint spark.

Again. This time, flame.

He held it near the sock — not touching yet. Breathing shallow. Waiting.

A door creaked somewhere in the distance.

He paused, flame still flickering.

Then, slowly, he let it die.

Not yet.

Not here.

He placed the bottle gently back into the bag and waited in the dark, listening.

Night of Fire

He saw her just as he was stepping into the open.

A woman leaving the building, keys in hand, coat half-zipped, moving quickly as if late. Her head was bowed, but he recognised the shape of her walk — the slight tilt to the left, the stiffness in her right shoulder. She paused under the blue light by the entrance, fumbled with her phone, then turned down the road.

He froze. The bottle was already in his hand.

She didn't see him. Just walked — steady, unremark-able. He crouched behind the bins, heart hammering now, breath shallow and fast. The sock was still damp. His fingers smelt of paraffin.

She moved past him, crossed the street under the flickering streetlight, and disappeared into the night.

He stayed there, hunched, trying to swallow the dry panic rising in his throat. He recognised the coat, and the posture was hers. That was his mother. It had to be.

He tried to stand but stayed crouched. The adrenaline, the not-quite-certainty, the lurching sense that the line had shifted — all of it pinned him to the concrete.

He waited.

Ten seconds.

Thirty.

A full minute.

Then he lit the sock.

It caught quickly, the flame small but eager. He stood. Walked to the edge of the path. The building looked hollow now, windows dark, the light above the door buzzing quietly.

He pulled back his arm.

Hesitated.

And threw.

The bottle arced lazily, like something released from thought. It struck the brick just left of the door, shattered with a brittle pop. The flame leapt up fast, unnatural, licking the wall and gutter, curling into a crude blossom of orange and blue.

He turned and ran.

Not fast — not like a fugitive. Just steady. Purposeful.

Behind him, the fire crackled against the wall. No alarm. No sirens. Not yet.

The road stretched open in front of him, wet underfoot, wind rising.

He didn't look back.

Not yet.

Not ever.

He didn't stop running until the noise of the fire faded into the hum of traffic. At the edge of town, near the industrial estate, he slowed to a walk, chest tight, breath fogging in short bursts. The rucksack bounced lightly on his back — empty now, a hollow shell that still smelt like something dangerous.

He found a skip behind an abandoned warehouse and shoved the bag deep into it, under damp cardboard and plastic wrap. He wiped his hands on his jeans. The smell wouldn't leave. It was in his skin now.

The streets here were dead. Security lights buzzed. A train passed in the distance, low and slow, like a machine thinking. His stomach rolled with something sour. He ducked into a side path between two units and leant against the corrugated wall.

In his mind, the image of the fire replayed. It hadn't spread quickly — just clung to the brick like it was waiting to be believed. He didn't know if it had reached the door. He didn't wait to see if anyone came out.

But he'd thrown it.

Even after seeing her.

That was the part he couldn't unstick.

He slid down the wall, crouched in the dark, and let the night breathe around him. No one called. No one followed. The act was done, and the world hadn't cracked open.

His hands trembled. Not from fear, exactly. From something else. Something closer to recognition.

He pulled out his phone. No signal — still no data. He scrolled through old screenshots: the group messages, the building photo, the address. Then the invite link — now expired. Beneath it: *This chat no longer exists*.

Gone.

They'd vanished.

He swallowed hard. The rush was over. All that remained was him — damp hoodie, burnt fingertips, and the echo of glass hitting wall.

He stood. Stretched his back. Walked toward the main road like a man returning from something no one would ask about.

A bus passed, empty. Its lights blurred across the wet tarmac.

The night didn't care.

Truth

The news came quietly, through a muted TV in a café window. Lewis had been walking, aimless, hoodie pulled low, hood strings clenched between his fingers. The screen caught his eye. Flames licking brick. Police tape sagging. The headline: *"Blaze at Housing Site — Staff Member Escapes Injury."*

He stopped.

A still image appeared. CCTV. Grainy. A woman leaving the building moments before the fire began. Coat flapping, keys in hand, phone pressed to her ear.

He stepped closer.

His breath caught.

It was her.

Not a doubt, not a guess. His mum. The work coat she always wore, navy with the stitched-on badge. Her lanyard, her shape, the stiff right shoulder from years of care shifts. He saw it all.

And he'd thrown the bottle anyway.

He turned, walked fast, didn't know where to. His mouth filled with heat. Shame climbed his throat. He cut down a side road, then another, until the shopfronts gave way to shutters and silence. The first open door was a pub. He pushed through without thinking, didn't meet the barman's eye, headed straight for the toilet.

The cubicle lock jammed twice before it slid home. The door didn't fully shut, but it didn't matter. He dropped to his knees, hands on the rim of the toilet, chest heaving.

The bile came up hard — thick, acrid, yellow. He gagged again. Nothing left. Just the echo of his breath and the trickle of water through the pipes.

His eyes stung. His body shook. He tried to stand but fell sideways, hitting the tiled wall with a thud. He sat there, legs curled beneath him, as if braced against a wave.

She had been in the building.

He'd seen her. Had seen her leave.

And still—

His stomach lurched again, dry and convulsive. His hoodie clung damp to his spine. The sour taste coated his teeth.

When he finally rose, he didn't look in the mirror. He splashed water on his face, used too much soap, rubbed until his skin went red. Paper towel stuck to his fingers. He scrubbed harder.

Then he stopped.

His reflection waited, blurred by steam.

Not a man.

Not a monster.

Just something in between.

Fallout

By morning, the group had vanished.

The Reklaimers no longer existed. No icon, no feed, no usernames. Just a grey screen and the message: *This chat is unavailable or has been deleted.* He refreshed. Searched. Nothing. Gone like smoke.

Lewis sat in his room, phone on the pillow beside him, eyes red from no sleep. He didn't move much. His hoodie still smelt faintly of fuel. His hands were scrubbed raw. But it lingered — under the nails, in the seams of his thoughts.

He scrolled through old chats, half-formed threads, videos saved in the hope of meaning. Faces he didn't know, words that once felt sharp — now dulled. The invite that had changed everything was dead. The usernames he'd watched night after night had logged out without warning. No parting word. No claim of responsibility. No message of success.

Just silence.

And he was still here.

He looked out the window. The road was quiet. A bin truck groaned past. Someone's dog barked once, then stopped. No sirens. No reporters. No knock at the door.

He hadn't been caught.

He hadn't been named.

No one was coming.

The CCTV image on the news hadn't shown the attacker — only his mother, leaving. He'd watched the segment three more times, without sound. Her keys jangling. Her face half turned.

She hadn't looked back.

He closed the curtains.

Sat down on the carpet, legs crossed.

The group had promised retribution, brotherhood, action.

They gave him nothing. Used him for the moment. Let him do the thing they wouldn't. Then disappeared. No explanation. No follow-up. Just an empty feed and a sick taste in his mouth.

He'd expected something.

Anything.

A sign, a signal, a reckoning.

Instead, he had the memory of a bottle leaving his hand, and the knowledge that if she'd been two minutes slower, he might have killed her.

He thought about texting her.

Then didn't.

His phone buzzed once — a bank alert.

He turned it over.

Face-down.

Dark.

He waited for them to come.

Each knock made him flinch. Each siren in the distance froze his chest for a beat. He stayed close to the door those first few days — not to answer it, but to hear them coming. But they never did.

No officers.

No call.

No letter.

The police hadn't linked him to the fire. Or hadn't tried. Or didn't care. He wasn't sure which was worse.

By Monday, the news had moved on. The fire was now "under investigation," with no suspects named. A community leader gave a statement outside the building. Lewis recognised the backdrop — the door still scorched, the new lock gleaming silver. The man spoke of unity, of resilience, of vigilance. Lewis muted the sound.

That night, he walked past the building again. No tape now. No press. Just a faint black trace on the brick and a CCTV camera newly affixed to the corner. The light in the window upstairs was back on.

He stood across the street and watched for a while.

No one came out.

He crossed to the alley, crouched low near the fence where he'd stood the night it happened. His legs ached from the cold. The silence felt thicker now. He wanted something — not forgiveness, not even punishment. Just proof that it had mattered.

But the building looked unchanged.

And he was still free.

He walked home slower than usual. The lights were on in his house. His dad's silhouette moved behind the curtains — flicking the kettle, pulling on the cord for the blinds, checking the oven without putting anything in.

Inside, the air smelt stale, faintly of toast and plastic.

'You're out late,' his dad said, not looking up from the sink.

Lewis shrugged. Took off his shoes. Stood in the doorway too long.

His dad dried a mug and placed it gently on the counter. 'No word from anyone?' he asked, tone too casual.

Lewis shook his head.

His dad didn't push.

The silence between them settled again — not empty but crowded with everything unsaid.

Lewis sat down on the floor near the radiator and let the heat pool around his knees. Outside, a car passed. Inside, the mug steamed quietly.

No one had come.

But someone would.

Surely.

Confession

He tried three times.

Once at breakfast, while his dad was spooning instant coffee into a chipped mug. The words hovered at the edge of his mouth, but he swallowed them with the toast. Too early. Too exposed.

The second time was in the hallway, as his dad bent down to tie his bootlace. Lewis stood behind him, hands clenched into his sleeves, heart pounding. He opened his mouth — nothing came. His dad looked up, nodded, and stood. 'You alright?' he asked. Lewis nodded back. They both pretended it meant something.

The third time, it was dark. The telly played low in the living room, some rerun with canned laughter he couldn't stand. His dad sat in the chair by the window, face lit by the screen, beer half-finished on the floor. Lewis stood in the doorway again.

'I need to say something,' he said, quietly.

His dad muted the TV.

Lewis hesitated, throat tight.

'I did something,' he said. 'I mean—I was part of something. Not just online. It... I threw it.'

His dad turned in the chair. His face was tired, blank, unreadable.

Lewis looked down. Couldn't continue.

Silence.

Then:

'I know,' his dad said.

Softly. Without weight.

Lewis blinked. Looked up.

His dad's eyes were on the wall now, not him.

'You knew?' he asked.

His dad nodded once. Slowly. 'Not all of it. But enough.'

The room held still. Even the telly seemed to freeze in its loop.

Lewis waited for a lecture, a shout, a blow — something.

But his dad just sipped his drink.

'So... what now?' Lewis asked.

His dad didn't answer. Just turned the volume back up.

The laughter came again. Too bright. Too false.

Lewis stood there, mouth open.

Then closed it.

Turned.

Left the room.

Lewis sat at the top of the stairs, knees tucked against his chest. The carpet was thin and rough beneath him, frayed near the banister where the dog used to scratch before it died. He traced the edges of the threadbare patch with one finger, slowly, as the voices from the telly rolled up the staircase.

He hadn't expected calm. Not this kind. It unsettled him more than shouting would have. There had been no disbelief. No demand to explain. Just the quiet weight of something already known.

Downstairs, his dad laughed at something on the screen. A single chuckle, short and sharp. Then nothing.

Lewis leant his head back against the wall. The paint was cool. He closed his eyes.

It made sense now — the long silences, the way his dad hadn't asked questions. Not out of trust, but because he'd seen it in him. The same shape. The same fire behind the eyes. Not surprised. Just tired.

He remembered being younger, watching his dad come home from the warehouse, hands black with grease, eyes bloodshot, saying nothing about anything. Just sitting in that same chair, beer in hand, foot tapping a rhythm no one else could hear.

Maybe this had been waiting in both of them.

He didn't know what to do next.

The group was gone. The messages erased. No charges, no headlines. His mother hadn't said anything. Maybe she didn't know. Maybe she did.

He heard the clink of a glass being set down.

Then the creak of the recliner.

His dad would fall asleep in that chair again.

And Lewis would stay here, halfway down the stairs, stuck in the middle of a story no one would tell.

Part 10: Critical Essay

Radicalisation of the Fatherless

In the architecture of contemporary radicalisation, the absence of the father functions less as a singular cause and more as a structural vacuum — a space where grievance, shame, and yearning fester unchecked. Lewis, the central figure in this narrative, embodies this hollowness. His father's physical presence — embodied in the quiet act of asking him to turn off the Wi-Fi — is not authority but resignation. There is no guidance, no redirection, only tacit knowledge of collapse. This dynamic, unspoken but palpable, is where extremism finds its footing.

Lewis's online indoctrination is not militant in the traditional sense; it is intimate, domestic, almost banal. He joins *The Reklaimers* not with ideological fervour but with inertia — a desire for belonging where institutional life has failed. The group's language mimics familial cadence: codes, tests of loyalty, private chats masquerading as rites of passage. They offer, in effect, a surrogate initiation into manhood for boys left unparented by both family and state.

Unlike traditional narratives of radicalisation which rely on political grievance or religious zeal, Lewis's drift is motivated by nothing so coherent. It is affective rather than intellectual: a swirl of loneliness, resentment, and a desire to be *seen*. In this, the father's absence is mirrored by the mother's distance — not emotional, but circumstantial. She is working — literally and symbolically — within the very system her son is taught to oppose.

The figure of the "fatherless radical" is a familiar spectre in the post-industrial West, yet Lewis complicates the trope. He is not animated by racial supremacy nor explicit hatred, but by an inability to metabolise loss. The bomb he prepares is not just a weapon — it is an expression. A misdirected lament. The moment he recognises his mother as the building's final occupant is not a plot twist, but a revelation of tragic symmetry: the system he sought to punish is embodied in the only person who still shows up for him.

Radicalisation here is not ideological acquisition — it is emotional inheritance. The vacuum becomes the vector. And in the space where the father should have stood, a screen glows. A username beckons. A fire is lit.

The Mother as Contradiction

The role of Lewis's mother is delicately poised between care and complicity — not in action, but in symbol. She is a worker at the migrant housing centre, a site of political contestation and moral projection, yet to her son, she is simply absent. Not emotionally distant, perhaps, but structurally unreachable — consumed by the demands of a system that both needs her and neglects her. In many ways, she represents the last functioning node of liberal institutionalism: underpaid, overworked, and unable to choose between profession and parenthood.

Her presence in the building Lewis targets reframes the entire narrative. She is not merely collateral damage but a silent axis around which the story turns. Her existence disrupts binary readings of 'enemy' and 'victim', 'native' and 'migrant'. She is both insider and outsider: native-born but increasingly alien in her son's worldview, public servant yet privately invisible. In burning the building, Lewis does not just commit violence against the other — he assaults the mother figure, the embodiment of labour without recognition.

This contradiction — mother as both nurturer and enforcer — cuts to the heart of Britain's fractured moral economy. The very structures that employ women like her to uphold social order also erode the domestic sphere they once anchored. She is tasked with compassion under constraint, asked to mediate crises she did not cause, and blamed (by implication) for policies she cannot influence. Her silence in the aftermath is telling. There is no confrontation, no breakdown, just a mute recognition between her and her son — a grief beyond words.

In many depictions of political extremism, women are marginal — mourning mothers, passive victims, or symbolic abstractions. Here, the mother resists all three. She is instead a hinge — holding together the broken, if only barely. Her son's act is not just one of rage but of misrecognition: the belief that she serves a foreign cause, when in fact she is serving everyone, and no one. Her labour is not honoured, her personhood not fully seen — by the state or her own child.

The contradiction is not hers alone. It is national. To nurture in a system that cannot protect, to serve a public that has turned private in its grief — this is her inheritance. And in Lewis's flame, we see the cost.

Online Incitement, Offline Collapse

Lewis's descent does not occur in a public square or place of worship, but in the glare of his screen. *The Reklaimers* exist not as a physical organisation but as a digital whisper

— a Telegram group, ephemeral and encrypted. Their influence is diffuse yet binding, trading in memes, slogans, and directives stripped of complexity. Here, the internet functions not as a space for dialogue, but as a funnel — narrowing thought, accelerating grievance, and eroding any remaining boundaries between fantasy and action.

This is not radicalisation in the traditional sense. It is collapse — psychological, civic, and narrative. Lewis is not drawn into a well-defined ideology but pushed along a gradient of frustration, nudged from alienation to arson by a culture of ambient extremism. There is no manifesto, no public claim of responsibility, no formal initiation. Just a slow and silent education in despair, punctuated by emojis and half-truths. The incitement is aesthetic as much as ideological — anger rendered into aesthetic form: flames, broken glass, the righteousness of destruction.

Offline, the collapse is quiet but profound. The target is not symbolic; it is literal — a housing centre, sheltering people Lewis will never speak to. There is no direct grievance, only the sense that this building represents something he is not part of. The violence, then, is not protest but projection: a desire to make visible the pain he cannot articulate. This is the key transformation — from feeling forgotten to insisting on being remembered, even if through fire.

What makes this collapse particularly modern is its disconnection from consequence. The group vanishes the next day. No arrests are made. The news cycle moves on. There is no reckoning, no explanation — only the enduring knowledge that something burned and no one noticed quite enough. The internet, having incubated the act, now erases its fingerprints. Digital footprints dissolve; emotional scars remain.

This is the new topology of incitement: decentralised, deniable, and devastating. No leader to arrest, no pamphlet to ban. The state is left chasing ghosts, while the victims live among the ruins — or work in them, as Lewis's mother did. The story offers no catharsis, because none exists. The screen goes black. The system stutters. And somewhere, another boy logs on.

Masculinity and Shame

The fire Lewis sets is not born of dominance but humiliation. His act is not a demonstration of power, but a cry to be perceived. In this, *The Firestarter* diverges from traditional narratives of male aggression. Lewis is not asserting manhood — he is pleading for it to exist. The shame that drives him is quiet, cumulative, and largely unspoken: the shame of economic redundancy, emotional inarticulacy, and social invisibility. In burning something down, he believes, however briefly, that he might be *seen*.

Masculinity here is not toxic, but eroded. Lewis is a young man in a culture without clear rites of passage, no dignified labour to inherit, no moral anchor to resist the pull of extremism. The old templates — protector, provider, patriarch — have crumbled, and what remains is improvisation. The online world offers substitute scripts: brotherhoods formed through grievance, purpose modelled through destruction. The flame he ignites is, in effect, his initiation ritual. It marks his passage — not into maturity, but infamy.

Crucially, the shame that underpins his act is compounded by personal contradiction. He learns, too late, that the building he attacked housed his own mother. This is not just a mistake, but a profound betrayal of self. His target becomes his origin. The maternal figure he never voiced allegiance to was, all along, the one actively serving others.

The burn is no longer political — it is oedipal, internal, and irreparable. When Lewis vomits in a public toilet, it is not guilt alone — it is the physical extrusion of shame.

There is a cultural truth embedded in this arc: young men who feel ashamed will either vanish or explode. Lewis does both. He disappears into the anonymity of an unclaimed act, but not before making a spectacle of collapse. His father, aware yet inactive, represents a broader failure of intergenerational transmission. No wisdom is passed on, no boundaries enforced. There is no hand on the shoulder, no reckoning in the shed — only a dead screen and a bedroom door ajar.

The story renders masculinity not as threat, but as question. What remains when all scripts are voided, all symbols burned? For Lewis, the answer is tragic. To be noticed, he must destroy. To confess, he must confront the only man left in the room — who already knows, and says nothing.

The Vanishing Group

The Reklaimers, like many modern extremist cells, vanish without climax. They do not issue statements or take responsibility. Their chat thread evaporates, their members disperse, and their trace dissolves into the digital ether. This vanishing is not incidental — it is central. The group's power lies in its impermanence. It is the perfect structure for a collapsing world: weightless, deniable, and entirely disposable. For Lewis, the disappearance is both a release and a further unravelling. He is left not as a comrade, but as residue.

In this formulation, ideology is no longer durable — it is viral. These online communities are not built to endure, but to incite. They exist for the act, not the aftermath. Once the deed is done, the group recedes, like a wave that leaves the beach scarred but dry. There is no community to return to, no shared reckoning. Radical belonging is revealed as conditional and performative: solidarity only for as long as you serve its destructive script.

The moment the group disappears, Lewis's isolation becomes total. The only thing worse than being radicalised, the story suggests, is being radicalised and then abandoned. His guilt has no outlet, his remorse no audience. He is not pursued by police, but by silence. This is the cruelty of modern extremism — it demands total buy-in for a single moment, and offers nothing in return. No support, no doctrine, no moral defence. Just wreckage, and memory.

The vanishing group also mirrors the broader political culture. Movements rise and fall in hours; attention shifts before the smoke clears. Moral intensity flares, then flickers out. The online space facilitates this with clinical efficiency — groups form, swell, splinter, and dissolve. What remains is not cohesion, but exhaustion. Lewis is emblematic of this cycle: primed, ignited, and then discarded. He is not a soldier, but a symptom.

And yet the consequences are real. The building still burned. The shame still lingers. The woman who survived the attack is still his mother. The group's vanishing absolves no one. It merely refuses responsibility. In the vacuum left behind, Lewis is forced to reckon not with ideology, but with self. He was recruited by ghosts and left behind by cowards. What he carries now — unlike them — will not disappear.

Race, Class, and the Local

Violence, when it emerges from the local poor, is rarely read with empathy. In the media, the arson is either ignored or attributed to 'fringe elements', with no effort to

understand the social architecture that produced it. Lewis
is not granted complexity. He is white, working-class, angry
— a profile easily dismissed or pathologised. His pain is not
narrated, only recorded. The burnt building becomes an
image of disorder, not a symptom of decay.

In Britain, the intersection of race and class has long
shaped who is allowed narrative depth. The migrant centre, though not a character itself, is symbolically overde-
termined: a proxy for state failure, multicultural anxiety,
and policy outsourcing. Yet it receives the protection of
moral clarity — it shelters, therefore it is good. The boy
who attacks it, by contrast, becomes a moral void. But the
story complicates that. Lewis's act is unforgivable — but
not inexplicable. The story refuses to render him as either
martyr or monster. He is a boy shaped by systemic attrition.

Class is central to this refusal. Lewis does not live in
the England of commentary and commissions. He lives in
the England of shut libraries, temp contracts, and pater-
nal withdrawal. His local reality is not multicultural, but
fractured — with no script for coexistence, no language for
resentment that isn't instantly disqualified as hate. His violence is not racially motivated in any coherent sense, but it
will be read that way, because there is no other interpretive
grammar available.

This disjunction — between act and analysis, cause and
coverage — is itself a form of abandonment. The local working class, especially its young men, are either
weaponised or erased. When they implode, they are prose-
cuted; when they disappear, they are not missed. And when
they burn something, the fire is treated as pathology, not
protest. But this fire was not ideological. It was personal.
Confused. Shame-born. A cry mistaken for a war-cry.

That Lewis's mother worked in the centre undoes easy
narratives of racial antagonism. This is not 'us vs them', but

'us against ourselves'. The tragedy of the fire is not just in its target, but in its misrecognition. A local boy burns down a lifeline, unaware it was his mother's. That no one covers this with nuance is not surprising. In Britain, some kinds of collapse are too local to be legible.

Children of Collapse

Lewis is not an outlier — he is a product. A child of institutional fatigue, moral confusion, and cultural entropy. His story is less about deviance than drift. He does not storm the barricades; he follows a Telegram link. He does not shout slogans; he listens. This is the posture of a generation raised amid contradictions — told they are privileged, yet economically precarious; warned against offence, yet steeped in ambient hostility; promised inclusion, yet met with algorithmic neglect.

Generation Z in this Britain do not inherit a coherent nation. They inherit fragments: a shuttered job centre, a polarised feed, a parent who no longer believes in the system. For Lewis, there is no grand betrayal, only accumulated absences. School did not prepare him. Work did not stabilise him. Home did not hold him. The extremism that finds him is not persuasive — it is available. In a cultural moment defined by irony and exhaustion, his sincerity is easily weaponised.

This makes him vulnerable in ways that are rarely acknowledged. Lewis is not hardened — he is porous. He cries, he hesitates, he vomits. There is no glory in his act, only recoil. His descent is marked not by ideological certainty but emotional vulnerability. He is not filled with hate but emptied of orientation. The fire he sets is not a battle cry — it is a question: *do I matter enough to be stopped?*

That no one answers is part of the tragedy. His radicalisation occurs in a vacuum of adult authority. The father
is inert. The mother is occupied. The state is absent. Only
the group, momentary and faceless, provides structure —
and then vanishes. This is what collapse looks like: not
spectacular, but ambient. Not revolution, but rot.

Lewis is one of many children of collapse. They do not
march. They meander. They burn things not because they
believe, but because belief is no longer on offer. And when
they seek to confess — as Lewis does — there is no ear
waiting. Just a father who already knows and says nothing.
The intergenerational handover fails. Not with a shout, but
with a shrug.

The question that remains is not *how did this happen?* but
*how many more like him are there — waiting, watching, burning
quietly inside?*

Aftermath as Story

There is no trial. No headline. No catharsis. Lewis is not
arrested, and the event fades from public consciousness almost as swiftly as it entered. In this, the story refuses the arc
of justice or redemption. What remains is not resolution,
but residue — a quiet ruin that continues without reckoning. The aftermath is not an epilogue; it is the story. The
building still stands. The family still lives there, perhaps.
The mother still works, or doesn't. Lewis still breathes.
Nothing ends, but everything is altered.

This is a profound structural choice. Most narratives of
political violence seek closure: a court scene, a confession, a
punishment. *The Firestarter* offers none. Instead, we are left
with a kind of narrative dissonance — the knowledge that
something grave has occurred, and that nothing will come
of it. It mirrors, precisely, the way contemporary Britain

metabolises trauma: quickly, superficially, with no systemic correction. The news moves on. So does the boy. But the fire, symbolically, continues to burn.

The refusal to frame Lewis as either terrorist or victim underscores a wider moral fatigue. Society no longer seems interested in causation. Stories are flattened into hashtags, policy debates truncated by fear of misreading the room. The housing centre is re-painted. The system resets. But something critical has been lost — not just a sense of justice, but a capacity to *remember*. The aftermath exists, but it is unstoried. This, too, is a form of collapse.

And yet, in the ruins, there is still the potential for witness. The father's knowledge — his quiet recognition — is one such moment. It is not dramatic, but it is significant. In saying nothing, he confirms everything. The circle of silence holds: around the act, around the motive, around the home. This silence is not peace. It is stasis. And it is through this stasis that the narrative resists both sentiment and scapegoat.

Ultimately, the story becomes its own form of indictment. Not of a boy, or a group, but of a culture that no longer knows how to make meaning from collapse. Lewis's act was misguided, cruel, and senseless. But the greater violence may be this: that no one will ever speak of it properly. No trial. No inquiry. No memorial. Just a boy, a father, and a scorched wall where a window used to be.

Part 11: The Translator

Market Day

Fawad heard the voice before he saw the man.

It carried — not loudly, but clearly, lifted above the market hum like something rehearsed. The fruit stalls buzzed with chatter and the dull slap of courgettes into brown paper bags. Somewhere, a radio played 'Dancing Queen' in tinny defiance of the cold. But the voice threaded through all of it — low, deliberate, rising and falling with the cadence of authority.

Fawad froze by the olives.

'And do not be among the heedless,' the man said.

Not shouted. Just said — like a fact being offered.

The words struck something deep. Not the content, but the rhythm. That pause before the final word. That turn in the throat, half a breath too long. He'd heard it before. A decade ago. In a compound outside Lashkar Gah. That same voice, offering mercy in one tongue and commands in another.

He turned, slow.

The stall beside the butcher had become a kind of congregation. Five or six men, some with beards, some not, stood close to the speaker. He wore a dark coat, clean trainers. No robe. No fanfare. Just presence. The kind that draws gravity without asking.

Fawad stepped back behind a stack of plantain crates. Watched. Waited.

The man continued: 'We must remain awake. You see what is happening. You know who brings it.'

No one interrupted. A few nodded.

It wasn't a sermon — it was a warning.

Fawad's hands trembled slightly. He hadn't heard that voice in over ten years. But it hadn't changed. Not the tone. Not the certainty.

He moved away, quickly, weaving between stalls, breath shallow, blood thudding in his ears. At the end of the row, by the bus stop, he pulled out his phone. The screen reflected his face, washed pale in the morning light.

He opened the voice recorder app. Tapped once. The red line blinked to life.

Then he walked back.

This time, from a distance. He held the phone low, screen down. The voice continued — speaking now of trials, of purity, of the weakness of men who bent for the unbelievers.

Fawad pressed stop.

Saved the file.

Named it: *FridayMarket_001*.

Then he walked home, slowly, past the car park and the empty post office, the wind tugging at his coat, the voice still echoing in the folds of his mind.

He didn't say the name out loud.

Not when he reached his flat. Not as he set down the shopping bag and peeled off his gloves. Not as he boiled water and placed a single teabag in a cracked mug. The name stayed in his throat, coiled and silent. But the recognition was total.

Samiullah Khan.

He'd been younger then. Leaner. The beard shorter, voice harsher. But it was him. Same rhythm. Same eyes — flat, unreadable. Back then, he was translator and executioner both. Preacher and pragmatist. The man who spared Fawad's life with one hand, and ordered another man's death with the other.

And now he was in a Yorkshire market, quoting scripture beside a butcher stall, wrapped in the vocabulary of reform.

Fawad sat at the kitchen table, steam rising from the mug, phone on the placemat in front of him. The recording sat there, a digital weight. Proof. Or close enough.

He tapped play.

The voice filled the small room. Fainter than in the moment, but still sharp. Measured. Each word dropped like a stone. There was no outright incitement — nothing that would raise legal eyebrows. Just insinuation. Implication. Warnings delivered with the calm of someone already certain they're right.

He paused the file. Listened to the quiet.

The radiator ticked.

His fingers tapped the tabletop once, twice.

Then he opened a browser.

Typed in the counter-terror contact form.

Paused.

The page asked for details. Names, dates, specific threat indicators. There was a section for "supporting audio or documentation."

He stared at it for a long time.

He did not upload the file. Not yet.

Instead, he typed a short message: *Known individual resurfaced. Former Taliban recruiter. Seen speaking at local market. Possible grooming language used.*

He didn't sign his name. Just ticked the box marked "former government contractor."

Then he hit send.

The page thanked him for his vigilance.

No case number. No follow-up.

Just: *Your message has been received.*

Fawad leant back. Looked at the mug. Cold now.

The wind rattled the glass.

He closed the browser. Pressed the power button on the phone. The screen went black.

Then, finally, he said it. Low, almost a whisper: 'Samiullah.'

And for the first time in years, his hands didn't stop shaking.

Denial

The call came two days later.

A withheld number. Fawad answered on the second ring, voice steady.

'Is this Mr Fawad Rahimi?'

'Yes.'

'This is Sergeant Collins from North Regional Counter-Terror Intelligence. You submitted a report regarding a potential extremist speaker in your area. Do you have a moment?'

Fawad sat down. 'Yes.'

The voice was polite. Controlled. Almost apologetic. It asked him to recount what he saw. He did — clearly, concisely, with none of the urgency dulled. He mentioned the voice, the location, the past affiliation. He gave the name.

There was a pause.

'Samiullah Khan,' he repeated. 'He recruited in Helmand. I saw him speak again this week. He's changed his look, but not his message.'

'And how long ago was your last interaction with this individual?'

'2011. But I'm certain.'

Another pause.

'Mr Rahimi, we appreciate your attentiveness. From what you've described, it doesn't meet the threshold for immediate escalation.'

Fawad blinked. 'He's not shouting threats, no. But he's laying foundations. The language is coded. This is grooming.'

The sergeant's tone softened. 'I understand your concern, but unless there's direct evidence of incitement or a verifiable security threat, there's a limited scope for intervention. Was there any explicit mention of violence?'

Fawad paused. 'No. Not in the recording.'

'And you say this is based on vocal recognition from over a decade ago?'

'I would bet my life on it.'

A polite breath on the other end. 'That's noted. We'll log your report. If you see anything further, or if the messaging becomes more overt, please do get back in touch. We appreciate your time.'

Click.

No case number. No follow-up. Just another report filed somewhere under "monitor."

Fawad stared at the phone in his hand. Then pressed play again. Listened once more to the clipped delivery, the subtle charge in every phrase.

He knew that voice.

But knowing, it seemed, was no longer enough.

The next morning, frustrated by the lack of follow-up, Fawad walked into the community liaison centre.

The man behind the desk offered him tea and a smile that didn't reach his eyes.

'We're grateful you came in, Mr Rahimi,' he said, fingers steepled, a file unopened on the desk between them. The room smelt of printer ink and surface cleaner. A poster on the wall behind the man read *"See It. Say It. Sorted."* beneath a cartoon CCTV camera.

Fawad didn't sit. 'I gave you a name. I gave you a voice-print. I gave you context. And still—'

The man lifted a hand, diplomatic. 'I've reviewed the audio. I understand your concern. But with respect, what you're describing is — at this point — hearsay. There's no confirmed identity match. No actionable threat language.'

'You're waiting for him to say *kill*?' Fawad asked, quiet but firm.

A pause. The official smiled again. 'We're guided by thresholds. Legal ones. It's not that we don't believe you—'

'But you don't.'

The silence hung like condensation.

The man sat back in his chair. 'I'm not here to challenge your integrity. I respect your past service. But we have to work with evidence. Surveillance resources are stretched, and sermons — however uncomfortable — are protected under religious expression.'

'Not when they radicalise.'

'If they radicalise.'

Fawad laughed once. Not out of humour.

'He's already recruiting boys in the park behind the flats. He speaks like an uncle, but what he offers isn't belonging — it's direction. He's doing what he used to do. Only now he's wearing Nike and quoting Hadiths about patience.'

The man scribbled something on a notepad.

Fawad leant forward. 'You'll wait until someone leaves. Disappears. Then you'll ask where they went. By then, it'll be too late. Again.'

The man closed the file gently. 'We take all reports seriously. If more information becomes available, we'll reassess.'

Fawad stared at the closed file. Nothing inside it had changed.

He turned, left without shaking hands. Outside, the wind pulled at the lapels of his coat. The air was sharp, the street too quiet.

He didn't go home.

He walked.

And the name beat in his ears with every step:

Samiullah.

Still free.

Still speaking.

Still heard by everyone — except the ones who were meant to listen.

Flashback

Afghanistan, 2010.

The light inside the compound was harsh — fluorescent strips nailed to wooden beams, buzzing with static. Dust hung in the air, lit like fog. Outside, the wind carried the thud of distant movement — not gunfire, not yet, but the kind of stillness that comes before it.

Fawad stood between two British soldiers, notepad in hand, headset looped around his neck. The room reeked of stale sweat, diesel, and heat. Across the table sat Samiullah Khan.

He wasn't shackled. That was part of the strategy. Make it feel like a conversation, not an interrogation. He sat with his legs crossed, calm, hands folded in his lap. His beard was shorter then, dyed slightly with henna. His eyes watched everything.

One of the soldiers — Corporal Haines — nodded at Fawad. 'Begin.'

Fawad translated the question. A test one — benign, procedural.

Samiullah smiled. 'Your accent is Kabul. But you've been here a while.'

Fawad didn't answer.

'You think you're safe because they're behind you,' Samiullah continued, in Dari. 'But you'll always be between us. Neither here nor there.'

He answered the question, eventually. Politely. Precisely. No delays.

An hour passed. Then another.

Nothing concrete. No confession. No defiance. Just calm, polished speech, framed with just enough ambiguity to stay off the radar.

Later, outside, Haines lit a cigarette with shaking hands. 'What do you think?' he asked.

Fawad looked out at the mountains. 'He won't tell you anything. But he's not guessing. He's measuring. He already knows what matters to you.'

'Should we hold him?'

Fawad hesitated. 'If you let him go, he won't come back here. But he won't disappear.'

'You think he's real?'

'I think he's patient.'

They released him that night. Lack of evidence. Pressure from above. Too many files. Not enough time.

As Samiullah passed through the gate, he turned once, looked directly at Fawad, and offered the faintest nod.

Not gratitude. Recognition.

A mark.

The alley smelt of blood and damp cloth.

It had been a mistake — a checkpoint crossed at the wrong hour, a name misunderstood, the wrong radio code at the wrong moment. Fawad had been pulled from the convoy and shoved into the back of a battered van. His hands tied. His mouth dry.

They hadn't blindfolded him.

That was what scared him most.

The compound was nothing like the military base. It was quieter. The quiet of decisions already made.

He was knelt in the corner, beside a plastic chair. His legs cramped. His heart stuttered in rhythms he couldn't control. Someone had questioned him — a boy, barely out of adolescence, wearing a scarf too loose to be taken seriously. But the boy had held a knife.

Then Samiullah entered.

No fanfare. No fury. Just presence, cold and absolute.

He asked no questions. Just looked.

Then he crouched down, resting his elbows on his knees.

'You're the one who speaks both ways,' he said. 'The one who changes words for money.'

Fawad didn't answer.

Samiullah tilted his head. 'You translated me once, didn't you? Outside Lashkar Gah.'

Fawad nodded, slowly.

Samiullah considered that. 'You did it well. You didn't mock. You didn't flatten.'

He stood, stretched, then turned to the boy with the knife.

'Let him go,' he said. 'He's not the target.'

The boy looked confused.

Samiullah didn't repeat himself.

The ropes came off.

No parting threat. No lecture. Just a nod again, the same faint mark of awareness.

As Fawad was led back to the van, he glanced over his shoulder once.

Samiullah stood in the doorway, hands behind his back, gaze steady.

It was not mercy.

It was a pause.

A deferral.

Pattern

The park was too quiet for a Saturday.

Fawad sat on a bench near the bandstand, the kind with peeling paint and a missing slat. The trees above him rustled faintly in the wind, branches bare. Across the footpath, by the swings, he saw them again — the boys.

Three of them. Young, maybe thirteen or fourteen. One wore a backpack far too heavy for his frame. One bounced a football, nervously, tapping it against his heel. The third just listened, eyes locked on the man in front of them.

Samiullah.

No robe now. No script. He wore a raincoat, plain trainers, and carried nothing but a takeaway coffee cup. He stood with the relaxed weight of someone entirely at home. His hands moved gently as he spoke — not preaching, not scolding. Conversational. Measured.

Fawad strained to hear, but the words didn't carry. Still, he knew the structure. It was in the posture, the distance, the circle they'd formed — boys drawn in just enough to feel chosen.

He pulled out his phone. Opened the recorder again. Tapped once.

The red light blinked.

Fawad angled the microphone, kept the screen low. He couldn't hear everything, but snatches reached him.

'...not about hate. It's about duty.'

'They'll laugh at you until they need you.'

'You're not lost — just not yet found.'

The boys nodded. Said nothing. The man smiled, touched one on the shoulder.

Fawad gripped the phone tighter.

This wasn't recruitment in the old sense — not boots and banners, not training camps and manifestos. It was subtler. A long game. Preparing the ground, not planting the seed. Familiar. Effective.

He kept recording.

Watched until the boys turned to leave — the one with the football kicking it lightly along the path, the others following. Samiullah stayed behind, sipping from his cup, gaze drifting up to the grey sky.

For a moment, he looked straight at Fawad.

Not startled. Not curious.

Just aware.

Then he turned and walked the other way.

Fawad ended the recording.

Saved it.

Named it: *ParkCircle_ 002*.

He sat back.

The wind passed through the bandstand again, quiet and cold.

He sent the file that same evening.

Attached it to a follow-up email marked *URGENT* — *ongoing pattern of ideological grooming*. Included the date, location, time. A brief transcript. The same name, bolded now: *Samiullah Khan.*

He waited.

No reply came that night. Or the next.

On Monday morning, a message finally landed. A generic address. A shorter response.

"Thank you for your submission. Your observations have been noted and shared with relevant partners. At this stage, no further action is being taken."

No signature. No reference number. Just polite disappearance.

Fawad stared at the screen. Read it twice. Three times.

Then he closed the laptop. Sat still.

A siren passed outside. Distant. Disinterested.

He stood, walked to the bookshelf, and pulled down the old journal he hadn't touched in years — a slim black notebook from his service days. Inside, neat lines of translation practice, unfamiliar words once learned by repetition.

He flipped to the back.

Wrote a date.

A time.

A phrase from the recording: *"Not lost — just not yet found."*

He capped the pen.

Returned the book to the shelf.

The flat felt colder. Not physically, but in atmosphere — like something vital had been removed. Trust, maybe. Or utility.

Fawad opened the voice recorder again. Listened to the park exchange once more. Then again. Let the man's calm voice curl around the sentences like silk hiding a blade.

He could feel it happening — not just the recruitment, but the forgetting. The system slipping back into its patterns. Polite nods. Logged concerns. Apathy made efficient.

The danger wasn't just what Samiullah said.

It was what no one else did.

The Raid

It happened on a Thursday.

No warning. No knock. No polite preamble.

At dawn, the mosque was surrounded — unmarked vans, men in tactical gear, radios murmuring clipped code. Streets cordoned. Doors battered. Windows lit up in flats across the estate.

Fawad watched from the other side of the car park. Arms crossed, collar high. The cold air sharpened every sound — the crack of boot against doorframe, the metallic thump of a bin overturned, the sharp bark of an officer calling for confirmation.

It was quiet. Brutally efficient.

He didn't feel vindicated.

Just late.

Inside the mosque, a boy was led out first — maybe fifteen, maybe younger, in a hoodie too big for him. Then another. Pale, shaking, hand pressed to his ribs like he'd been winded.

Then Samiullah.

Still calm.

Still composed.

He didn't resist. Didn't look for anyone in the crowd. Just walked between the officers like a man late for a train.

The imam stood outside, barefoot, gesturing, pleading — not for the man, but for the building. 'It is a place of prayer,' he shouted. 'Not a battlefield.'

No one listened.

The vans filled.

The officers withdrew.

The tape came down.

Fawad stayed where he was, unmoved. A woman next to him whispered, 'I thought it was drugs. Or maybe a visa raid.'

He said nothing.

Just watched as the doors closed.

A final figure stepped into the last van — a boy he hadn't seen before. No coat. No shoes. His eyes wide, but not frightened.

Empty.

As if he'd already been somewhere else.

The van doors shut.

The silence that followed was worse than the noise.

Not because it was peaceful.

But because it had taken this much — this long — for anyone to hear what he'd said from the beginning.

By nightfall, it was confirmed: two boys were missing.

Not detained. Not arrested. Just... gone.

Their names weren't released. The police spokesperson used the phrase *"unaccounted for at time of intervention."* The news anchor softened it further: *"possibly relocated without guardian notification."*

Fawad watched it on the small TV in his kitchen. The sound was low, almost irrelevant. The captions told the story in fragments. *"Raid... concerns... influence of radical speech... minors..."*

But no blame. No names. No mention of Samiullah.

He turned the volume up — hoping, absurdly, that one detail might appear that hadn't been scrubbed of urgency.

Nothing.

The file he'd sent. The recordings. The descriptions. Weeks of warnings. None of it had made it into the official narrative.

Just a place of worship "under review."

Just two boys "not yet located."

He stood up. Crossed to the window. The mosque was visible from here — just its minaret over the rooftops, half-lit in the orange spill of streetlight. It looked unchanged.

But it wasn't.

Not now.

Not for him.

He picked up his phone, scrolled back through the recordings. *FridayMarket_001. ParkCircle_002.* Others unnamed. Others unsent. They blurred now. Not because they'd lost meaning — but because they'd proven themselves futile.

The boys were gone.

And the state had arrived only when it was no longer useful.

The doorbell rang.

He froze. Waited.

It rang again.

Slowly, he stepped to the door, looked through the peephole.

It was no one official.

Just a boy — not one of the missing, but close in age. Eyes red, trainers soaked from the rain.

He said nothing. Held something out.

Fawad opened the door.

It was a folded prayer mat. Still damp. Torn at one corner.

'I think you dropped this,' the boy said.

Fawad shook his head.

'I didn't.'

The boy nodded once, turned, walked away.

Fawad stood in the doorway for a long time, the mat heavy in his hands.

Prayer Rug

He laid the rug in the garden just after midnight.

The grass was slick from an earlier rain, the sky still low with cloud. No stars. Just the heavy quiet of a town trying not to look at itself. He unrolled it carefully, smoothing the corners, flattening the creases.

It wasn't the same rug. The one from service was long gone — lost in a box, or folded into a move no one remembered. This one was newer. Lighter. A gift from a neighbour, once.

But it had absorbed enough.

He knelt beside it, not on it.

Just close enough to see the pattern — geometric, delicate, the arch pointing east like a compass for the soul.

He struck a match.

Held it to the fabric.

It caught quickly, more smoke than flame at first. Then a curl of orange, a slow bloom. He knew what it meant to burn something sacred. But some things, once marked, couldn't be sanctified again.

He stepped back. Let it burn.

The fire climbed through the stitching with quiet efficiency. It wasn't angry. It wasn't defiant. It was a ritual — not of rejection, but of recognition.

He watched it all.

The blue edge. The border fading to black. The final flicker that left only shape, and then ash.

When it was done, he stood in the smoke.

Removed his shoes.

Stepped forward.

And knelt on the earth.

No barrier. No fabric. No symbol.

Just ground.

Cold and real beneath his knees.

His forehead touched soil. Damp, unspectacular.

The wind passed over the fence. A hedgehog snuffled under a nearby bush.

And in that stillness — stripped of language, country, and expectation — Fawad whispered the only thing he still believed in:

'I saw.'

Not for God.

Not for anyone listening.

Just to say it.

So that something, somewhere, might remember.

He stayed there a long time.

Knees pressing into the softened mud, hands resting on his thighs, back straight not out of pride but habit. The smoke had thinned, carried off by the early wind. Only a faint black ring remained on the grass, barely visible in the dark.

His breath slowed.

No words now. No verses. No recitations.

Silence, honest and uncluttered.

Not defeat. Not faith.

Just the moment after truth has nowhere else to go.

A neighbour's light flicked on, briefly, then off. A siren sounded far away. Somewhere behind him, a door creaked open. He didn't turn.

The soil was cool beneath his palms. He pressed them into it, as if to ground himself, or to test what was still real. No rug. No echo of sermons. Just this patch of earth, indifferent to allegiance, to memory, to men who speak and are not believed.

A bird called once from a rooftop.

Then nothing.

The house behind him waited. Empty of movement. The world went on.

He didn't rise.

Didn't pray.

Didn't cry.

Just remained, still and alert, kneeling where the rug had burned, eyes open to the dark.

As if witnessing might still mean something.

Even if no one listened.

Part 11: Critical Essay

Betrayal of the Loyal Migrant

Fawad is a man Britain promised to protect — then forgot. His life story is shaped by loyalty, not ideology: a former interpreter for British forces in Afghanistan, now a quiet resident in a northern town. He has no demands, no protest placard. Only a memory he can't shake and a truth he can't bury. That truth — a voice from the past now preaching in a local mosque — is met not with action, but dismissal. The country he served no longer hears him.

This betrayal is not explosive, but procedural. When Fawad informs the authorities of what he's recognised, he is not met with interest or inquiry. He is met with bureaucracy. The word "hearsay" becomes a wall. His past, once seen as useful, is now suspect. His experience, once essential to military strategy, is now inconvenient. There is no ceremony to the betrayal — only paperwork, protocol, and indifference.

Fawad's story underlines a particular cruelty within the British institutional psyche: it accepts the loyal migrant when he is useful, and discards him when his knowledge complicates the narrative. His familiarity with threat — with the shape and cadence of radicalism — should make him a valuable informant. Instead, it renders him unstable in the eyes of the state. He knows too much. He remembers what others would rather forget.

The betrayal is also personal. The man he once spared now recruits others. There is no gratitude, no recognition — only erasure, doubled by the state's silence. The trauma is not just in what Fawad hears, but in who refuses to listen. This is the essence of institutional betrayal: not violent suppression, but quiet discrediting. The very act of speaking becomes dangerous.

When MI5 finally raids the mosque, it is too late. Two boys have already disappeared. The gesture is reactive, performative, hollow. Fawad, who saw it coming, is left with ashes. The rug he burns in his garden is not just an object of faith — it is a symbol of exhausted allegiance. A final ritual for a contract broken without acknowledgement.

Britain's promise to men like Fawad was never merely legal. It was moral. To break that promise without ceremony is to write a new chapter in collapse — one where even loyalty, once the firmest ground, turns to smoke.

Trauma of the Remembering Witness

Fawad's trauma is not located in a singular event, but in a recurring condition: the burden of memory in a culture that no longer believes in the past. He is not haunted by what he did — but by what he saw, what he understood, and what no one else now wants to hear. His knowledge becomes contamination. His recall, a threat.

He remembers the voice — not its accent or tone, but its rhythm. The way it broke in the middle of a sentence, the pause before invocation. This is not paranoia; it is recognition, precise and involuntary. In a just world, that memory would be a warning. Here, it is treated as delusion.

The trauma of the remembering witness lies in the dissonance between truth and reception. Fawad's memory is clear, but the state's attention is fogged by indifference, suspicion, fatigue. His role — once central in war — is now bureaucratically inconvenient. He is no longer an asset, but an interruption.

This form of dismissal is not benign. It corrodes. The institutions that once relied on Fawad to interpret danger now regard his insight as unstable. His reports are filed, ignored, then lost. His concern is reframed as grievance. There is no room in this new Britain for his kind of memory — the memory that bridges war zones and housing estates, that links foreign policy to local radicalisation.

Fawad does not collapse publicly. He does not rage. His breakdown is internal, precise, ritualised. It culminates in the burning of the prayer rug — a gesture not of apostasy, but of grief. Not grief for God, but for truth. A world where witnessing was once a civic duty has now made it an emotional liability.

The failure is not just institutional, but epistemological. What does it mean to know something in a system that no longer values knowing? Fawad's knowledge is not hearsay. It is lived, cross-referenced, emotionally bonded to survival. But the authorities need video, not testimony. Bodies, not patterns. The trauma, then, is double: not only was he right — but being right changed nothing.

To witness in this world is to suffer twice: once in the moment, and again in the telling. Fawad survives the war. But not the forgetting.

Radicalism Reborn Locally

The voice Fawad hears in the mosque is not foreign. It is embedded. Embedded not just in accent, but in geography — on British soil, in a local sermon, to a local congregation. The threat is no longer distant, flown in, or smuggled through channels. It has grown roots. Radicalism has adapted to its environment. It now wears local shoes.

This is the unsettling truth the story reveals: the home-grown is indistinguishable from the imported. The man Fawad once encountered under desert skies now speaks behind a lectern two streets from his own. The past has not returned — it has been waiting. And the place where the rhetoric lands is no longer a battlefield, but a park, a prayer room, a bus stop.

What gives this form of radicalism its potency is not volume, but subtlety. There is no shouting, no flag-waving, no easily captured image. It is layered into casual speech, dripped into cultural grievance, framed as moral correction. It does not resist British life head-on. It reinterprets it, repurposes its freedoms as weaknesses, its diversity as division. It doesn't burn — it soaks.

Fawad's alarm stems not only from the speaker's identity, but from the passivity of the surroundings. The mosque council shrugs. The parents look away. The police decline to act. Everyone sees something, but no one sees enough to risk reputation. Radicalism thrives in this gap — not where power is strong, but where resolve is weak. It does not need secrecy when silence will do.

The story draws attention to how such movements flourish not despite integration, but alongside its failure. The speaker is not an outsider. He knows the codes, the cadences, the cultural soft spots. He recruits not with fire, but with certainty — offering identity where institutions now offer only process. In a landscape of managed decline, radical clarity becomes seductive.

This is what Fawad fears most: not just the man, but the soil in which he now stands. The ground has changed. Britain, for all its rules and oversight, no longer possesses a firm grasp of its own moral borders. Surveillance watches for explosions. It misses the sermons.

Radicalism's new passport is local. Its route: already walked.

And the door, politely, is open.

Children and Grooming Revisited

Two boys disappear. That is the quiet climax. No explosions, no alarms — just the absence of young lives absorbed by something larger and unspoken. The method is not new, only reframed. Britain has lived this pattern before: the slow co-opting of children under the watch of institutions too paralysed by risk to act. But here, the grooming is not sexual — it is ideological. The shape remains; the language changes.

Fawad watches it unfold in real time. He sees the man — the recruiter — speaking in parks, loitering near school gates, smiling at boys who have not yet learned to distrust kindness. It mirrors what happened in other towns, in other decades, with other predators. Yet the response is the same: delay, deferral, denial. To act is to offend. To wait is to manage. Until it's too late.

The tragedy is not just institutional, but conceptual. The British state still struggles to hold ideological grooming in its moral frame. Sexual exploitation is now understood — belatedly — as power repackaged as care. But radicalisation remains compartmentalised: a "threat," not a seduction. Something foreign, rather than familial. The idea that extremism begins with kindness — that it might feel good, feel safe, feel like belonging — remains too complex for policy briefings.

These boys do not vanish into shadows. They walk there. Led by someone who promises them certainty in a world that offers none. Fawad recognises it instantly — the re-cruitment pattern, the soft instruction, the quiet segrega-tion of thought. But his warnings are swallowed by the same fog that once obscured other scandals. The desire not to see.

This section's moral echo is clear: what happened before, is happening again. And still, we don't have the language. We fear naming, because naming sounds like blame. But silence is not neutrality. It is complicity. And children pay the price.

Fawad is not trying to indict a community. He is trying to save it. The boys could be anyone's — his neighbour's, his own, himself years ago. The loss is personal. The rage, held back by decorum, sits in his eyes.

When they are taken, there is no camera. No appeal.

Just names left unspoken.

And one man, again, not believed.

Systemic Deafness

Fawad is not dismissed violently, or even rudely. He is listened to politely, then set aside. His concern is noted. His report is logged. And then — nothing. This is what systemic deafness looks like in contemporary Britain: not antagonism, but procedural indifference. The system hears him. It simply doesn't respond.

Deafness, in this context, is not about sound but about selection. The state listens where it chooses to listen. It acts where there is political cover to act. Fawad, with his accent, his history, and his uncredentialed concern, falls outside the zone of urgency. His warning is not loud enough, not quantifiable. It does not come with evidence that fits the form.

The irony is suffocating. Fawad was trained to listen — to decode, to anticipate, to relay. As an interpreter for British forces, his judgment once saved lives. Now, that same judgment is considered unreliable, tainted by emotion or bias. His memory is labelled subjective. His warnings, premature. The system that once depended on his clarity now finds it inconvenient.

This failure is not one of individual malice. It is systemic architecture. Risk is no longer assessed morally, but administratively. If the threat doesn't tick the right box, it isn't real. And until there are bodies, there is no budget line. Fawad lives in that fatal gap — between knowledge and action, recognition and risk management.

Worse still, his identity becomes part of the state's excuse. He is brown. Muslim. Local. Perhaps he has an axe to grind. Perhaps he misunderstood. Perhaps — the quiet implication goes — he is too close to the story. The result is paralysis by optics. The fear of being wrong outweighs the cost of inaction.

Systemic deafness breeds two things: repetition and despair. Fawad is not the first man to warn of danger and be ignored. But he may be among the last to try again. The silence he encounters is not just frustrating — it is corrosive. It teaches him, and others like him, that loyalty is not rewarded, and that knowledge — especially when uncomfortable — is best buried.

When the raid finally comes, it proves him right. But no one returns to say so.

The deafness is broken by force — not by trust.

And trust, once broken, does not come back.

The Voice That Wasn't Believed

In the end, Fawad's greatest injury is not inflicted by violence, but by doubt. He speaks clearly, repeatedly, and without embellishment. He names what he hears. He names who speaks. He even records a conversation — but it isn't enough. His voice, though calm and certain, is marked by a disqualifying quality: it is inconvenient.

To be disbelieved when you are unsure is painful. To be disbelieved when you are right is annihilating. Fawad doesn't lose faith in Britain overnight. It erodes with each unanswered call, each cautious shrug, each moment where institutional discomfort outweighs public safety. His truth doesn't fit the national mood. It carries the wrong accent. It threatens the wrong narrative.

There's a particular violence in being dismissed with kindness. No doors are slammed. No voices are raised. Instead, the rejection is bureaucratic, ambient. A file marked "not actionable." A polite nod that says: thank you, now go. The gaslighting is not personal — it's procedural.

The voice that isn't believed becomes, in time, a burden. Fawad hears it in his own head, questioning his certainty. Did he misremember? Did the voice change? Was it truly the same man? This is the cost of disbelief: it corrodes even the reliable narrator. It makes memory suspect — not because it is faulty, but because no one else will hold it with him.

And still, he continues. He records. He reports. He insists. Not because he believes it will work, but because he has to. Bearing witness is not optional for him. It is a duty, even when it becomes a wound.

The final silence, when the police acknowledge the threat only after it has borne fruit, is the cruellest echo. No apology. No restitution. Just belated confirmation. Fawad does not scream. He burns the rug, not in defiance of God, but in mourning for what truth has become — something weightless, unactioned, half-heard.

The story doesn't dramatise this. It doesn't need to. The quietness is the point. Fawad doesn't die. He just stops speaking.

Because eventually, every unheard voice learns the same truth:

You are only believed when it's too late.

Migrant vs. Migrant Conflict

The story shatters the monolith. It refuses the comforting simplicity that "migrants" are one bloc, one voice, one collective experience. Fawad's story is a direct confrontation with this flattening. He is Afghan, Muslim, a former interpreter — and the man he recognises is also Afghan, also Muslim, but a recruiter for the very ideology Fawad risked his life resisting. Both men occupy the same postcode. Only one is trusted.

This tension is rarely addressed in public discourse, which prefers its narratives tidier — the grateful migrant, the dangerous outsider. But reality, as the story insists, is messier. Conflict doesn't vanish at the border. It travels. It embeds. And it evolves.

What Fawad experiences is not just fear of extremism, but betrayal within a presumed community. He is not targeted directly, but he is undermined. The recruiter operates freely, cloaked in plausible respectability, while Fawad is sidelined for being *too alert*. His vigilance is read as overreach. His motives questioned. The unspeakable implication: maybe he's the problem.

This kind of intra-migrant tension is politically fraught, and thus culturally unspoken. But it is real. The story lays bare the fissures within diasporic life — tensions shaped by class, war experience, ideology, and gender roles. Fawad is not a mirror of the man he opposes. He is his opposite: wary of political theology, bound by civic trust, shaped by military collaboration. And it is precisely this difference that isolates him.

The institutions that should parse this nuance don't. To the state, they are both just "community members." One is radicalising boys. The other is pleading for help. But the system sees ambiguity and chooses stasis.

This is the cruelty of flattening. It fails everyone. It fails the boys recruited. It fails the man who warned them. And it fails the wider public by mistaking politeness for safety. When you make all brown men the same, you make no one safe — least of all those who are trying to speak against violence.

Fawad never wanted to be a spokesman. He wanted to be heard.

Now he is neither.

And his silence, unlike his warning, fits neatly into the state's filing system.

Language, Truth, and Fire

The story closes not with a confrontation, but with a ritual: Fawad burns the prayer rug, then kneels on bare earth. It is a symbolic act, and a linguistic one. The rug — woven with memory, prayer, repetition — represents a covenant between belief and speech. Its destruction is not apostasy. It is protest. Not against God, but against the silence of men.

Language is central throughout. Fawad is a translator by profession and by disposition. His life has been built on interpretation — of danger, of meaning, of motive. He translates not only words but contexts: war into testimony, threat into alert, trauma into articulation. But by the end, language fails him. He speaks, but is not heard. He records, but is not believed. The truth, once clear, becomes volatile. Unwanted.

This breakdown is not internal. It is systemic. Truth has become something that must be branded, endorsed, cross-verified, stripped of subjectivity before it can be acknowledged. A man's memory — even a professional one — is no longer enough. And so, fire becomes the final vocabulary. In Britain's new order, nothing is believed until it burns.

The act of kneeling on the earth is loaded with paradox. It evokes both surrender and return. Without the rug, there is no barrier between Fawad and the ground — no text between him and what he remembers. The gesture is pure. And devastating. It is a final form of witness. Not a plea, not a warning. Just presence.

This is where the story leaves us: not with resolution, but with ritual. Not with violence, but with scorched fabric and unspoken names. The fire does not cleanse. It marks. It draws a line between what was hoped for and what has been allowed to happen.

Language failed to protect. Truth failed to persuade. And so, like so many before him, Fawad turns to flame.

Not to destroy.

But to prove that something once mattered.

Part 12: The Vanishing Bank

The Walk

Sandra walked past three shuttered shops before she reached the square.

The butcher had gone first — a note in the window that simply read *"Thanks for all the years."* The café followed, then the charity shop. Its mannequins had stood inside for months, blank-eyed and unchanged, until someone removed them in the night. Now the windows stared back at her, clean and empty, like teeth with nothing left to chew.

She didn't walk fast. The mornings had become quieter lately, and there was no reason to rush. The buses came late now, if at all. She passed a man in a high-vis vest sweeping leaves into a pile no one would collect. He didn't look up.

The bank loomed ahead — a once-proud stone façade, blue sign faded to grey, cashpoint long removed. Two men stood outside, not customers but contractors, pulling off the last of the metal lettering with flat tools. *"-oyal Bank"* now, the crown crest already discarded.

Sandra paused across the road. Watched.

No ceremony. No final customer. Just the slow dismantling of another part of the town's spine. She thought of her father queueing inside on Fridays, cap in hand, wallet ready. Thought of her daughter, once small enough to lift onto the counter. Thought of nothing in particular, really

— just the way time folds when there's nowhere left to put it.

One of the men looked over. Nodded.

She nodded back.

Carried on.

At the corner, the bin outside the bookie overflowed with scratch cards and crushed cans. Someone had chalked *"HELP US"* on the pavement. The letters were faint, as if scrubbed once and forgotten.

A gust of wind caught her coat. The hem flapped. She reached up to tighten the scarf at her neck and kept walking.

At the crossing, the lights blinked amber, then red. She stopped. Not because of traffic — there was none — but because that's what you do. The habit of waiting. Of obeying rhythms that no longer applied.

She stepped across slowly.

The pavement was cracked at the edges. The hardware shop beside it had closed in winter and never reopened. Someone had taped up the keyhole, as if that might stop the cold from getting in.

The bus stop was taped off.

Not cordoned with authority — just a single strip of weathered plastic, fluttering from one post to the next like caution offered without commitment. The timetable was still there, faded behind its cracked plexiglass. No service listed after March.

Sandra stood for a moment beside the bench, hand resting on her bag. The tape fickered softly in the wind. The bus shelter's roof was cracked. Moss crept in along one edge.

She remembered waiting there in better shoes, holding a carrier bag with fresh rolls inside, her daughter kicking her feet beside her. Back then, it had seemed like everything might still grow.

Now it just waited to be removed.

The bench was damp. She didn't sit. Instead, she looked at the notice someone had pinned up — the paper had curled, the ink bled slightly. It read: *"Rerouted to Central. No replacement planned."* There was no contact number. No apology.

She followed the road with her eyes. It led nowhere now. Just to the roundabout, then the bypass. The routes had shifted, just like everything else. Convenience redefined. Service remeasured.

A boy cycled past, hoodie up, rucksack lopsided. He didn't glance at the stop. Probably never had to use it. Or knew better than to expect it to come.

Sandra crossed to the other side and stood for a while, looking back at the taped bench, at the closed shops beyond it. A woman with a pram passed, coat pulled tight, eyes ahead. The baby slept, mouth slack.

The quiet held.

There was a sound once — the engine rumble, the hiss of air brakes, the creak of old shocks as the door folded open. She could still hear it, somewhere, tucked behind memory.

She turned and walked on.

There was no hurry.

Nothing coming.

Nothing to meet.

The Closure

The bank closed without ceremony.

No farewell notice. No final hours. Just blinds drawn down midweek and a single printed sheet taped inside the door: *"This branch is now closed. Please use our nearest facility in Millstone, 14.6 miles away."*

Sandra stood outside it again, the following Monday. The window caught her reflection — pale coat, scarf still twisted from the walk, a carrier bag creased in her hand. She didn't look in. Just stood, as if expecting something to unlock by presence alone.

The cash machine had been removed months earlier. The small alcove now filled with a sheet of plywood, painted a shade too bright. Someone had scrawled *"Why?"* into the surface with a key.

She tried the handle.

Locked.

A flicker of something — not surprise, but confirmation.

The town had lost other things. The GP. The post office. The florist. But the bank felt final. Not because she needed it — she hadn't used the counter in years — but because it had *meant* something. The building had weight. Stone, not plastic. A door you could lean on. She'd once queued behind five people there and not minded.

Now it was gone.

Across the street, a couple stood outside the pharmacy, arguing quietly. One of them gestured toward the notice on the door. *"Closed for stock review. Reopens Tuesday."* Their voices blurred with the wind.

Sandra stepped back. Looked up at the crest above the door — a lion barely visible in the carving. Faded. Forgotten. Like a flag no longer hoisted.

She walked on.

Two turns later, she found herself outside the refugee intake centre.

It used to be the library.

Now the sign read *"Community Support Hub – East Entrance."*

A line stretched from the door, people clutching forms and folders, some with children in tow. The glass was clean. The lights were on. Inside, staff moved behind desks with plastic screens and branded lanyards.

Sandra stood opposite the queue for a while, not out of bitterness but disorientation. The only open building in town was no longer for her.

She didn't cross.

Just turned and walked back the way she came.

The sky above the bank was the same as it had always been — flat, indifferent.

But the door beneath it would never open again.

The line moved slowly.

Sandra watched from the other side of the street, beneath the shadow of the old hairdresser's awning — the one with the faded pink lettering still ghosted on the window: *"Shear Bliss."*

Outside the refugee centre — the library, as it still was in her head — the queue bent gently around the corner. Families, young men, women with prams. Some held clipboards. Others carried folded paper under their arms like fragile maps. One woman stood in silence, her son clinging to her leg, thumb in mouth.

The glass doors opened every few minutes. A staff member stepped out, cheerful voice rehearsed: *"Next three, please."*

No one complained. No one raised their voice.

Inside, the fluorescent light pooled across the floor in hard rectangles. Desks divided by screens. A waiting area with chairs bolted to the ground. Leaflets in neat stacks. Posters offering support in six languages.

Sandra didn't cross over. She couldn't have said why.

It wasn't resentment. Not exactly. More like distance. Not between her and *them*, but between her and *usefulness*. That building was active. Staffed. Funded. It had a printer that worked. It had doors that opened. It answered questions.

The bank hadn't done any of those things in years.

A boy broke from the queue to chase something — a windblown crisp packet, a dare — before his mother called him back with a soft word Sandra couldn't place. The boy obeyed. Rejoined the queue. As if even he knew this was something not to be missed.

Sandra looked at the sign: *"Community Support Hub."* The words sounded right. Looked right. But she couldn't remember the last time she'd queued for something that wasn't a reduction. The last time someone behind a desk had said *"How can I help?"* and meant it.

Behind her, the wind lifted again. Carried the scent of something fried from the takeaway near the square. Her stomach turned, not from hunger — just memory.

She crossed the street, not towards the building, but away from it.

No one stopped her.

The glass doors slid closed again.

The line moved forward.

And she walked home, hands deep in her pockets, telling herself, not unkindly:

This part isn't for me anymore.

Questions

She returned on a Wednesday.

No queue this time. Just one man with a pushchair, rocking it gently while scrolling on his phone. A cleaner swept the pavement near the bins. The air had that dull, post-rain thickness — not wet, just reluctant to dry.

Sandra stood outside the intake centre for a full minute before entering.

Inside, it was warmer than expected. The walls were painted an optimistic blue. Plastic plants in corners. A laminated sign near reception read: *"Welcome to the Hub – Please be patient. We're here to help."*

A young man at the desk looked up. Maybe early twenties. Close-shaved hair. Lanyard with a name she didn't catch.

'Hello,' she said, quietly. 'I just had a question.'

He smiled the way people are trained to. Kind, but hollow. 'Of course. What can I help with?'

She hesitated. 'I was wondering... how long this place will be here?'

He blinked. 'Sorry?'

She gestured vaguely around them. 'The centre. Is it permanent? Or just until... things settle?'

He tilted his head slightly, as if recalibrating. 'Well, we're funded on a rolling basis. Depends on demand and government priorities. But for now, we're here to stay.'

She nodded. Didn't know what that meant.

'Why do you ask?'

'I used to work across the road,' she said. 'Back when this was still the library.'

He smiled again, softer this time. 'Oh, I think we kept a few books. In the back somewhere.'

'That's something,' she said.

They stood in silence a moment. Behind him, a printer whirred. Somewhere further inside, a child laughed. A different language — sharp, bright.

She looked at him again. 'It's just... the bank's gone. The GP's gone. The bus, mostly. But this—this is still here.'

He nodded. 'We're quite lucky, I suppose.'

Lucky.

She smiled. 'Thank you. That's all I needed.'

He said, 'Have a good day.'

She walked out into the grey light. The glass doors sighed shut behind her.

No answer. Not really.

But not a lie, either.

Just a shrug.

Wrapped in a smile.

****

He had meant well.

Sandra knew that. The young man at the desk — he hadn't been rude, or evasive. Just trained. Smiling through every uncertainty, calibrated to deflect without ever quite saying no.

She replayed his shrug as she walked home. It stayed with her longer than expected. It wasn't dismissive. It was structural. A gesture learned in a system where no one could give a straight answer because no one had one to give.

We're quite lucky, I suppose.

She turned the phrase over. Lucky. As if permanence now came down to lottery. To timing. To headlines. As if buildings stayed open not because people needed them, but because someone in a department remembered they were still there.

She passed the school — the gates locked, though it wasn't late. Graffiti stretched across one panel: *"WE WERE HERE."* The paint had started to fade.

At her front door, she fumbled with the key a moment too long. The lock stuck, again. Inside, the hallway smelt of polish and old fabric softener. Familiar. Thin.

She sat on the bottom stair, coat still on, and placed her bag beside her.

The rug in the hall had curled at one corner. The post still lay unopened by the radiator. A single envelope read: *"To the Occupier."* The others bore no name.

She thought about the boy at the desk. The lanyard, the softness in his voice. She didn't dislike him. He was doing his job. And he did it well — made her feel seen for a minute. Not helped, exactly, but acknowledged.

That was rare now.

She leant back, listened to the quiet. The fridge kicked in with a groan from the kitchen. Outside, a car passed. Distant. Forgettable.

The shrug stayed with her.

Not because it was cruel.

But because it had replaced answers.

Departures

Her neighbour sold the house for cash.

No sign. No fuss. Just a van that arrived one morning, its driver quiet and efficient. A few cardboard boxes, no furniture. By noon, the windows were bare and the front garden had been stripped of the rose bush he used to trim every spring.

Sandra watched from her kitchen window, kettle in hand. The man — Brian, or Bernard, she could never remember which — didn't wave. He didn't look back. Just got into the passenger seat and was gone.

The house had been his since '89. His wife died three years ago. After that, he mostly sat out back with a crossword and tea, nodding at passersby like punctuation marks in his day.

She sipped her tea. It tasted like cardboard.

By evening, a small sign had appeared in the window: *"Private Sale. No Viewings."* She didn't know who had put it there.

Later, she stepped outside, walked slowly past the fence line. The path was swept clean. The empty windows gave nothing back.

She stood for a while. Not long. Just enough to notice how quickly a life could be folded up. How fast it became someone else's turn to forget.

Back inside, she peeled a satsuma. The kitchen light flickered once, then steadied. Somewhere in the house, a pipe groaned.

She thought of the intake centre again. Its lights. Its queue. Its warmth.

And then of the houses, one by one, with their curtains drawn in daylight.

Not everyone moved away.

Some just stopped appearing.

Her daughter rang on a Sunday. Not the usual day.

Sandra sat in the armchair by the gas fire, knitting half-finished on her lap, television muted. She answered on the third ring.

'Mum, I've done something — not big, just... I thought I should say.'

Sandra smiled before the sentence was finished. 'Go on.'

'We've applied for German passports. For the boys, too.'

There was a pause. A small one.

'You said we should, years ago,' her daughter added quickly. 'While we still could.'

'I did.'

'It doesn't mean we're leaving tomorrow. But it's a safety thing. Just in case. With everything going on.'

Sandra looked at the framed photo on the shelf: her daughter, mid-thirties, eyes like her father's, hair tucked under a wool hat. The boys were grinning, arms flung wide on a beach Sandra had never visited.

'It's alright,' she said.

'You're not cross?'

'No.'

A rustle down the line. A kettle maybe, or paper. Then: 'You could come too, you know. You'd be eligible, through Dad. Dual. We could help.'

Sandra didn't answer right away. She looked at her living room — the doily on the side table, the faint stain on the carpet where the dog used to lie, the curtain she'd meant to hem.

'I think I'd rather stay,' she said gently.

'Why?'

'Because someone should.'

There was silence. Not cold, just distance. A small sea between them.

'I'll send you the forms anyway,' her daughter said.

Sandra smiled. 'Alright.'

They spoke for a few more minutes — school, heating bills, something about a friend moving to Lisbon. Then they hung up. No drama. No goodbye heavy with meaning.

Just a line gone quiet.

Sandra sat a while longer.

Then turned the television back on. The news. Something about markets. A distant flood. A minister apologising.

She reached for her knitting.

The stitches no longer matched the row before.

The Drowning

It began with rumour.

Someone at the pharmacy said a woman had walked into the sea at Lowmere. No note. No explanation. Just left her coat on the railings and stepped out past the rocks.

Then another. Two towns over. Then three.

No headlines. Just mentions — in corner-shop whispers, in half-heard conversations on buses, in Facebook posts that vanished after a few hours. No pattern, officially. Just sad coincidence. Unconnected tragedies.

But Sandra noticed.

They were all women. All of a certain age. Not young. Not quite old. All local. Not from elsewhere. Not part of anything you could name.

She didn't speak of it. Just watched.

On the Thursday, she walked to the edge of town. Past the old depot, down the back lane lined with rusted fences and thistles, to where the sea path used to be maintained. It hadn't been trimmed in years.

The tide was halfway out.

She reached the rocks, stood still. The wind had teeth in it. A gull screamed overhead and wheeled inland.

No one else there.

Just sky. Just the cold rhythm of the waves.

She didn't go in.

Just stood.

And looked.

She thought of the women. Not as victims. Not as stories. Just as people who had come to the end of something, and seen no doorway back.

The world hadn't taken anything from them in one blow. It had taken *everything*, piece by piece, until even leaving felt like a form of loyalty. A final act of attention.

The wind pulled at her sleeves.

She stayed until her fingers went numb.

Then turned back.

The ground behind her held no trace of her feet.

She left the house just before dusk.

No coat. Just the cardigan she wore inside. The buttons done up wrong. A scarf tucked into her sleeve, out of habit more than need. The street was quiet — bins out, curtains drawn, the neighbour's house still empty. She closed the door behind her without locking it.

No one saw her leave.

The walk was slow, deliberate. Not hesitant. Not hurried. She passed the old bus stop, still taped off, and the shuttered café with its menu still sun-faded in the window. No one looked out. No one called her name.

She took the path behind the estate, through the nettle-strangled verge, past the rusted gate that once led to the allotments. The wind was low. The sky folding from grey into slate. She heard a dog bark far off, then nothing.

At the edge, where land stopped pretending to belong to anyone, she reached the sand. Cold underfoot. Damp through the soles of her shoes. She didn't stop. Walked straight to the line where the sea began to speak again.

It was further out than yesterday.

She stepped forward.

The tide met her ankles — a shock at first, then something else. Memory, maybe. Or the absence of it.

She looked ahead. No lighthouse. No buoy. No destination.

Only the flat line between water and sky.

Her hand brushed her thigh. The scarf still in her sleeve slipped loose, caught the wind, fluttered once, then dropped into the foam.

She followed.
Not quickly. Not dramatically.
Just continued.
Until the water reached her knees.
Then her waist.
Then her chest.
And the town behind her became no heavier than breath.

Afterlight

The room was quiet.

Inside the intake centre, fluorescent lights cast a steady hum across the vinyl floor. The waiting area was empty now — chairs in neat rows, leaflets untouched, posters curling slightly at the corners. A mop leant against the wall beside the cleaner's cupboard. No one had bothered to put it away.

At the reception desk, a monitor flickered. A message blinked: *"Auto update complete."* The lanyards still hung on their hooks. The printer tray was full.

It was after hours, but the lights stayed on.

No storm. No intrusion. Just silence.

Outside, the town darkened window by window. The street lamps buzzed into life. No cars passed. A fox crossed the roundabout, unnoticed.

The library sign, long painted over, still showed faintly beneath the gloss. You had to know where to look.

Inside, a fan switched on, though the room wasn't hot. A screen saver bounced across the monitor: *"Together, We Support."*

No one was there to read it.

And yet, the building hummed — quietly, dutifully, as if still waiting for someone to ask for help.

Somewhere, far off, a siren rose.

Not urgent. Not fast. Just a single note, climbing slowly, then tapering out across the rooftops. It didn't belong to anything in particular — not an ambulance, not fire. Just sound. Just proof that somewhere, a machine still responded.

Inside the intake centre, no one moved.

The automatic lights in the corridor blinked once. Reset. Stayed on.

Outside, the sea rolled in again, unhurried. The tide reclaiming what it always had.

On Sandra's street, a curtain fluttered in a house where no one now lived. A porch light clicked on, then off again, sensor triggered by a cat or a falling leaf.

The siren faded.

And then, nothing.

No footsteps.

No return.

Just the hum of a building with its lights still on.

And a town that no longer waited for anything at all.

Part 12: Critical Essay

Economic Retreat

The slow death of a town rarely makes headlines. It does not arrive with sirens or flashpoints, but in absences: the shuttered shop, the taped-off bus stop, the final bank closure that seals the community's fate. In *"The Vanishing Bank"*, this retreat is chronicled with precision and restraint. Sandra's walk through the high street is not just local observation — it is national diagnosis. The infrastructure of the town isn't failing; it's leaving.

What unfolds is not simply economic decline, but a systemic extraction of civic viability. Once, a bank signified permanence, credibility, rootedness. Its disappearance signals more than lost services — it marks the withdrawal of belief. With it goes the last illusion that this place still matters to the state.

There is no riot. No protest. Just queues at the refugee centre, a building that now serves as proxy government, distributing not interest or investment, but subsistence and intake assessments. Cash flow hasn't stopped — it has been redirected. The town isn't bankrupt. It's been reallocated.

This process, the story suggests, is not a failure of policy but the result of one: neglect repackaged as inevitability. No investment plan, no consultation. Just disappearance. A kind of invisible austerity in which towns are not closed, but hollowed. Public goods are not dismantled, but left to fade. The result is a form of ambient abandonment — not violent, but suffocating.

Sandra's experience reflects the quiet grief of those who remember when the town had a pulse. Her walk is a navigation of ghosts: old bus routes, former post offices, neighbours already gone. The geography remains, but its meaning has been stripped. Her story is not nostalgic — it is elegiac. The town doesn't need to be idealised to deserve preservation. It simply needs to be recognised as still inhabited.

The story resists sentimentality by refusing redemption. No new initiative arrives. No glossy regeneration plan is announced. The lights remain off. The silence deepens. Economic retreat, here, is not just spatial — it's moral. It reveals which places the nation considers expendable.

What's left behind is not just a physical vacuum but a psychological one. No doctor, no cashpoint, no point. When the structures go, so does the sense of belonging. People don't simply leave. They vanish. One by one. Quietly.

Just like the bank.

Refugee Centres as the New Government

Power, in this story, has not vanished — it has moved. Where once it lived in council offices, banks, or civic halls, it now resides in the intake centre. Bureaucracy hasn't collapsed. It has been concentrated. In *"The Vanishing Bank"*, the refugee centre becomes the new site of authority — not through coercion, but by default. It is the only building still lit.

Sandra walks past queues not for groceries or train tickets, but for access — to housing, benefits, healthcare advice, Wi-Fi. The centre does not offer empowerment; it offers mediation. It has absorbed the functions the state once distributed across an ecosystem of institutions. Now, there is only one door left to knock on.

The symbolism is quiet but precise. The bank closes, and a population gathers outside another queue. One form of capital — financial — is replaced with another: humanitarian. And with that shift comes a redefinition of who the state is for. Those outside the centre look in. Those inside it wait. But the town itself no longer hosts governance. It hosts processing.

The presence of the refugee centre is not framed with hostility. The story resists cheap antagonism. It does not pit Sandra against the centre. Rather, it observes how both are held in suspension — she by memory, the centre by mandate. But one is slowly dimming. The other is brightly lit, constantly staffed, funded from elsewhere. In a town where everything else is closing, the centre's permanence becomes a kind of provocation. Not because of what it does, but because it is allowed to exist.

This inversion — where the only remaining structure of care is one imported by crisis — forces a reckoning with policy priorities. The town has not been forgotten; it has been deprioritised. What flourishes is not development but triage. The refugee centre does not replace the post office or the doctor. It simply endures, and in its endurance, reorders the civic hierarchy.

Sandra's unease is not ideological. It is existential. She stands in a town that once had functions, now reduced to symbolism. The centre signals that administration still exists — just not for her. The message is subtle but loud: services have not vanished, only been rerouted.

The government still governs.

Just somewhere else.

Vanishing Infrastructure

Collapse doesn't always sound like breaking glass. Sometimes, it is the gentle click of a door closing for the last time, never to re-open — the bus stop taped off, the chemist boarded, the lights off at the surgery where no GP came back. In *"The Vanishing Bank"*, infrastructure disappears not in a fire or under a hammer —but in neglect. The town's skeletal remains are intact, but its living tissue is gone.

Sandra's journey through the high street reads like an inventory of absences. Each closed shop is a former function. Each taped entrance a severed nerve. The cumulative effect is not shock but erosion — the kind that hollows identity from the inside. She walks streets that still carry names, but no longer offer purpose.

This is not decay by chance. It is the product of strategic retreat. Investment has been withdrawn, maintenance deferred, services centralised to cities whose names carry political weight. What remains in towns like Sandra's is not just loss, but ghost logic — buildings that hint at a former coherence, now repurposed or rotting.

In this context, infrastructure is not merely physical. It is psychological scaffolding. The post office, the GP, the town hall — they were once points of orientation, grounding people not only in geography but in belonging. Without them, space becomes abstract. The town shrinks — not in size, but in meaning. Residents lose more than access. They lose anchorage.

What's chilling is the normalisation of it. Sandra's response is not fury, but weariness. She does not shout or campaign. She notes. She absorbs. Her reactions are muted because the retreat has been slow, deliberate, and dressed in the language of efficiency. Rationalisation. Digital transition. Budget realignment. But the result is the same: silence where there was once service.

The remaining structures — a single supermarket, the refugee centre, distant signs to a retail park — do not form a town. They form a holding pattern. No place for continuity, only subsistence. The gap between memory and present stretches wide. And no plan arrives to bridge it.

Vanishing infrastructure marks more than decline. It marks a withdrawal of care. It is not simply the loss of utility. It is the loss of recognition. The buildings are still there. But their purpose has departed.

And with it, the future.

Local Womanhood and Rootedness

Sandra is not simply a witness to decline — she is its remnant. A woman in late middle age, neither activist nor outlier, she remains in a place others have left because that is what she has always done: stayed. In *"The Vanishing Bank"*, this act — of remaining — takes on the weight of resistance, even as it begins to crumble under her.

The story centres female endurance without romanticising it. Sandra is not heroic. She is tired. She walks streets she has memorised, past houses she once visited, past a bus stop now cordoned off like a warning. Her rootedness is not a political statement. It is a default position — the last one standing when all others have moved on.

The story makes a quiet but sharp observation: in many towns like this, it is the women — especially older women — who hold what remains of the civic fabric. They organise the food bank, keep the community centre keys, check on neighbours, maintain the family garden. They do the unnoticed work that holds frayed edges together. And when they disappear, the town goes with them.

Sandra's daughter applies for a German passport. Her neighbour sells his house for cash. These are rational acts.

Sensible ones. But Sandra stays — out of habit, maybe out of memory. She asks the intake officer a question not because she expects an answer, but because once, questions led to conversation, and conversation led to change. Now, the officer shrugs. She is not seen. She is managed.

Rootedness, in this story, becomes a kind of grief. Not only for what's gone, but for what no longer seems to matter. Sandra's presence in the town is not an anchor; it is a reminder. And the state has no script for that. Policy speaks of growth, targets, metrics. It does not speak of women like her, who remember what the library used to be, who know whose house once had the daffodils in front.

Her walk is not nostalgic. It is forensic. She is cataloguing loss by walking through it. Not as protest, but as posture — the body still present where the state has receded.

When women like Sandra go, they leave no monument. Only silence.

And an outline of a town that once held.

Policy by Neglect

In *"The Vanishing Bank"*, no single villain emerges. There is no speech, no budget announcement, no plan stamped and enforced. The collapse comes not from action, but from inaction. From delay, drift, and decision-making dressed in passive voice: *services have been paused, resources reallocated, departments consolidated.* This is policy by neglect — governance through absence.

The town is not declared redundant. It is simply no longer considered. Its needs are not debated in Parliament. Its name does not appear in strategy documents. Instead, it is managed through attrition. A GP retires; the surgery closes. A bus route is cut; the stop disappears. A bank underperforms; its branch vanishes. Each step justified on paper. Each step subtracting from the lived world.

Neglect here is not incidental. It is structured. It masks itself as rationality. The market decides. The numbers don't lie. But beneath that lies a deeper truth: when a place is no longer seen as useful, its decline becomes self-fulfilling. The state no longer invests, so services falter. Services falter, so people leave. People leave, so the state withdraws further. And so the cycle turns.

Sandra walks through this logic without naming it, because it has never been explained to her. She simply sees the consequences: the queue at the intake centre, the shuttered windows, the house on her street quietly emptied and listed as "sold subject to contract." No one told her this was the plan. Perhaps because it wasn't. Not officially. That is the cruelty of neglect — it doesn't announce itself. It simply stops showing up.

There is a peculiar violence in this form of disappearance. Not overt, but administrative. Not loud, but legal. The post is still delivered. The bins are still collected. But everything else that gives a place texture — the counter clerk who knows your name, the bus driver who waits an extra minute, the pharmacist who remembers your prescription — fades.

Sandra senses it, even if she cannot define it. The feeling that her postcode has slipped off the map. That decisions are made far away by people who do not walk where she walks. That her community is no longer in crisis — it is in quiet conclusion.

No one needs to demolish a town like this.

They only need to stop returning its calls.

Psychological Erosion of Community

What collapses first is not always the building. It is the sense that anyone still cares if it stands.

In *"The Vanishing Bank"*, the psychological toll of retreat is subtle but cumulative. Sandra doesn't articulate her despair. She walks through it. Each closed door, each unstaffed counter, each unanswered question chips away at the belief that her community is real — not just materially, but emotionally. What remains is not grief in its dramatic form, but a kind of civic numbness.

The town does not mourn in unison. It fragments. One neighbour leaves. Another sells. A third stops waving from across the road. There are no funerals for towns. No public rituals for when the last cash machine goes dark. The result is disorientation — not chaos, but the quiet erosion of shared time, shared space, and shared meaning.

Community, in its most durable sense, is built on routine: the post office queue, the greetings at the newsagent, the borrowed sugar from next door. In this story, these routines are not disrupted violently — they are dissolved. Sandra doesn't shout about it. She internalises the rupture. Her questions go unanswered, not because they're unimportant, but because there's no longer anyone tasked with answering them.

The refugee centre remains lit, but it is not a community space. It is a triage station — impersonal, temporary, configured for throughput, not rootedness. It is not a place where people gather; it is where they are processed. It cannot replace the emotional infrastructure that has disappeared — it can only highlight its absence.

Sandra's observations are small, domestic, precise. But they point to something larger: the sense that she is now living in the outline of a place, a former town hollowed by years of quiet exits. Even her daughter's departure becomes

part of this erosion — a next generation seeking somewhere else to belong.

The psychological impact is not spectacular. It is weary-
ing. Hope doesn't break. It seeps away. Sandra does not
speak of abandonment. But her silence says it. Her stillness
says it. Her walk through the empty square is not a protest
— it is a kind of private elegy.

In a country that often confuses visibility with value, the
unspoken truth is this:

When no one sees you anymore, you start to disappear.

Suicide as Protest

The sea does not roar. It waits.

In the penultimate chapter of *"The Vanishing Bank"*,
women begin walking into the water. One by one. Without note, without banners, without visible rage. No media
coverage. No explanation. Only absence. This, the story
implies, is protest in its most distilled and desperate form:
not to be heard, but to make it impossible to ignore that
something is dying.

Sandra does not speak of it. She watches it. Feels it.
Recognises its shape in the air, in the finality of small goodbyes. There are no slogans here. Only gestures. This is not
martyrdom, and it is not madness. It is the last act left when
all forms of civic expression have failed. The women do not
shout. They do not strike. They step forward. Into water.
Into silence.

The framing resists sentimentality. There are no poetic
waves, no tragic lighting. The sea is not a metaphor. It is
geography — steady, inevitable, absorbing. Its neutrality
makes the act even sharper. The state has grown used to
complaints, to petitions, to dissent wrapped in data. It does
not know what to do with this: an act of erasure that speaks

not through violence, but through the refusal to keep waiting.

Suicide here is not pathology. It is politics — not in the party-political sense, but in the moral indictment it delivers. It says: *you made it unliveable*. Not suddenly, not spectacularly, but slowly, over years, through every withheld service and every quiet decision to dis-invest. These deaths are not personal. They are cumulative. Inheritances of despair, passed hand to hand.

The fact that it is women — middle-aged, local, embedded — matters. These are not the usual agents of revolt in public narratives. They are often written out. Their griefs deemed private. Their anger rendered irrational. But here, they become the final custodians of protest, precisely because they stayed the longest. Their deaths do not scream. But they mark.

Sandra's steps toward the sea are not framed with drama. They are measured. She follows. Not out of imitation, but conclusion. There is nothing left to hold.

The town has already gone.

The lights still shine in the intake centre.

But the civic heart is gone.

And the sea waits.

Feminine Disappearance

They leave without spectacle.

No farewell notes. No recorded testimonies. No media profiles. The women of the town disappear in a manner the story treats not as tragedy, but as culmination. In *"The Vanishing Bank"*, disappearance becomes a gendered act — not because women are more fragile, but because they held the fabric together the longest, and now, in leaving, mark its final undoing.

The story offers no forensic explanation. It does not delve into pathology. It understands that what happens is not individual crisis, but collective exhaustion. These women are not fleeing domestic lives, but civic ones. They have outlasted everything: the shop closures, the withdrawal of doctors, the departure of their children. They vanish not because they want to escape, but because escape is the last civic act available.

Feminine disappearance, here, is neither dramatic nor theatrical. It is deliberate and quiet. The antithesis of masculine protest, which so often relies on noise, fire, and spectacle. The women do not ask to be seen. They ask to be missed. Their withdrawal is the final audit: *What happens when the caretakers stop caring?*

Sandra does not plan a departure. She absorbs one. Her movements echo theirs. A kind of call and response formed not by agreement, but by atmosphere. Her walk to the shoreline is not framed as an ending, but a yielding. There is no resistance left to give. The institutions are gone. The houses are emptying. The town is a shell. What remains cannot hold.

The narrative structure reinforces this. There is no voiceover, no interior monologue. Just stillness. And then absence. The kind that confirms something essential has shifted. These are not suicides of despair alone — they are acts of record. Of saying: *This happened. And no one came.*

The story denies us any return. There is no search party. No policy reversal. The final image is of the intake centre — lights still on, functional, impersonal. It survives because it was never part of the community. It was built on top of it.

What disappears is not just a woman, or a street, or a service. What disappears is an entire way of life: local, shared, unglamorous — and no longer deemed worth sustaining.

The last protest is silence.

And the last light is not in a home, but in a building no one was ever meant to belong to.

Part 13: The Inheritance

The Arrival

The church stood on the edge of what had once been a town.

Half-submerged, its stone walls streaked with salt, its windows long since emptied of glass. The sea had crept inland over years, not storms — just tide and time. Roads now ended in marsh. Shops were hollowed. The sign that once said *WELCOME TO ELMRIDGE* hung sideways from a bent pole, rusted into unreadability.

But the church remained.

No bells. No services. Just structure.

One by one, they arrived.

Not together. Not from the same direction. They didn't speak. They didn't nod. Some came walking, slowly, with eyes trained on the path. Others stood for a while before entering, as if to ask permission from a building no longer owned by anyone.

Nora was first. She stepped in with her coat zipped to the chin and a candle in her hand. She placed it on the floor near the altar, unlit.

Then Amira. Quiet, pale. Her hands trembled only once — when she touched the back of a pew. Then she sat. Didn't look around.

Lewis came next. Hoodie up, gaze low. He moved like someone used to watching windows. He took a place at the edge and stared at the floor.

Fawad entered without stopping. Sat halfway down the aisle. His coat was still damp from the walk. He carried nothing.

Sandra came last. No coat. Just a scarf drawn over her shoulders, her shoes muddy at the edges. She looked up once, saw the beams sagging above, then chose a pew near the middle. She didn't sit straight. She just folded into it.

No one spoke.

No one asked why the others had come.

The church made no noise.

Wind moved through the cracks like breath.

Outside, the water lapped softly at the foot of the stairs.

Inside, silence held.

They did not look at each other.

But they did not leave.

They came without names.

No introductions. No reunions. Just presence. Each figure entered the church like someone returning to a place they'd never seen but somehow remembered.

Alfie slipped in unnoticed, small and wide-eyed, his school badge still pinned to his coat. He didn't sit. He wandered the aisle, tracing lines in the dust with one foot.

Kev followed — older now, shoulders rounded from ycars of shiftwork and waiting rooms. Hc pauscd at thc threshold, eyes adjusting to the dim. His ambulance jacket was gone. Just a plain windbreaker, zipped halfway. He sat near the back, near the door.

Rachel entered shortly after, her face unreadable. She held a folder — closed, battered — and placed it beside her before sitting, arms folded tight against her chest. Her hair had greyed. She did not look up.

Malik stood just inside the entrance, glancing over the pews like scanning a list. He didn't walk far. He sat in the last row, as if still on duty.

David appeared at the side door, the one no one remembered being unlocked. His eyes darted, unsettled, until they rested on the altar — then softened. He carried a notebook, water-warped, spine frayed. He clutched it like a map.

Each figure bore the marks of their own story, but none brought it forward. They did not recount. They did not explain. They simply arrived. One by one. Like pieces of a puzzle no one had chosen to complete.

The space between them was not awkward. It was respected.

At the front, Nora adjusted her coat, folded her hands.

Amira glanced sideways once — at Alfie, then away.

Fawad exhaled, low and steady.

No one broke the silence.

They did not sit like a congregation. They sat like remnants.

The church, such as it was, held them without judgement. It did not ask them to speak. It did not promise warmth. But it stayed upright. Just enough.

Outside, the sky dulled. The sea whispered against the stone.

Inside, something had gathered.

Not peace.

Not purpose.

Just presence.

Babel

They spoke, eventually.

Not in unison. Not in conversation. Just small sounds, scattered like pebbles across the room.

Rachel murmured a line from Orwell, almost under her breath. Nora asked, quietly, if anyone had a light for the candle. Fawad spoke in Dari — one sentence, soft, directed at no one.

Alfie said a name — maybe his brother's, maybe imaginary. Amira whispered a prayer, unfinished.

None of them responded to each other.

Not because they were unwilling.

Because they couldn't.

Each sentence landed in the air and dissolved. The sounds did not clash. They simply passed each other, like trains in opposite directions with no station between them.

Kev said, *"I didn't mean to be late,"* to no one in particular.

Lewis muttered, *"I tried,"* but didn't finish the thought.

Sandra opened her mouth once, closed it again.

Fawad looked across the room at Malik, recognition flickering — then fading.

Even those who shared a language couldn't meet in it. The cadence was wrong. The weight behind the words too different. They might have once lived in the same country, spoken the same civic tongue. But that tongue no longer held.

They were not hostile.

They were simply unreachable.

The space filled with near-speech — phrases shaped by memory, lost in translation, uttered without expectation of reply.

No argument. No agreement.

Just voices, failing to connect.

And still, no one left.

In the back pew, David opened his notebook. Wrote one line. Closed it.

The wind moved through the broken windows like a sigh.

The church listened.

But did not interpret.

No one understood.

The words floated, but never landed. Like radio signals caught in fog — audible, but directionless.

Amira spoke again, this time in English. *"It was the third baby."* No one turned.

Nora reached for her handbag, then seemed to forget why. Her hands settled in her lap, empty.

Alfie stood in the aisle, drew shapes in the air with his finger. A box. A cross. A door.

Fawad tried once more — *"Do you remember?"* — but he said it in the wrong language, and his voice carried like mist rather than meaning.

Rachel looked straight ahead, jaw tight. Her folder rested on her lap like a wound no one asked about.

Kev adjusted his collar. Whispered, *"All that time, and no call back."*

No one answered.

Not because they didn't want to.

Because something had frayed too deeply to hold meaning.

This wasn't miscommunication. It was post-communication. The point after listening stops being possible — not for lack of effort, but for lack of shared ground.

Words had become personal effects — carried, but no longer exchanged.

They did not look confused. Only distant.

As if they were each sitting in their own room, watching the same storm from different windows.

Outside, the sea rose a little further.

Inside, no one moved.

Fire and Water

Someone lit the candle.

No announcement. No ceremony. Just a hand — maybe Nora's, maybe not — striking a match and lowering the flame to the wick. The light took slowly, flickering into shape like it wasn't sure it was welcome.

No one clapped. No one prayed.

But they all saw it.

The candle stood near the front, where the altar would have been, beside a basin that leaked steadily onto the stone floor. No one knew where the water came from — a broken pipe, maybe. Or the sea itself. It pooled and spread, inching forward one slow ripple at a time.

The light and the water didn't clash. They simply co-existed — one rising, one flickering. A strange, quiet pact between the elements. No drama. Just inevitability.

Alfie moved closer to the candle. Sat cross-legged on the floor, watching the flame with the quiet devotion of a child too young to carry language but old enough to feel its absence.

Malik leant forward in his seat, hands clasped loosely, like he was listening for something just out of reach.

Sandra looked at the basin, then at her shoes. She didn't step back.

Fawad pulled his coat tighter. Not from cold, but instinct.

The candle glowed steadily. The water continued to spread.

No one moved to fix it.
No one named it.
It was not metaphor. Not anymore.
Just fire.
And water.
Side by side.

Someone began to clean.

No instruction. No request. Just movement — slow, quiet, almost unconscious.

It was Amira.

She rose from her pew, removed her scarf, and bent down near the spreading water. She didn't speak. Didn't announce herself. Just used the cloth to press against the edges of the puddle, blotting it back.

The gesture wasn't desperate. It wasn't effective either. The water kept coming — slow, steady, indifferent. But she kept at it, as if the act itself held meaning, even if the outcome did not.

Fawad joined her. Took a handkerchief from his pocket, folded it once, and knelt beside her. They didn't look at each other. Didn't speak. They just wiped what could not be stopped.

Sandra watched. Her fingers gripped the edge of the pew, then released. She did not move.

Kev sat still, gaze fixed on the candle, as if willing it not to go out.

Rachel stood up, briefly — then sat back down, as if the weight of everything pressed her spine back into the wood.

Lewis blinked slowly. Muttered something no one heard. Stayed seated.

Alfie dipped a finger into the water and drew a circle.

The church didn't respond.

No voice from above. No thunder.

Just the sound of fabric against stone. And water against fabric. And the steady insistence of people doing something, even if nothing could be done.

They were not trying to restore the church.

They were not trying to save it.

They were simply acting, because action was the last thing left that could be shared.

Even if it was wordless.

Even if it wouldn't hold.

Witness

They sat in the pews, silently.

Some with hands folded. Others with arms crossed. No one slouched. No one prayed. They weren't waiting for anything. They weren't listening. They were simply *there*.

No phone screens. No whispers. No glances exchanged.

Not unity.

But not disarray either.

It felt like the inside of a paused clock — stillness stretched across space like wire, delicate, electric. A room full of people who could no longer speak to each other, but who had not yet left.

Outside, the light shifted. The sky, somewhere behind cloud and sea-mist, thinned to a dull violet. The church's interior dimmed. No one stood to switch anything on.

The candle still burned at the front. The basin still dripped, slowly.

The water now touched the front row.

David sat with his notebook closed, spine outward, as if to suggest it was finished. Or never started.

Sandra stared straight ahead.

Rachel blinked only once in a long while.

Fawad's eyes were closed, but not in sleep.

Amira's scarf — damp and crumpled — rested on the windowsill like a flag laid down.

Alfie curled up along the pew, head against his knees, breathing quietly. No one told him to sit up. No one shushed him.

In another place, it might have looked like waiting.

Here, it was witness.

No judgement. No narrative. Just people, assembled not because they belonged to something, but because there was nowhere left that belonged to them.

They did not move.

They did not flee.

They held still.

Together.

Not to change anything.

But to see it end.

A baby cried.

Softly at first — a gurgle, a sharp intake — then louder, the full-throated sound of small lungs testing space.

It came from the back, near the door. No one turned to look. Not because they didn't care, but because there was no surprise left in them. A baby meant something had continued. Or arrived. Or simply endured.

No one moved to hush it.

The crying carried through the room like a ripple in still water. It echoed off the stone walls, filled the vaulted ceiling, curled around the candle's flame.

Sandra blinked. One hand clenched briefly, then settled.

Nora closed her eyes. Just for a moment.

Rachel exhaled. Not deeply. Just enough to register sound.

The others remained still.

The baby did not wail. It cried like someone announcing themselves to no one in particular. Not in fear. Not in demand. Just there.

It was the only sound in the room besides the candle's faint sputter and the slow drip from the basin, now too wide to contain.

No one went to lift the child.

No one asked whose it was.

It didn't matter.

Not here.

The crying softened, then faded.

Not silenced — just spent.

And the silence returned, gentler now. As if it had been heard. As if that one voice — small, wordless — had said everything the rest of them couldn't.

They did not nod.

They did not move.

They simply sat.

Bearing witness.

To what had been.

To what remained.

To what might, quietly, go on.

Outside

The sea had risen higher.

It reached the stone steps now, licking the lowest one with each pulse of the tide. Foam curled between the cracks. Moss clung to the walls like a slow, silent warning.

The town beyond the church was already half-forgotten. Roads blurred into marsh. Street signs leant at impossible angles. Lampposts blinked in daylight as if unsure of their purpose. A swing set in the old park moved on its own — wind or memory, it was hard to say.

A post box stood at the end of a submerged lane, red paint blistered. No letters. No collection times. Just a hollow shell where messages used to pass.

In one upstairs window of a terraced house, curtains still fluttered. The house leant slightly, as though listening for something.

No sirens. No orders. No announcements.

Just the steady insistence of water moving inward.

The shoreline had lost its edge. What had once been barrier was now suggestion — blurred, soft, creeping.

Birds wheeled above, quiet.

The air carried salt and rot and something sweeter underneath, like old blossom or forgotten bread.

Inside the church, the candle still burned.

Outside, the world made no argument.

Only advance.

Still they stayed.

No signal passed between them. No pact. No shared vow. Just stillness — held like breath, like ritual, like memory unwilling to scatter.

The water had reached the doorway. It whispered against the threshold, slid inward inch by inch. But no one stood. No one blocked it. The flood wasn't sudden. It was slow. Familiar. Like grief you'd already lived with.

The candle remained lit.

A bird struck the window, lightly, then flew on.

No reaction.

They stayed.

Not out of fear.

Not out of faith.

But because leaving would have made it meaningless. Because movement now would break something — not the silence, but the shape it had taken. They sat not in hope, but in recognition.

There was nowhere else to go.

Nothing else to return to.

And still — still — they did not despair.

It wasn't resistance. It wasn't surrender.

It was something quieter, older.

Witness, perhaps.

Or waiting, without asking what for.

The water moved past the pews.

The air thickened.

And they sat.

Together.

Final Light

The roof gave way with a sound like breath held too long.

Not a collapse — a yielding. One beam bowed, then splintered. Dust rose. Light spilled in, sudden and grey. The candle flickered once, then steadied, as if acknowledging the change.

No one moved.

Dust swirled in the shaft of pale sky, circling like ash that had forgotten what fire was.

A tile fell near the aisle. Then another.

Rain, thin as thread, began to slip through the gap, dappling shoulders, catching in Nora's hair, dampening the hem of Rachel's coat. Still they sat.

Fawad looked up.

Not startled. Not afraid. Just present.

Alfie stood slowly, one hand resting on the pew, eyes wide but calm. He didn't speak. He just looked at the light coming in through the wound in the ceiling, as though he had seen it before — in a drawing, or a dream.

Sandra closed her eyes. Let the water reach her ankles.

Lewis raised his hood, too late to matter.

No one cried out.

No one fled.

The light grew as the hole widened, revealing beams weathered by time and rot. Above them, the sky continued — unremarkable, uncaring.

A single feather drifted down through the break.

It landed on the back of the pew in front of Malik.

He didn't touch it.

He just watched it settle.

No one spoke.

The rain continued.

The roof continued to fail.

But the building held.

Just enough.

The light remained.

The rain thickened.

The candle burned low, wick drowning slowly in its own softened wax.

No one moved.

The pews, half-submerged now, creaked softly as the water shifted. Outside, the town disappeared inch by inch beneath the rising tide — shopfronts swallowed, fences erased, the last streetlight flickering once before going out.

Inside, the church stood open to the sky.

The roof no longer held. The ceiling was gone.

But no one screamed.

No one ran.

The last voice had already spoken — the child's cry, echoing into memory.

Now only breath.

And then, even that quieted.

No last line.

No music.

Just stillness.

Not peace.

Not despair.

Only silence.

Thick enough to hold them all.

Part 13: Critical Essay

Post-Nation as Setting

By the time *"The Inheritance"* begins, Britain — as place, as idea — has already collapsed. What remains is not dystopia but residue: a derelict church, a submerged town, and a slow convergence of figures from stories we've already known. They arrive not in search of shelter or salvation, but of meaning. Or perhaps memory. The landscape no longer offers answers. It offers witness.

The story's opening scenes mark a decisive shift: no longer is collapse depicted through institutions, services, or specific injustices. Instead, it becomes spatial. Environmental. Existential. The nation has not exploded — it has dissolved. There is no centre to hold. What replaces it is not chaos, but stillness. The country is not in flames. It is underwater.

This framing suggests that Britain's undoing was not sudden but slow, almost geological. A retreat, not a rupture. Institutions atrophied, speech frayed, solidarity drained away in polite increments. Now, at the end, all that remains is this last building — part sanctuary, part ruin — where characters gather without knowing why. It is not a site of refuge. It is a stage for final presence.

What defines this space is its post-national quality. No flags. No politics. No policies. Just human beings in proximity, unable to speak across the distances history has created. The church is not holy. The town is not governed. Language circulates, but does not connect. This is Britain after the map has been erased. The post-nation — not a rebirth, but a reckoning.

The absence of national identity is deliberate. These characters do not assemble in defence of the state. They are not loyalists or rebels. They are remnants — survivors not of war, but of disconnection. Their inheritance is not wealth or tradition, but disorientation. They do not resist the sea. They do not rebuild. They sit.

In doing so, they mark the end of a particular fantasy: that cohesion can be restored through policy, or that fragmentation is temporary. What this final setting presents is a more haunting truth — that the nation can disappear without ever declaring it. That a country can remain geographically present, yet morally uninhabitable.

No one proclaims its end.

They simply stop speaking.

And gather in silence.

Language Death

In *"The Inheritance"*, the most profound failure is not institutional, but linguistic. The church fills with figures from prior stories — Nora, Amira, Lewis, Fawad, Sandra, and others — yet none of them speak to each other. Or rather, they speak, but nothing lands. Their words hover, untranslated, unanswered. Dialogue has been replaced by monologue. Meaning slips through the gaps.

This is not merely symbolic. It is terminal.

Language death in this context is not about silence alone. It is about mutual unintelligibility: the end of shared reference, the collapse of common ground. Every character carries trauma, memory, position — but none can hear or house the others. There is no longer a mother tongue, nor a civic one. Just a series of utterances suspended in air.

This, the story suggests, is the endpoint of the fractures traced across the previous twelve narratives. Each story held within it a breakdown: of housing allocation, medical trust, school discipline, radicalisation, emergency response. But in the final gathering, these discrete failures coalesce into something more final — a linguistic entropy. The characters are no longer just isolated by circumstance. They are isolated by syntax.

Their inability to speak across difference is not for lack of vocabulary. It is for lack of recognition. Words have become private. Identity markers, emotional flares, accusations, or prayers. They no longer build bridges. They defend islands. What should be a shared grammar has been reduced to static. A Babel without ambition.

The silence that follows is not peace. It is aftermath.

The story refuses resolution through speech. There is no final speech, no monologue that unites the room. No translation offered. No misunderstanding cleared. This refusal becomes the point: if there is to be inheritance, it will not be in the form of words.

In this post-national, post-discursive space, the tragedy is not that people have nothing to say. It is that they no longer believe the saying will matter. Language itself has been exhausted — not censored, not forbidden — just worn to dust. A slow erosion of meaning.

And so, they sit.

Not as actors in a final play.

But as remnants of a language no one speaks anymore.

Ritual Without Religion

The final setting — a derelict church on the edge of a drowned town — might suggest spiritual reckoning. But *"The Inheritance"* withholds transcendence. There are no prayers spoken, no sermons given. The pews are filled, but not in worship. What remains is not faith, but form: bodies gathered, gestures repeated, silences observed. Ritual survives, even when belief has collapsed.

This is not accidental. It speaks to a deeper condition — that humans cling to shape when meaning falls away. The architecture of the church, hollowed but intact, frames the characters' movements. They enter. They sit. They face forward. One lights a candle. Another begins to clean. None of it is instructed. None of it is explained. These are not acts of doctrine, but instinct — post-religious gestures, drawn from memory rather than conviction.

The absence of God is not mourned. Nor is it defied. It is simply accepted. There is no bitterness in the hollow. Only a recognition that the space still holds a gravity of its own. Not sacred, but remembered. Not holy, but heavy.

This is the story's meditation on post-belief society — not one of militant atheism or spiritual crisis, but of ritual detachment. The forms remain because they are the last coordinates in a collapsing map. When language dies and institutions retreat, what endures are these faint, physical repetitions: lighting, kneeling, sitting, waiting.

Ritual here is not redemptive. It does not restore what has been lost. But it allows for witness. And in a world without coherence, that alone is meaningful. The act of sitting together, even in mutual incomprehension, is itself a kind of record. Not communion, but co-presence. Not ceremony, but marking.

There is a quiet defiance in this. To remain in a ruined place, to perform gestures without promise — this is not futility. It is a refusal to vanish completely. The church does not become a sanctuary. But it becomes a stage for memory. A frame that, though emptied of original content, still holds the shape of gathering.

In this way, *"The Inheritance"* suggests that the final ritual is not prayer — but presence.

They do not believe.

But they arrive.

And that, for now, is enough.

Collapse of Cohesion

The characters in *"The Inheritance"* share no dialogue, no common aim, and no path forward. And yet they sit in the same room. This is not solidarity — it is residue. What unites them is not a project or belief, but proximity. The final collapse is not dramatic. It is conceptual. There is no more "we."

This is not the chaos of civil war, nor the anguish of exile. It is something quieter and harder to resolve: a slow disintegration of the collective imagination. These people — once teachers, carers, officers, children — no longer belong to a shared story. They recognise one another dimly, but not deeply. Their suffering is mutual, but not communal.

The church becomes a kind of failed ark — a place that might once have sheltered a common purpose, but now houses only parallel griefs. No one explains why they came. No one instructs them to stay. The cohesion that once held neighbourhoods, schools, institutions, and values together has frayed beyond repair. What's left is choreography without contact.

The collapse of cohesion is not depicted through violence or betrayal. It is shown through inaction. No one reaches for another. No one calls for help. They sit. Still. As though awaiting something — a flood, a light, a sound that never comes. They don't flee. But they do not move toward one another, either.

This is the end of the social contract. Not in anger, but in fatigue. Not in disillusionment, but in distance. The nation, as idea, no longer binds them. Identity offers no bridge. Pain does not generate kinship. All the promises — of multiculturalism, unity, justice, future — have receded, not in crisis, but in slow retreat.

And yet, they are here. Together, but apart.

The story does not mourn this collapse. It does not beg for reconstitution. It simply records the moment when cohesion can no longer be presumed — when sitting in the same room does not mean sharing the same world.

This is what remains after the shared project ends.

Not rebellion.

Not reconstruction.

Just a room full of people who do not speak.

And do not leave.

Stillness as Resistance

They do not flee.

In *"The Inheritance"*, as the sea rises and the church crumbles, none of the characters run. This stillness — quiet, unspectacular — becomes the story's final political act. Not defiance, not faith. Simply refusal. To stay. To remain. To witness.

In a culture obsessed with action, stillness is often misread as surrender. But here, it is something else. These characters have already been through motion: migration, protest, resignation, collapse. What remains is not paralysis. It is presence. Their bodies stay rooted while everything else has given way.

This decision is not rhetorical. No one announces it. There are no speeches, no justifications. But it is deliberate. As water climbs the pews and the sky darkens, they do not seek higher ground. They do not plead. They sit, side by side, in a silence that refuses spectacle. It is not that they have hope. It is that they will not disappear unseen.

This is resistance of a different register — not aimed at winning, but at witnessing. The characters do not resist the flood, but they resist erasure. Their presence in the space, however fragmented, marks a line between collapse and nothingness. It says: *we were here, even if you looked away.*

The story treats this stillness with reverence. Not romanticism, but seriousness. No one is saved by it. No redemption arc emerges. But it lends dignity to people who have been denied it at every level — denied service, belonging, comprehension, legacy. Their sitting becomes a form of protest that needs no slogan. A gesture that carries no demand, only meaning.

Stillness becomes the last form of agency. The world will do what it does — retreat, submerge, forget. But they will not contribute to their own disappearance. They will stay, even if they are no longer heard. Especially because they are no longer heard.

This is what remains when language, nation, and cohesion are gone: the body, choosing not to flee. The self, choosing not to collapse inward. A collective presence that does not speak, but marks.

In this silence, they are not waiting to be saved.

They are refusing to vanish without being seen.

Inheritance as Burden
The title of the final story carries weight — *"The Inheritance"* — yet what's inherited here is not legacy or pride.

It is burden. A wreckage passed on not through intention, but through abandonment. These characters do not receive tradition, wealth, or wisdom. They receive silence, fragmentation, and the responsibility to bear witness to a country that no longer functions — or pretends to.

There is no estate to divide. No generational triumph to protect. Instead, they gather amid the ruins, inheriting a set of conditions no one asked for: disconnection, dislocation, and the residue of systems that once promised continuity. Each person in the church arrives with their own losses — but none of those losses have been grieved together. Inheritance, here, means carrying what could not be resolved.

This burden is not individual. It is structural. It's the weight of unafforded housing, closed hospitals, empty classrooms, broken promises, and unspoken grief. The story suggests that this is what modern inheritance increasingly looks like — not opportunity, but debt, emotional and social. The younger ones are left without tools. The older ones, without voice. Both are asked to continue. Neither can.

What deepens the tragedy is that no one chooses this inheritance. It arrives by default. Because no one cleared it. Because no one was brave enough to name what had gone wrong early enough to stop it. So the characters sit, with hands that cannot pass anything on except presence. Even the gesture of lighting a candle — a flicker of continuity — is fragile, unsustained.

The story gives us no answer to this burden. It doesn't call for revolt or healing. It doesn't offer vision or redemption. It simply holds the weight with them, lets us feel it — the dead momentum of a country that once imagined itself proud, now unable even to explain what happened.

In this space, inheritance is not gift.

It is residue.

And the fact that they remain — that they have not left, not exploded, not erased themselves — is itself the only thing passed on.

They inherit collapse.

And they sit with it.

Together.

Architecture of Memory

The final gathering place is not chosen — it is what's left. A church, half-submerged, crumbling at the edges, offers no salvation but holds significance. In *"The Inheritance"*, architecture becomes memory made visible. Not sacred space, but remembered space. Not functional, but symbolic. The nation is gone. This is what remains of it: buildings once meant to hold meaning.

Throughout the project, certain structures carried the burden of collapse — the council flat, the school, the ambulance depot, the mosque, the bank. By the end, all are gone or hollowed. The church stands not because it endured, but because it was simply not useful enough to dismantle. Like so much in this country, its survival is the result of neglect, not reverence.

Yet the characters arrive. One by one. Not to pray. Not to plan. But to sit in this skeleton of collective memory. The walls hold their pasts, even if the words for those pasts have disappeared. The building becomes archive — of language, of loss, of rituals once shared. It is not home. But it is known.

This is how the story treats architecture: not as shelter, but as mnemonic. A holding frame for lives that have been increasingly unheld. The church means something different to each person — for some, a site of faith; for others, of exclusion. But all acknowledge it, however unconsciously, as the last public space that still seems to mean something.

It is telling that no new building has replaced it. The story resists futures that promise sleek solutions or glass-panelled utopias. There is no "new civic centre," no smart hub. What remains is old, cold, and crumbling — but still locatable. The building, like the people inside it, is scarred but visible.

In a nation that has increasingly replaced permanence with utility, this church is a stubborn relic. Its pews, its stone, its rotting beams all refuse to adapt. In doing so, they allow memory to accumulate. The building remembers what the country has forgotten.

This is what architecture can do, even in collapse: hold presence. Witness gathering. Provide shape, when meaning has gone.

It does not save them.

But it proves they were here.

Ending as Gesture

"The Inheritance" does not conclude with resolution. It ends with a gesture — quiet, ambiguous, and deliberately incomplete. A roof caves in. A candle flickers. A baby cries. And no one moves. The sea continues to rise. The silence deepens. What remains is not closure, but presence.

In this refusal to conclude, the story mirrors the condition it records: a nation that has not ended cleanly, but eroded into fragmentation. The characters gathered do not stand up. They do not speak. They do not flee. Their presence is not heroic. It is elegiac. The final gesture is not forward-looking. It is observational. They witness, and in witnessing, they become the record.

This is the story's final defiance: it denies catharsis. There is no redemption, no sudden common purpose, no new manifesto rising from the ashes. The project does not circle back with optimism. It circles in on itself — a closed system of accumulated grief, memory, and structural abandonment. To end with gesture, rather than transformation, is a deliberate act of realism.

The final silence is not absence. It is verdict.

There are echoes of ritual — the church, the gathering, the light. But nothing transcends. The characters do not rebuild. They do not forgive. They do not narrate what comes next. The gesture is all that's left. And it is enough. Because at the edge of cultural collapse, articulation is not always possible. Sometimes, it is enough to be still.

Stillness becomes the act. Presence becomes the meaning.

The roof falls in. They do not run. Not out of apathy, but out of principle. They stay, together, in the last lit place, bearing the full weight of what was lost.

There is no lesson.

There is no plea.

Just this gesture:

We were here.

We saw.

We did not look away.

After the Smoke

On Witness, Ethics, and Refusal

There is always a danger, in writing collapse, of turning it into performance. To observe brokenness too beautifully. To make poetry out of failure. This book is not innocent of that.

The stories in these pages are attempts — not answers. They fail in some ways. Too neat. Too sharp. Too stylised. But that is the cost of trying to tell truth sideways, when truth direct is no longer heard.

In pairing narrative with essay, the aim was not explanation, but double exposure. To show both the emotional interior and the systemic frame. Story without argument can become sentiment. Argument without story becomes abstraction. Together, perhaps, they approach something like clarity.

There are limits, of course.

A story cannot change a policy.

An essay cannot stop a boy from burning something.

A paragraph cannot rebuild trust.

But what it can do is record. And that matters. Especially now, in a country where erasure comes dressed in politeness — in forms not returned, budgets renamed, silence outsourced.

These pages do not offer redemption.They offer recogn ition.They say: this happened. This is happening. You are not alone.

In the end, the only ethical claim this book makes is this:

To refuse silence is not enough. But it is something.

Even if no one listens.

Even if the lights are already off.

Even if it's too late.

Author Bio

Edward Myles writes from the edge of what remains.

A British writer exploring the fractures of modern life —
from institutional decline to cultural disinheritance.

His fiction and criticism examine what becomes of a
nation — and its people — when policy replaces meaning
and institutions forsake their purpose.

Working across fiction and nonfiction, he focusses on the
lived consequences of political silence and social upheaval
— blending narrative, analysis, and memory into a form
that is both literary and urgent.

Disinherited marks the beginning of a longer cycle of
hybrid creative-critical works on Britain in transition.

Printed in Dunstable, United Kingdom

68558832R00221